Hippocrene Language and Travel Guide to

BRITAIN

Hippocrene Language and Travel Guide to

BRITAIN

Catherine M. McCormick

HIPPOCRENE BOOKS
New York

For information, address:
HIPPOCRENE BOOKS, Inc.
171 Madison Avenue
New York, NY 10016

Library of Congress Cataloging-in-Publication Data
McCormick, Catherine M.
Hippocrene language and travel guide to Britain/Catherine M.
McCormick.
    p.   cm.
Includes bibliographical references and index.
ISBN 0-7818-0290-3
    1. Great Britain—Guidebooks. 2. Americans—Travel—Great Brit-
ain—Guidebooks. 3. English language—Great Britain. 4. Great Brit-
ain—Civilization. I. Title. II. Title: Britain.
    DA650.M24   1994   94-39042
    914. 104'859—dc20   CIP

Printed in the United States of America

For Jerry and Joshua

Contents

They One and the Same? — Perpendicular? What's That? (A Listing of British Architectural Terms) — U.K. Regions, Counties, Islands and Capitals — Meanings of Suffixes on British Town Names — Barton-in-the-Beans! What's That? — Welsh Names and Their Meanings — Some Welsh Greetings — Heraldic Badges and Their Associations — Britain's Tradition of Labor and Invention — How the U.S. Acquired the Potato, the Sandwich, the Apple and the Christmas Card

Health — Health Words — Health Sayings — Organizations — Death

Acknowledgments

This book has only been made possible by the grace of God and the invaluable assistance of my husband Jerry who, when our home was being inundated with shoeboxes filled with three-by-five cards of British and American words, provided me with a computer and printer, adapted all the necessary computer programs, exhibited enormous patience while teaching me how to use them, and solved all problems as they occurred. He's been an "all around support group." I can't thank him enough!

I am also enormously indebted to Margaret Watson of Leicester, England, teacher and historian, who shares my interest in history and archaeology. While we lived in England, she set up itineraries for weekly trips to places of historic interest and has since provided answers to questions when my sources ran dry.

She has also **vetted** (checked) every chapter of this book to eliminate archaic and obsolete words and expressions and is my authority on cricket and fox hunting.

I am also very indebted to my dear friend, Anita Barone, of Saddle Brook, N.J., an English major and teacher, who has always been very supportive of all my literary efforts. She also checked the book for grammar and proper American expressions.

I want to thank Frieda Gates, artist and author, of Monsey, N.Y., for her monthly "Writer's Roundtable" meetings at Rockland County Community College. The necessity of having something prepared to share at each meeting gave me the impetus to change my British-American/American-British dictionary into a travel book.

A special debt is owed to Dr. George Blagowidow, president and publisher of Hippocrene Books, who encouraged me to extend the scope of my original book; that is, to include the many phases of British life.

A special thanks also goes to Michelle Gagne, travel editor, for her probing questions, and her editing "par excellence," which was of great help in tightening up the text.

A grateful thanks to Linda Kramer, librarian of the English Speaking Union in New York City, who made a considerable contribution by allowing me the freedom of the library; and Sharon Bernard, secretary, for her efficient and courteous library assistance.

I also wish to thank the following for their assistance: Patrick Smith, curator of Noah Webster Birthplace, 227 South Main Street, West Hartford, Connecticut, for information dealing with Webster's books; Sally Marthaler of the New York office of British Information Services for providing up-to-date information on British life and recreation; and Ann Jones, Wales marketing assistant, of the British Travel Authority in New York for information on the Welsh language.

A special thanks to Russell Baker and John Mortimer, who graciously allowed me to use information from their interesting books; and to the Hampshire, England, publishers of Dr. P.H. Reaney's excellent book, *Origin of English Place Names*, Routledge and Kegan Paul, 1960 edition.

Preface

One of the pleasures of traveling in Britain is that Americans and the British share a common language; but the word "common" is deceptive because American and British versions of the English language have been diverging since before the American Revolution. When one adds to this the numerous regional idioms that have developed on both sides of the Atlantic, it can make for difficulties in communication in particular situations. This need not concern the tourist who takes a conducted tour; but if one strikes out on one's own, it would do well to be aware of some of the language problems that one may encounter.

This book will serve to ease many of these language difficulties. You will be helped with automobile travel (road signs and conventions), shopping (clothing sizes and names), restaurants (names of foods), pubs (names of drinks), telephone use, tea matters, health matters, and places to visit plus an overview of British history, customs, government, educational system, and recreational activities. There is also a generous measure of colloquialisms and slang, all-occasion words covering many aspects of British life and a liberal sprinkling of interesting words and expressions found in British mysteries.

These words and expressions were collected during my two trips to the United Kingdom, one lasting a year, and subsequently from hundreds of British books, and many British television programs, magazines and newspapers.

This is not a definitive study. A definitive study of everyday language is practically impossible because new words are coined to fit new situations almost daily; enough examples are given here to show that the everyday language used in Britain is just as colorful and full of zip and zing as American English.

Disclaimer

Great pains have been taken to corroborate the facts in this book; however, inevitably errors may occur. Readers are advised that these are times of rapid change. So many varied factors can influence the travel industry and can make up-to-date information change right after publication. Neither the author nor the publisher should be held responsible for any changes that are encountered but we would appreciate being apprised of them for future editions of this book.

How to Use This Book

When I explain what my book is about, most people look at me surprised. "Don't they speak the same language over there?, they ask. My answer is, "Yes they do, but with a difference."

Russell Baker, the much acclaimed New York Times "Observer" columnist, discovered that difference immediately when he was assigned to a London post by his newspaper. On his first visit to a restaurant, he relates in his book "The Good Times," he "didn't dare try ordering anything as complicated as food" because he was "unable to understand English"...and "was going to need English lessons."

Chapter 1 will give you some "English lessons."

Chapter 2 will arm you with information you will need before you get on the plane.

Chapter 3 is for reading on the plane to prepare you for British ways.

Chapters 4 through 11, and 21 and 22 will help the short-time tourist get the most out of his/her trip:

Chapter 4: Explanations, abbreviations and derivations

Chapter 5: London and its environs

Chapter 6: Driving tips

Chapter 7: Places to visit on your own

Chapter 8: A short history of the U.K.

Chapter 9: Shopping

Chapter 10: Pubs

Chapter 11: Restaurants, food shops and tea

Chapters 20 and 21 give actual trips taken by the author as examples of how one's interests can be served.

Chapters 11 through 19 are especially for those who will be renting self-catering homes or apartments or who want to go more deeply into British life: The British people, their homes, work, customs, recreation, government and politics, education and system of law.

Polonius: What do you read, my lord?
Hamlet: Words, words, words.
—William Shakespeare, *Hamlet*, II, ii

CHAPTER ONE

SO YOU THINK YOU SPEAK ENGLISH?

Any American who has visited England, watched British movies, British TV and read British books will admit to not always being able to comprehend what apparently is English, his/her own language. It's not surprising. Take any language, separate the people using it by an ocean, and after a period of time, there are bound to be differences in spelling, punctuation, pronunciation and accentuation even though the grammar remains the same. George Bernard Shaw understood this very well when he wrote, "We're two great nations divided by a single language."

Some examples follow:

1. **"We'll be clear away before they sort out the dog's dinner on their plates."** (We'll be a long way from here before they straighten out the messy situation they're in.)

2. This refers to an actor: **"He was aging and a bit breathless if second house patter was demanded too soon after the interval."** (He was getting older and would be a little breathless if the second act came too soon after intermission.)

3. **"The butcher served her a half pound of streaky."** "Streaky" is short for **"streaky bacon"** (lean bacon).

4. **"There were trippers everywhere waving orders to view."** (There were tourists everywhere waving entry passes or vouchers.)

5. **"She was being asked to act as a dogsbody."** (They were treating her like a drudge.)

6. **"I told him he could have his cards and get out."** (I gave him his walking papers.)

7. **"If they weren't so scatty and such an absolute hoot, I'd begin to think they were sinister."** (If they weren't so scatter-brained and such an amusing bunch, I'd begin to think they were dangerous.)

8. **I found young who's-your-father.** (I found young what's-his-name.)

How's That Again?

"How's that again?" is the question you'll ask yourself after hearing a familiar phrase. It sounds right but something's just not quite right. Let's take: **"As sure as God made little apples."** Sounds right but one word is missing, **"green."** The familiar American saying is: "As sure as God made little green apples." Now take, **"Ask me no questions, hear no lies."** The first part is exactly the same, but the second is usually "I'll tell you no lies." Then there's, **"I wouldn't touch it with a barge pole."** Americans wouldn't touch it with "a ten-foot pole." And how about getting ready **"in two shakes of a duck's whisker?"** In America it would be a "lamb's tail."

"If the shoe fits" becomes **"If the cap fits."** Others in the same vein are: **"The boot is on the other leg."** (The shoe is on the other foot); **"That's another pair of shoes."** (That's another story.), and **"I'll eat my boots if it isn't so."** (I'll eat my hat if it isn't so.), and **"Put the boot in!"** (Kick him when he's down!).

To **"turn an honest penny"** (earn an honest dollar) while waiting for one's **"boat to come in"** (ship to come in), one can get **"black in the face"** (blue in the face) from putting one's **"back to the wheel"** (shoulder to the wheel). **"Working like drayhorses"** (working like a horse) may not be **"up one's street"** (up one's alley) but it's no reason for **"chucking up the sponge"** (giving up).

One **"chews the cud"** (chews the fat) or **"chunters"** (chats) with a **"chatting acquaintance"** (casual friend); and gets **"bored rigid"** (bored stiff) in certain situations. One can also be **"innocent as a babe unborn"** (innocent as a newborn babe) **"thankful for small mercies"** (grateful for small favors), **"square and aboveboard"** (honest and aboveboard) and have **"skeletons in one's cupboard."** (skeletons in one's closets).

If you ask how after one's health, you'll hear: **"I'm right as a trivet,"** (right as rain), **"fit as a flea"** (fit as a fiddle), **"right as ninepence,"** or **"sound as a bell"** (sound as a dollar).

If one **"goes off at half-cock"** (goes off half-cocked) and **"drops a spanner in the works"** (drops a monkey wrench in the works); one may be called to task with, **"That's torn it!"** (That did it!), **"Now no back chat."** (Now no back talk.), **"I'm fed up to the back teeth!"** (I'm fed up to here, Americans say, with the top of one's hand held flat under the chin). **"Don't come the innocent"** (Don't play the innocent), **"You're cleverer than you look."** (You're smarter than you look.) This may lead to a **"mother and a father of a row"** (grandfather of a fight).

There are many more phrases which sound right but have a word change here and there:

a big **pot** — a big **shot**

all the same — **just** the same

anti-clockwise — **counter**clockwise

as queer as **the next fellow** or as queer as **a coot** — as queer as **can be**

at a pinch — **in** a pinch

at cost price — **at cost**

base minded — **dirty** minded

black as **ink**, black as **soot** or black as **night** — black as coal

bootbutton eyes — **shoe**button eyes

bottomless **well** — bottomless **pit**

breast the tape (at end of race) — **break** the tape

by the sly — **on** the sly

call**over** — **roll**call

call over the coals — rake over the coals

can't make top nor bottom or top nor tail of it— can't
make heads or tails of it

can't see the wood for the trees — can't see the forest
for the trees

can't stick it — can't take it

catch one up — catch up to someone

caught out — found out

chance found — found by chance

chokey (gaol) — pokey (jail)

dog sick — sick as a dog

Fire ahead! — Fire away!

footmarks — footprints

get it off pat — get it down pat

give one the toe of one's boot or sack some one —
give one the boot

go to jelly — turn to jelly

go straight out — go right out

hang about — hang around

I take your point. — I get the point.

I wouldn't trust him as far as I could see him. — I
wouldn't trust him as far as I could throw him.

in due course — in due time

It doesn't amount to a row of beans. — It doesn't
amount to a hill of beans.

It doesn't click. or It won't wash. — It won't work.
or No soap!

It's above my head! — It's over my head!

neat as a new pin — neat as a pin

set one's face against something — set one's mind
against something

storm in a teacup — tempest in a teapot

The grass is always greener on the other side of the
hedge. — The grass is always greener on the other
side of the fence.

tread upon eggs — walk on eggs

There are many, many more. Look for them in the Appendix under Chapter One.

The slight changes shown above might give one momentary pause; but using the following words and phrases incorrectly could cause some confusion or embarrassment.

Strangely Enough

U.K. "A backwoodsman" is a peer who rarely attends the House of Lords; apparently staying at his country estate.

U.S. "A backwoodsman" is a person who lives in a woods or forest or is a "hick from the sticks."

U.K. "A bomb," theatrically speaking, is what in the U.S. would be "a hit."

U.S. "A bomb" is "a dud" or failure.

U.K. "A cracker" is a party favour (favor).

U.S. "A cracker." The British would call this a thin, crisp biscuit.

U.K. "A crib" (slang) is a house or a job.

U.S. "To crib" (slang) is to cheat or steal, as well as slang for a house or apartment.

U.K. "A guy" is a joke. "To guy" is to mock.

U.S. "A guy" is a fellow.

U.K. "A hayseed" is a grain of seed from a haystack.

U.S. "A hayseed" is a country bumpkin, what the British call a chawbacon."

U.K. "A hooker" is a rugby player whose job is to hook or gain possession of the ball.

U.S. "A hooker" is a prostitute.

U.K. "A jumper" is a pullover called "woolly pulli" or just "pulli."

U.S. "A jumper" is a one-piece sleeveless dress under which one wears a blouse or sweater.

U.K. "A shake down" is an improvised bed.

U.S. "A shakedown" is forcing someone to pay you money.

U.K. "A stickup" is a stand-up collar on a shirt.

U.S. "A stick-up" is a robbery.

U.K. "Chips" are french fries.

U.S. "Crisps" are to the British what we call potato chips.

U.K. "Corn" is any grain, but especially wheat.

U.S. "Corn" comes on a cob and is what the British call **maize.**

U.K. "Crummy" (slang) means plump, lousy or a cow with a crumpled horn.

U.S. "Crummy" (slang) means cheap, feeling ill or under par.

U.K. "Graft" (slang) is hard work.

U.S. "Graft" or "Grift" (slang) is illicit profits.

U.K. "Half and half" is a drink: half porter, half ale; also known as "Mild and bitter" as it's a mix of ales.

U.S. "Half and half" is half milk, half cream.

U.K. "Homely" means pertaining to the home, friendly, cosy, comfortable.

U.S. "Homely" means a person is not attractive.

U.K. "Macs" are short for mackintoshes or raincoats.
U.S. "Macs" are a variety of apple.

BR. "Mean" means careful with money.
U.S. "Mean" describes a person who hurts others by word or deed.

BR. "A milk run" is the milkman's morning round or any routine assignment.
U.S. "A milk run" is a pilot's routine flight.

U.K. "Nervy" means nervous or excited.
U.S. "Nervy" means one is bold and has impudent self-assurance.

U.K. "Oil cloth" is canvas covered with linseed-oil paint or linoleum.
U.S. "Oil cloth" is cloth treated with oil or paint and used as a table and shelf covering. It's what the British call **"American cloth."**

U.K. "Paraffin" is kerosene.
U.S. "Paraffin" is wax for candles or coating.

U.K. "Pavement" is a sidewalk and "footway" is a path.
U.S. "Pavement" is a paved street or road. It's the British name for **"roadway."**

U.K. "Pot Head" is a stupid person.
U.S. "Pot Head" is one who takes pot (marijuana).

U.K. "Queer" means odd-looking.
U.S. "Queer" means one favors his/her own sex. This

definition is rapidly catching on in the U.K., as is "gay."

U.K. "Rough-stuff" is coarse paint laid on after priming.
U.S. "Rough-stuff" is a fistfight.

U.K. "Squash" is a drink made from fruit syrup and water.
U.S. "Squash" or "zucchini" is a cucumber-shaped vegetable. The British call them **"courgettes."**

U.K. "Stores" is the name for a warehouse.
U.S. "Stores" are what the English call **"shops."**

U.K. "Sweetie or Sweety" is a sweetmeat (candy).
U.S. "Sweetie" is an affectionate name for a loved one.

U.K. "To be two-fisted" is to be clumsy.
U.S. "To be two-fisted" is to be virile, vigorous; or pertaining to a drink, large.

U.K. "To knock someone up" is to arouse someone, that is, to knock on someone's door.
U.S. "To knock someone up" to make a woman pregnant.

Confusing Usages

"Should have done" is a phrase that is confusing to Americans because it is missing a word, **"it."** as per: "I didn't feed the dog. **I should have done,** but forgot." We would say, "I should have done **it."** In an instance like the following, we would leave out the **"done."** "Conservation has no appeal to him. Perhaps **it should have done."** We would say "Perhaps it should have."

"Undertake" is a word we don't use much at all, perhaps because it's closely allied with **"undertakers."** We mostly use the word **"undertaking"** as in, **"a big undertaking"** meaning **"a big job."** The British also use it in the same sense but also as shown in the following sentences:

We don't **undertake** (take) divorce cases.

You can go if you **undertake** (can manage) to send the boat back.

"Chalk" is also used frequently. **"As different as chalk and cheese,"** we would understand but **"To walk one's chalk"** meaning "to go off" or "go away" is rather baffling. **"Not by a long chalk or chalkmark"** is comparable to our "not with a ten-foot pole," but why chalk? What is known is that chalk is used in scoring points and somehow it got into these baffling expressions.

"Up" is another word that would make Americans wrinkle their foreheads and say "Huh?" when it's seen at the beginning of words such as: **upfill** (fill up), **upgo** (go up), **upgrow** (grow up), **uproll** (roll up or close up), **upspeak** (start speaking), **upstumps** (pack up and leave) and **uptear** (tear up). These are mostly used by **press** (newspaper) people to save money on telegrams and cables.

But What Exactly Is "English?"

The English language, like many other European languages, is a branch of an **ancient Indo-European tongue**, the language used 5,000 or more years ago by the people who lived in Eastern Europe, in the valley of the middle Danube. It is also a blend of all the languages of the invaders: **Celtic** which survives as a form of **Gaelic** or **Scottish Erse** in Scotland, **Erse** or **Irish Gaelic** in Ireland, **Welsh** in Wales, **"Manx"** on the Isle of Man and **"Cornish"** in Cornwall; **"Germanic"** (Anglo-Saxon); **"Latin"** (Roman); **Viking** or **Old Norse** and **Norman-French.** After each invasion, new words were added to the language:

CELTIC: **bin** (box) **dun** (dark color) and many Norman place names: **Devon, Dover, Kent, Thames, Avon**

TEUTONIC: **street, tile, wine, bishop**

LATIN: creed, alms, disciple, monk, purse, pail, pot, cook, pear

NORSE: sister, egg, window, they, are, take, them

NORMAN: parliament, judge, soldier, gown, beef, chair, pheasant, poetry, surgeon, consideration

English is divided into three long periods: **Old English** (450-1150), **Middle English** (1150-1500) and **Modern English** (1500-present). In each period, some old words became obsolete and new words were added to the language. Word spellings also changed. Herewith some examples of early Old English and Middle English:

THE OLD ENGLISH-SAXON OF KING ALFRED'S DAY (848?-899):

"Way Gahr-Daynuh in yahr-dahgum ellen fremedon!"
(We, Spear-Danes were valorous in days of yore.)

CHAUCER'S "MIDDLE ENGLISH" (1340?-1400):
A description of the knight in his Canterbury Tales:
A knyght ther was, and that a worthy man,
That fro the tyme that he first bigan
To riden out, he loved chivalrie,
Trouthe and honour, fredom and curteisie.

There was a knight, a worthy man who
From the time he first began
To ride out into the world, loved chivalrous deeds,
Truth, honor, freedom and courtesy.

Concerning Dictionaries

Though by the close of the 14th century, English was taught in schools, there was no standard dictionary. Someone should have thought about putting one together when Gutenberg provided the means with his invention of the printing press in the 1400's, but it didn't happen for 204 years. When the first dictionary was published, it lacked all the words used in daily life. That took 400 more years of "dictionary evolution."

The first English language dictionary was published in 1604 by a schoolmaster, **Robert Cawdrey.** It was called *Table Alphabeticall* and listed only words from Latin and French texts. In 1721, **Nathan Bailey** published *An Universal Etymological English Dictionary* which included only words which were to his mind **"in good standing."** In 1755, **Samuel Johnson** also chose only words he considered proper for his great *Dictionary, with a Grammar and History of the English Language.* Even **Noah Webster's** dictionary included only words **"in good standing."**

It wasn't until **Richard Trench,** Dean of Westminster, read a paper in 1857 to the Philological Society in London entitled **"On some Deficiencies in our English Dictionaries,"** in which he said dictionary writers should not select only the words they considered good, they should include all the words in use by the people, that an all-inclusive dictionary was considered.

That admonition was taken to heart and research began on an all-inclusive dictionary. It was such a tremendous project that it had to be published in parts from 1884 to 1928 by the Philological Society and the Clarendon Press. It was called, *A New English Dictionary on Historical Principles*, and became what is now considered the greatest dictionary of all time, *The Oxford English Dictionary* published by Oxford University Press.

Noah Webster's American Dictionary

Noah Webster was a Yale graduate with a law degree who, to keep up with the new scientific discoveries of his day (the 1700s), was frequently exasperated when he couldn't find the words he didn't understand in any existing British dictionary. From his frustration came his *Blue-Back Speller* of 1783 (it was published by Hudson and Goodwin, Hartford, Connecticut and had a blue paper cover); and later, after 17 years of research and preparation, *An American Dictionary of the English Language*, which was published in two volumes in 1828 by F. Converse, N.Y.

It was a revolutionary idea to remove words from the dictionary concerning fox hunts and other British activities that weren't pertinent for the American colonists. Instead, Webster substituted new words that were continually springing up to describe the types of work the Colonists engaged in, the objects they used and their diversions. The differences in spelling between British and American words, in great part, can be laid at Noah Webster's feet. While careful to include all the scientific terms that interested him, he also made a number of changes to simplify the language, as for example, changing **"waggon" to "wagon," "develope" to "develop," "gaol" to "jail"** (used interchangeably in Britain today) and dropping the **"u"** from words ending in **"our,"** such as **"honour"** and **"labour"** and changing words ending in **"re" to "er"** as in **"theatre"** and **"centre."** Because his books were widely used, the New England dialect of the 18th century, grew to be accepted as Standard American English.

Here are most of the ways we differ with the British in spelling, punctuation and pronunciation. You will note that the British use **double "l's"** within words, Americans use them at the ends of words. For word endings, they prefer **"ise"** and **"our,"** we prefer **"ize"** and **"or."**

The word that causes the most confusion is **"practice."** In Britain, **"practice"** with **"ice"** is a noun, an actual doing or a professional person's business, that is, **"a practice." "Practise,"** with **"ise"** is a verb, that is, **"to practise."** In the U.S. **"practice"** with **"ice"** is used in both instances.

SPELLING DIFFERENCES

BRITISH		AMERICAN	
ae	anaemia	e	anemia
amme	programme	am	program
ce	offence	se	offense
dge	judgement	dg	judgment
em	empanel	im	impanel
en	encase	in	incase
iae	mediaeval	ie	medieval
iare	caviare	iar	caviar

ise/ice	practise/ practice	ice	practice
ise	dramatise	ize	dramatize
k	kerb	c	curb
l	enrol	ll	enroll
ll	jewellry traveller	l	jewelry traveler
oe	foetus	e	fetus
oeuvre	manoeuvre	euver	maneuver
ou	mould	o	mold
our	colour	or	color
ough	plough	ow	plow
py	pyjamas	pa	pajamas
que	cheque	ck	check
re	fibre theatre	er	fiber theater
ry	devilry	try	deviltry
sa	civilisation	za	civilization
sc	sceptic	sk	skeptic
yse	paralyse	yze	paralyze
xe	axe	x	ax
xion	connexion	ction	connection

PUNCTUATION DIFFERENCES

Although American grammar is the same, some British names for **punctuation points** (punctuation marks) are quite different:

colon	:	colon
semi-colon	;	semi-colon
inverted commas	" "	quotation marks
comma	,	comma
full stop	.	period
hyphen or **dash**	-	hyphen or dash
brackets	( )	parentheses
exclamation mark or **"screamer"**	!	exclamation point

indicates a pause   *   indicates a footnote

SOME PRONUNCIATION DIFFERENCES

	British	American
agile	ah-jile	ah-jill
been	bean	bin
bolero	bahl-er-oh	bow-ler-oh
bristles	brist-uls	bris-sles
cemetery	sim-ih-tree	sem-eh-terry
centenary	sen-teen-ary	sen-ten-ary
ceramic	ker-am-ik	sir-am-ik
charades	shah-rods	sha-raids
clerk	clark	clerk
compost	kom-pahst	kom-post
culinary	cull-in-ary	kule-in-ary
derby	darby	derby
digitalis	digi-tay-lis	digi-tal-is
Don Juan	Don Joo-on	Don-Wan
duodenal	duo-deen-al	doo-od-en-ul
epoch	ee-pock	ehp-uck
evolution	ee-volution	ehv-olution
facade	fuh-sade	fuh-sahd
forsythia	for-sythe-ee-ah	for-sith-ee-ah
fragile	frage-I'll	frage-ill
garage	gah-ridge	ghuh-raj
glazier	glass-ee-er	glaze-ee-er
grant	grahnt	grant
handkerchief	han-ker-cheef	hand-ker-chiff
herbs	herbs (*h* is pronounced)	erbs
innocuous	in-oak-shus	in-ock-you-us
iodine	eye-oh-deen	eye-o-din
issue	iss-you	ih-shoe
lather	lah-ther (as in la-la-la)	lah-ther (ah as in actor)

marquis	mar-kwiss	mar-key
metallurgy	meh-tal-urge-ee	met-ull-urge-ee
midwifery	mid-wiff-ree	mid-wife-ree
migraine	me-grain	my-grain
missile	miss-I'll	miss-ill
organisation	organ-eye-sation	organ-ih-zation
patent	pay-tent	pah-tent
patriotism	pat-rioh-tism	pay-trio-tism
privacy	priv-uh-see	pry-vuh-see
process	proh-sess	prah-sess
progress	proh-gress	prah-gress
schedule	shed-yule	sked-you-ull
simultaneous	sim (like Tim)	sim (like time)
solder	sold-er or saw-der	sod-er
theatre	theer-ter	thee-ahter
tomato	toe-mah-toe	toe-may-toe
vitamin	vit-uh-mean	vite-uh-min
zebra	zeh-bra	zee-bra

BRITISH PLACE NAME PRONUNCIATIONS

Alcester — Awlster
Aldeburgh — Awlbura
Belvoir — Beever
Bicester — Bister
Derby — Darby
Edinburgh — Edinborough
Featherstonehaugh — Fanshaw
Leicester — Lester
Marlyebone — Marl-bin
Mainwaring — Mannering
Norwich — Norch
Pall Mall — Pell Mell
Thames — Tems

Oh how I long to travel back,
And tread again that ancient track!
    —Henry Vaughan, *Silex Scintillans*, The Retreat, I, 1

CHAPTER TWO

BEFORE YOU LEAVE

There is no other country in the world like England. If you're an Anglophile or have studied British history, you may have a strong sense of de-ja vu, of coming home. Everywhere are places you've read about **"in situ"** (in their original locations)...living history: Bronze Age structures such as Stonehenge next to modern highways; the four-centuries-old Roman stamp on the country: Roman ruins juxtaposed to shining modern buildings, Roman roads, Roman baths, and Hadrian's wall; medieval **market crosses** (stone structures in centers of towns surmounted most times by a cross to insure fair dealing between customer and vendor); majestic cathedrals; fortress castles, stately homes as well as thatched houses with their welcoming appearance. One of Britain's greatest charms is its attachment to habit, tradition and original Celtic names with odd pronunciations.

It is truly amazing that such a small country, approximately 650 miles long and 300 miles wide (about the size of Montana, 556 miles by 322) has managed to exert such an enormous impact on the world at large, and in particular, on the United States. Britain's 1,000 year old traditions of granting personal freedom, its laws, and its court system are all the basis of our own. And like 12 other countries around the world, we also share the same official language. **Well...almost.**

Americans visit Britain in droves every year. Millions can trace their ancestry to England, Scotland, Ireland and Wales, are intrigued by its history, its pageantry, its Royal family, its literature, its arts, its courts, its castles, its stately homes, its gardens, its so many things rolled into one beautiful country.

Getting Ready

Order the travel booklets regarding the areas you want to visit (Note: The British Tourist Authority, 551 Fifth Avenue, Suite 701, N.Y., N.Y. 10176, has a booklet on how to trace your ancestors), check out all the books on Britain in your local library and if you're a computer buff, there are now software versions of familiar travel guides which provide users with maps of popular cities and the lowdown on their hotels, restaurants and attractions. As well, programs like Internet, OnLine America and the like offer direct correspondence with fellow Anglophiles or even the Brits themselves. Armed with all this information, it's time to see a travel agent to set up your itinerary. **Ready, Steady, Go.** (Ready, get set, go.)

Bed and Board

Tourist Boards regularly inspect the thousands of places to stay in Britain and they are classified according to the range of facilities and services provided. The maximum designation is **"Five Crown."** Those having higher quality standards will have **"Approved" ("Merit" in Wales), "Commended," "Highly Commended"** or **"Deluxe"** next to the Crown designation. Be sure that the price quoted is **"all found"** (all inclusive) so there won't be any extras on the final bill.

A travel agent can help you reserve accommodations while in America; but if you prefer to handle this yourself, in Britain you can make use of:

1. The network of **TICs** (Tourist Information Centres). TICs charge a modest fee for a service called **Book-a-Bed-Ahead.** There are over 800 TICs in Britain. They are usually in central positions in towns and on main roads. Look out for an arrow sign depicting a small box holding the letter "i" and next to it the words **Tourist Information.** To book, you must appear at a TIC office before 4 p.m. You cannot **book** (reserve) by phone or

mail. The British Travel Centre, 12 Regent Street, Piccadilly Circus, London SW1 also offers a TIC accommodation booking service.

2. **The British Travel Centre**, 12 Regent Street, Piccadilly Circus, London SW1 also books rooms.

3. **B&Bs (Bed and Breakfast)** homes offer real value besides allowing the visitor a chance to meet the people. In summer, book in advance, otherwise, just look for a B&B sign and knock at the door.

4. **Guest Houses** are more expensive as they have more bedrooms and bathrooms.

5. **Farmhouse Bed and Breakfast** is another alternative offering the chance to stay at numerous farm houses offering B&B; or having a **self-catering** (do-it-yourself) accommodation.

6. **Hospitality Home-Stay** enables one to stay with a British family and join in some of their activities.

7. **Holiday Homes:** You can rent an apartment, house or cottage with all the household requisites supplied.

8. **University and College Accommodation:** There are over 50 low-cost locations during summer and other student holiday periods. Contact the British Universities Accommodation Consortium Ltd., Box 744A University Park, Nottingham NG7 2RD, England; or Higher Education Accommodation Consortium, 36 Collegiate Crescent, Sheffield S10 2BP, England.

9. **Youth Hostels**, located across the country in various cities.

10. **Canal-Boat Holidays:** There are 2,000 miles of picturesque canals (3,220 kms) in England. No boating experience is necessary.

11. **Home Exchange**

12. **Pubs** sometimes do have rooms and the food is usually good.

LODGINGS (ACCOMMODATIONS) WORDS

alarm call — wake-up call

bar man or **barmaid** — bartender
bed-sitter — studio apartment
commercial room — room set aside for **commercial** (business) travelers
desk porter — desk clerk
digs (slang) — furnished apartments or houses
doorkeeper — doorman
hotel attendant — bell-boy
liftman — elevator operator
lodger — renter
lodging house — rooming house
self-contained set — private suite
service flat — furnished apartment with linens and towels and a cleaning service
lifts — elevators
the ground floor — first floor

Visa Necessary?

No, U.S. citizens only need a passport. The same is true for citizens or nationals of the Commonwealth (Australia, Canada and New Zealand) and the Republic of South Africa. Your stays are usually limited to six months. Should you wish to stay longer or apply for work, you must contact the **Home Office**, 50 Queen Anne Gate, SW1, Telephone: 213-3000.

Customs

There are no restrictions on the amount of money you can take into the country. For duty and tax free allowances, check with your travel agent. You are prohibited from taking in: plants, perishable foods such as meats, meat products, eggs, fruit, firearms and ammunition (unless you've made a special arrangement), animals and obscene film or written material. Customs have **green and red channels** (lanes) at most ports and airports. The **Green Channels** are for people with nothing to declare over the allowances permitted to overseas visitors; but they are subject to security checks. Prescription drugs should be readily available. **Red Channels** are for people who have something to declare or are unsure.

Getting to London from the Airports

Stop first at the airport **Tourist Information Centres (TIC)** for a free package of useful and interesting information.

From Heathrow:

By underground or tube (subway) The Picadilly line goes direct and takes about 45 minutes. Its stations are Kensington, Knightsbridge, Park Lane (Hyde Park Corner) Picadilly, Covent Garden and Bloomsbury (Russell Square).

By Airbus Bus No. A1 goes to Victoria Station and Bus No. A2 goes to Euston station. Each takes about an hour and each stops at all the major hotel areas on the way.

By Taxi It is advisable to take the familiar **London "black cab"** or the fare may be higher.

From Gatwick:

There is no subway but one can reach Victoria Station by either train or bus.

By train It takes 30 minutes, and trains depart every 15 minutes during the day and then every hour round the clock.

Money Savers

THE GREAT BRITISH HERITAGE PASS The British Travel Authority (BTA) calls it "the most comprehensive ticket on the market; and the more you use it, the better value you'll get out of it." Included with it is a gazetteer with opening times of interesting tour sites, places you want to visit as well as maps showing their locations. You may want to plan your tour around the pass which is valid for either 15 days or one month; and can be obtained from your travel agent, the British Travel Book Shop (See address below.), BTA offices in the U.S. and Canada, and from the British Travel Centre (BTC) in London. The BTC is an excellent resource as it offers the most comprehensive travel information and booking service in London plus a high-class gift shop. It is located at 12 Regent Street, Piccadilly Circus, London SW1Y 4PQ.

THE BRITRAIL PASS The BritRail Pass is another travel bargain but it cannot be bought in Britain. **It must be bought in your own country before you leave. It offers unlimited rail travel in England, Scotland and Wales.** Other offerings are BritRail Flexipass, Youth Pass, Consecutive Day Pass, BritRail/Drive and the new BritFrance Pass which offers unlimited rail travel on all British Rail and French Railway Services. There's also a ScotRail Pass which gives unlimited rail travel in Scotland and a 20% discount on sailings to the Orkney and Shetland Islands. Full details on all of these can be obtained from a travel agent.

THE UK AIRPASS The UK Airpass is another discount fare card that **must be purchased in the US at least seven days prior to arrival in Britain.** It is for travel on British Airways, direct flights within Britain and the Channel Islands. **Reservations must be made when the ticket is issued.**

O.A.P. If you are 60 or over, look for **an "O.A.P." or "Concessions for Old Age Pensioners"** sign at ticket offices. By showing a proof of birth (a driver's license or passport) you can pay a lower price. **Students** also can get a break by showing their University student cards.

VISITOR TRAVELCARD Another travel bargain that must be purchased in your own country. This gives unlimited travel on almost all the London Bus and Underground systems and even the Piccadilly Line link to all terminals at Heathrow Airport, the Docklands Light Railway and British Rail Network SouthEast services within the London area.

ELDERHOSTEL Elderhostel, a non-profit educational organization, offers low-cost academic programs in Britain for people 60 and over. Accompanying spouse must be at least 50. It's a great opportunity to learn about the culture and traditions of Britain. The courses are not for credit and there are no grades. The classes include field trips and there's the opportunity of extending a stay with the purchase of an add-on sightseeing tour. Send for Elderhostel's International Catalog at Elderhostel, 75 Federal Street, Boston, MA 02100.

THE RIGHT TIME And finally, the "biggest bargain" of all according to the British Travel Authority: "You can save as much as 50% if you come between October and March — especially if a stay is for two nights or more. In B&B's and guest houses payment is generally required in cash — they do not usually accept credit cards."

Weather

The average daily temperature in Britain as furnished by the British Meteorological Office is:

	Jan	Feb	Mar	Apr	May	June	July	Aug	Sept	Oct	Nov	Dec
C°	4	4	6	9	12	15	16	16	14	11	7	5
F°	39	39	43	48	54	59	60	60	57	52	45	41

Britain has cool summers and mild winters. Prevailing SW winds, even in winter, bring warm air from the Gulf Stream allowing dwarf palms to grow in southwestern England. Palms can be also be seen growing outdoors in Wales and parts of Ireland.

It may rain or **spritz** at any time of the year so be prepared because it can get to be bone-cold even in summer on cloudy, rainy days. Clothing that can be layered is effective for keeping out the cold. An over-the-shoulder lightweight plastic bag filled with an extra long-sleeved shirt, a pullover or a sweater and a lightweight raincoat and folding umbrella would protect you **"if the weather is not too clever"** (if the weather doesn't cooperate) from **dirty, filthy or beastly weather** (bad weather). **"Raining like Billy-O"** means it is raining cats and dogs. Billy-O refers to William the Conqueror, who overran the country like a storm.

Don't expect full days of sunshine. In fact, the weather reporters on radio will say **"Outbreaks of sunshine expected**

this afternoon." much like "Showers expected this afternoon." is reported in America. Your camera should be at the ready whenever the sun is out because that may be the last bit of sunshine for the day.

OTHER WEATHER WORDS

lashing down — pouring down
pea-souper — a London fog
pelting rain — pouring rain
poor man's weather-glass — the scarlet pimpernel
    flower that loses its flowers when rain is near
rain-wash — soil washed away by rain
scud of wind — gust of wind
snow break — snow melt
sprat weather — name for the dark days of November
    and December
punishing rain — unending rain

Electricity Different?

Yes it is. A converter is necessary because **the standard voltage throughout the country is 240 volts AC, 50 HZ cycles** (America's is 115 to 120 volts AC, 60 cycles).

Medical Insurance Necessary?

Yes. Many people have the idea that if you become ill in Britain, your treatments will be free. **Not true!** The only treatment that is free is emergency treatment requiring out-patient treatment at **National Health Service Accident and Emergency Departments** of hospitals. The BTA strongly advises that one take out adequate insurance coverage before traveling to Britain. Check this out with your travel agent. Also, should you need more prescription drugs, you should carry a copy of your prescription plus a cover letter from your doctor. Drugs should be described by their generic names in case American brands are not available. Also, it may be necessary that the drugs be prescribed by a British doctor before a **chemist** (pharmacist) will fill the prescription. There is a fee for the dispensation of medicines on prescription.

If you're **"feeling poorly"** (feeling too sick), to see a **National Health Service doctor,** ask a telephone operator for the nearest **surgery** (doctor's office). For light ailments, a **dispensing chemist** (pharmacy) will be able to help.

They have window signs saying they have a **dispensary** inside. Some stores which only sell toiletries and related goods are called **Chemists or Drugstores** to distinguish themselves from **Pharmacies.** **"BOOTS"** are well known **"chemist's shops."** **For emergencies, dial 999** and ask for **"Ambulance."** If you can get there yourself, go to the nearest hospital **Casualty Department** (Emergency).

What to Do When Other Difficulties Arise

The U.S. Embassy, with phone service 24 hours a day, is your first line of defense.

1. They will replace a lost or stolen passport but you must have a police report and proof of citizenship.

2. If your money is stolen, you will be helped to contact relatives or friends who can send you money via the consulate; or they'll put you in touch with local groups who assist travelers.

3. If you have no way home, they will buy you an airline ticket for a promissory note. Your passport will be restricted until the ticket is paid.

4. If a friend or relative fails to arrive home on time, call **CITIZEN'S EMERGENCY CENTER, WASHINGTON, D.C. (202-647-5225)** and give the missing person's name and itinerary.

5. In case of illness, doctors and hospitals will be recommended.

6. If you are jailed for any reason, Consular officers can help to a degree. Someone from the Consular office will visit you to see that you are in good health and are being fed properly. You will also be advised regarding your rights and will be given a

list of lawyers. The Consulate cannot interfere, however, with the British legal process but will continue to be in touch with you until your case has been resolved.

Don't Forget Your Driver's License!

A usual driver's license or an International Driving Permit are allowed for driving in Britain for up to 12 months; and most rental companies usually require that you must have had your driving license for at least a year and that the rental charge (passenger liability, third party, fire and theft insurance) be paid in advance. Also, car rental conditions vary. Some companies will not rent to those under 21 or 25 and those over 70 or 75. It is wise to check in advance.

Important Tips

A computer is a great help in trip planning as information can be entered and altered easily. When your plans are complete, **make three copies**: Keep one in your pocket or purse, one in your luggage and give one to a relative or friend at home. You may want to include the following information in a form that is easy to read:

PLANE RESERVATION INFORMATION
Date Leaving................ Date Returning..............
Airport..................... Airport.....................
Terminal.................... Terminal....................
Check-in time............... Check-in time...............
Flight Number............... Flight Number...............
Flight Time................. Flight Time.................
Arrival Time................ Arrival Time................

PHOTO COPIES OF IMPORTANT PAPERS With a copy on hand of plane tickets, credit card and your passport's title page, time and worry will be saved should you lose your tickets, credit cards or passport.

USEFUL ADDRESSES IN THE U.S.:

British Tourist Authority (BTA)
551 Fifth Avenue, Suite 701
New York, N.Y. 10176
212-986-2200
There are also BTA offices in Atlanta, Georgia, Chicago, and
Los Angeles.

BritRail Travel Intl. Inc.
1500 Broadway
New York, N.Y. 10036
Phone: (212) 575-2667

British Travel Bookshop
Box 1224
Clifton, N.J. 07012
Phone: (800) 448-3039
Also: (212) 765-0890
This is a distribution center and has a brochure from which
you can order maps, videos and guides to all of Britain.

Northern Ireland Tourist Board
551 Fifth Avenue Suite 701
New York, N.Y. 10176
Phone: (800)-326-0036

USEFUL ADDRESSES IN THE U.K.:

British Travel Centre
12 Regent St.
London SW1

Wales Tourist Board
at the British Travel Centre
(071) 409-0969

Scottish Tourist Board
17 Cockspur St.
London SW1
(071) 930-8661

Northern Ireland Tourist Board
11 Berkeley St.
London W1
(071) 493-0601

Knowledge is of two kinds.
We know a subject ourselves, or we know
where we can find information upon it.
—Samuel Johnson, *Boswell's Life*

CHAPTER THREE

GOOD TO KNOW

This chapter deals with ways to make your stay in Britain more rewarding.

Look to the Right!

Remember to **look to the right first** before stepping off a **kerb** (curb) in the U.K. This warning is now painted at street crossings in London; an excellent safeguard for the many Americans tourists who are used to looking to the left first.

Post Offices

Post offices are open from 9 to 5:30, Mondays-Fridays and from 9 to 12:30, Saturdays. Stamps are also sold at **"Postal Centre"** stamp dispensers in large stores and major tourist attractions. **Newsagents** (newsdealers) who sell postcards, may also have stamps. For **posting** (mailing) letters, find a **red-painted letter-box** (mailbox).

POST WORDS (MAIL WORDS)

book-post — book mailing
carriage forward — payment on delivery
express messenger — special delivery man
G.P.O. — general post office
letter box or pillar mail box — mail box
ordinary letter post — regular mail
packet — package

recorded delivery — registered mail
shopping by post — mail order shopping
subpost office — post office branch

Telephone

British Telecom and Mercury Communications provide the telephones in Britain. The new pushbutton public phones accept coins of any denomination and there are also **Phonecard payphones** which accept pre-paid Phonecards. British Telecom Phonecards can be obtained from post offices and shops displaying the green Phonecard sign. **Mercury phones** are operated by your own credit cards or by special **Mercury telephone cards** obtainable from newsagents and nearby shops. It is cheaper to phone the U.S. from a **call box** (telephone booth) or a friend's home phone because some hotels, as in the U.S., can add hefty surcharges to phone bills.

TELEPHONE TALK

dialling tone — dial tone
directory enquiries — telephone book
engaged tone — busy signal
exchange line — telephone line
Give me a ring. — Call me.
hush line — hot line
I'll give you a tinkle. or I'll ring you up. — I'll call you.
internal telephone — in-house phone
INSTRUMENT OUT OF ORDER—PHONE OUT OF ORDER
Just ring up on the phone first. — Phone ahead first.
not on the telephone — unlisted
reverse the charges — call collect
rang off — hung up
rang through — called or phoned
telephone kiosk, box or call-box — phone booth
telephone talkers — obscene phone callers
Tell him I rang. — Tell him I called.

The Exchange — The Telephone Company
the blower (telephone) — the horn
The line is engaged. — The line is busy.
to put someone through — to put someone on
to ring someone soonest — to phone someone immediately
trunk call — toll call, long distance
trunks — long distance operator
was rung up — was called
work number — business number

Q: What Time Is 18 Hours? A: 6:00 P.M.

In Britain, as in all of Europe, the 24-hour clock is used on all official documents and timetables but not in general conversation. To use it, subtract 12 from any number greater than twelve. Example: **18-12=6**.

TIME WORDS

ack emma and **pip emma** — A.M. and P.M.
after the prescribed hour — after hours
alarm calls — wake-up calls
anti-clockwise — counter-clockwise
around half seven — around half-past seven
at the third stroke — at the third chime
B.S.T. — British Summer Time
backalong — a while back
between the lights, between two lights or **the half dark** — twilight
early on — early
evenfall — dusk
first light — dawn
five and twenty past — twenty-five after
fixed up — made a date
fixture — appointment
fortnight — two weeks
for donkey's years — for ages

getting past it — nearing retirement

Half a mo! — Half a sec!

He's knocking on for 60. — He's getting close to 60.

I shan't be a minute. — I won't be a minute.

in a tick — in a sec

in date order — in chronological order

in two two's — in two secs

It's coming up 11. — It's almost 11.

It's gone 11. — It's past 11.

It's just going 11. — It's just about 11.

It's just on 11. — It's 11 sharp.

like a clock — like clockwork

Mind the time! — Keep track of the time!

Monday week — a week from Monday

not beyond half an hour — not more than half an hour

on the instant — in a moment

overdated — out of date

seconds-hand — second hand (on clock dial)

sharp-on-the-button — on time exactly

since the year dot — since the year one

spot cash or **cash on the nail** — cash on the barrelhead

summer-tide — summer time

to take time by the forelock — to grasp an opportunity

the next day but one — in two days

"Tick-tack" says a small clock — "Tick tock" for both

"Tick-tock" says a large clock.

Banks

Banks are generally open from 9:30 to 3:30 weekdays (10 to 3:30 in Northern Ireland) but sometimes they stay open an extra hour. Most of the major banks are also open Saturdays. Some banks in Scotland and Northern Ireland take a lunch break of one hour. Automatic teller machines are also available. Check with your bank here whether it is linked to a British bank system.

If you need British currency and the banks are closed, remember that branches of banks are open 24 hours a day at all major airports. You can also be helped at any Thomas Cook office, exchange offices in major department stores, at counter desks in large hotels, at the many independent Bureaux de Change and at the British Travel Centre in London. You are advised to check in advance the rate of exchange and the commission charges. Bureaux de Change must show rates of commission at or near to the entrance of premises. Look for a **BTA Code of Conduct** display. Of all exchange locations, banks charge the smallest commission, so it is advisable to wait until they are open. If your bank is affiliated with a British bank, there will be no charge for **cheques** (checks) or other currencies.

BANKING AND FINANCE WORDS

Accounts Department — Accounting Department
banker's order — bank check
banking account — bank account
bullion van — armored truck
C.A. (chartered accountant) — C.P.A. (certified public accountant)
bullion bank clerk — treasury bank clerk
cheque — check
cheque clerk — accounts clerk
cheeseparing — cutting costs
City Guarantee Society — Banker's Insurance Company
clearing banks — bank clearing houses
the comings-in — income
corn rent — rent paid in grain
cost-free — free of charge
costing meeting — financial meeting
counter clerk — teller
crack credit — no credit

delinquent notice — overdraft
earnest money or **earnest penny** — a deposit
feeling the draught — bad economic conditions
financial boffins — financial wizards
going up the spout — going under
hedge buying — hedging
insurance scheme — insurance plan
investment firm subscribers — investors
keenest rates — lowest rates
a long figure — a high price
money pusher — bank clerk
peppercorn rent — nominal rent
Permanent Building Society — Savings and Loan
price held — price set or frozen
pricey — costly
pushed for ready — desperate for money
at short sight — payable on presentation
stand surety — vouch for
stock jobber — stock broker
strong box — safety deposit box
a swoop — a surprise audit
takings — net
three-monthly — quarterly
up to snuff — up to declared value

MORE BANKING AND FINANCE WORDS

Backwardation is a percentage paid by a seller of stock for keeping back its delivery until the following account.

Bill of Adventure is a note by a merchant stating that goods shipped by him in his name are the property of another who assumes the **"adventure"** (any risks involved).

A dripping roast is an expression meaning "a source of easy and continuous profit."

A letter of indication is a banker's letter requesting

foreign bankers to accept the bearer's **circular note** (letter of credit).

A **money scrivener** is one who does financial business for clients.

To waddle is London Stock Exchange slang for becoming a defaulter.

A **walk clerk** is one who goes around collecting the proceeds of banks.

British Money

In 1971, England adopted **"decimalization"** and the £ sterling (pound) was divided into 100 pence, known generally as **"p"** (pronounced **pee**) Coins are **1p, 2p, 5p, 10p, 20p, 50p and £1.**

All are round in shape except for the **20p** (small in size) and **50p** (large), which are seven-sided and silver in color. **Paper bills are £1 (Scotland only), £5, £10, £20, and £50.** A price is usually given as **"One-fifty"** meaning "One pound, fifty pence" Anything below a pound, is said as **"80p"** or **"80 pence."**

The British Tourist Authority advises that **credit cards are not widely accepted in Britain**, especially at **B & B's** (Bed and Breakfasts); and that retailers have the option to charge more for purchases and services obtained by a credit card.

MONEY WORDS

bawbee — half penny (Scotland)
be in low water — be short
crown or **crown-piece** — five shillings
bob — shilling
feeling chuft — feeling flush
fiddler's money — small coins (sixpences)
fiver — five pounds
guinea — 1 pound plus 5 pence
half crown — old coin that was worth 2 shillings, 6 pence

half-sovereign — old gold coin that was worth 10 shillings
lolly or **shekels** — moolah
lump of brass — pile of loot
making a good penny — making lots of money
monkey bag — small money bag hung round the neck
note-case — wallet
on tick or **on the slate** — on the cuff
pots of money — stacks of money
quid, nicker, sovereign, or quidlet — one pound
the queer or **slush** — counterfeit money
to run up a score — to run up a debt
shilling — 12 pence
stoney or **skint** — stoney broke
tenner — ten pound note
tuppence or tuppenny — twopence or two-penny

VAT: (Value Added Tax)

There is a national **VAT** charged on all hotel, restaurant and **car hire** (rental car) bills and as these are considered services, this VAT cannot be refunded. The VAT can be refunded on purchases made in **shops** (stores) that offer the **Retail Export Scheme** (Plan) or the **Over-the-Counter Scheme.** When purchasing something in these shops, ask for a **Retail Export Scheme Form** and how you can get a refund as refunds can be made by **cheque** (check) or credit card. Certain refunds can be obtained in cash on departure at **"VAT Refund Booths"** at London Heathrow, London Gatwick, Manchester, Glasgow and Stansted Airports. It is wise to keep all your purchases in a separate bag because customs may ask to see them.

Tipping

HOTELS The service charge included in a bill is usually 10 to 15%

RESTAURANTS A 10 to 15% service charge is usually added

to restaurant bills plus the VAT, so a tip requires some small change.

PORTERAGE (Porter service): 50 to 75p per suitcase.

TAXIS 10 to 15% of the fare. Generally one waits in a queue for a taxi.

HAIRDRESSERS £2 plus 50p to the assistant who washes your hair.

Facilities For the Disabled

Free information and advice on suitable hotels and other facilities is available from the Holiday Care Service, 2 Old Bank Chambers, Station Road, Horley, Surrey RH6 9HW, England. BTA offices have Holiday Care Service enquire forms.

The Chunnel

One can now cross over to France in 35 minutes from Folkestone, West Sussex, to Calais, France, 24 hours a day, every day of the year, by **Eurotunnel**, popularly known as the "**Chunnel**." The Chunnel was inaugurated on June 6, 1994 by Queen Elizabeth II and French President Francois Mitterrand. The trains run at speeds of up to 187 mph at depths of from 80 to 150 feet below the sea bed. They provide three types of service: **Cargo**, which **carries trucks** on double-decked train cars; **Le Shuttle**, which is a **car-, bus- and motorcycle-ferry service**; and **Eurostar**, train service for "**foot traffic**," that is, travelers without a vehicle. Le Shuttle will run every 15 minutes and each train carries up to 180 cars. No reservations are necessary. Passport and customs checks will be done before boarding.

This royal throne of kings, this scepter'd isle,
This blessed plot, this earth, this realm,
this England...
—Shakespeare's *Richard II*, Act II, Scene I

CHAPTER FOUR

EXPLANATIONS, DERIVATIONS, ABBREVIATIONS, EMBLEMS and INVENTIONS

There Are Over 5,000 Islands in "This Scepter'd Isle!"

The largest island consists of **England, Wales and Scotland,** the next largest consists of **Northern Ireland** and **The Republic of Ireland.** Then there are more than 5000 much smaller islands, the largest being the **Isle of Man** in the Irish Sea and the **Isle of Wight** at the southermost part. The rest are clumped into groups: the **Hebrides** (500), the **Orkneys and Shetlands** (190 altogether) Channel Islands (four main islands and innumerable islets) and the **Scilly Islands** (around 140). Total area, 120,755 sq. miles. The British Isles are separated from Western Europe by the **English Channel,** now traversed by the "Chunnel" and the **North Sea.**

"The U.K.," "Great Britain," and "The British Isles." Are They One and the Same?

No! **"The U.K."** and **"Great Britain"** are short for **"The United Kingdom of Great Britain and Northern Ireland"** which encompasses: **England, Wales, Scotland and Northern Ireland,** areas under British rule. **"The British Isles,"** is a geographic term that includes the independent **"Republic of Ireland."** All were separate countries until 1282 when England annexed Wales by conquest. Scotland was added in 1603 when James VI of Scotland became James I of England, however, Scotland kept its own parliament until Queen Anne's reign (1665-1714). Then an **Act of Union,** 1707, joined the two parliaments with the name **Great Britain.** All of Ireland joined Great Britain by another **Act of Union** in 1801, changing the name to **United Kingdom of Great Britain and Ireland**; but then, in 1922, when southern Ireland became a dominion with its own parliament, the name changed to what it is today, **The United Kingdom of Great Britain and Northern Ireland** or **The U.K.**

Perpendicular? What's That?

In viewing the beautiful buildings, churches, Roman ruins and stone and iron age artifacts in Britain, you will encounter many descriptions such as: "The Church of St. John the Baptist in Cirencester is one of the most beautiful **"Perpendicular"** churches in England." Other puzzling words associated with architecture would be **"Decorated," "Baroque,"** and **"Palladian."** Associated with Roman ruins are words such as **"Principium"** and **"Tessellated;"** and **"barrow"** and **"henge"** with Stone and Iron Age artifacts.

ARCHITECTURAL AND ARCHAEOLOGICAL WORDS

apse — a large semi-circular, arched recess usually found at the altar end of a church

bailey — usually the fortified courtyard of a castle.

barbican — an outer area, usually a tower, to defend the entrance to a castle

Baroque — meaning "irregularly shaped." It's an Italian style that was popular in 17th century Europe, and is characterized by extravagant ornamentation.

barrow or **tumulus** — a burial mound

cairn — a pile of stones atop a prehistoric grave

caryatid — a column in the shape of a female figure.

chancel — the altar area of any church.

Classical — a style borrowed from ancient Greek and Roman buildings

clerestory — the area above the main body of the church **(the nave)** which has a series of windows; these are often seen when a roof has been lifted to heighten the nave

corbel — a stone or brick wall projection to support a weight

crenellated — loopholes atop castles as defensive positions.

cruciform chamber — any church built in the shape of a cross

crypt — a burial chamber beneath the chancel of a church

curtain wall — the outer wall of a castle

Decorated — the second stage of English Gothic architecture, the 14th century, characterized by elaborate and rich decorations, particularly swirling or leaf-like patterns in the windows

donjon — or a **keep**, a strong central tower to which a garrison retreated when hard pressed

dykes — concentric ditches, similar to moats, around prehistoric forts.

Early English — the form of Gothic in which the pointed arch was first used in Britain...toward the end of the 12th century

Elizabethan — the mixed style that succeeded Gothic, a sort of Renaissance/Gothic mixture; often Tudor.

folly — a structure with no architectural purpose, built just for decoration

gallery-graves — oblong underground graves

gargoyle — a projecting waterspout usually from a

roof gutter, carved in the form of a grotesque human or animal

Georgian — the period of the four Georges (1714-1810) which brought a return to architecture with beauty of form and proportion

Gothic — a style of architecture with high pointed arches and clustered columns. It became subdivided into **Early English, Decorated** and finally to **Perpendicular**

Gothic Revival — revival of the Gothic in the late 18th and 19th centuries

ha-ha — a sunken ditch edging a park or garden

half-timbered — having walls with wooden frames and brick or plaster fillings

henge monuments — stones set into the ground, the name "henge" is taken from Stonehenge

Jacobean — of the period of James I of England (1603-25), often a mixture of Gothic and Classical

keystone — a wedge-shaped stone crowning an arch.

Lady Chapel — a chapel dedicated to the Virgin Mary, usually behind the high altar

lancet — tall narrow pointed arches or windows.

loggia — a covered open arcade or colonnade

lich gate or **lych gate** — a roofed churchyard gate under which biers are rested before going to the cemetery. Originally, the priest met the coffin here for the first part of the burial service; now he usually meets the coffin at the church porch.

megaliths — large blocks of stone

menhirs — ancient monumental standing stones

mosaic — Roman Age designs for walls and floors composed of small colored tesserae (fragments) of marble, glass or pottery

nave — the main body or central aisle of a church.

Neo-Classical — mid-18th century revival of the Classical style

ogam or **ogham script** — ancient Celtic alphabet of straight lines meeting or crossing the edge of a stone.

oriel window — a sort of bay window supported by **corbels** (brackets) projecting from an upper floor.

Palladian — a style of architecture introduced to England by **Andrea Palladio** (1518-80). These houses are very symmetrical and often have a **pedimented** (triangular gable over the portico) central block. Some also have wings.

passage graves — circular mounds of earth or stone which are entered by a long, narrow passage

Perpendicular — the last stage of English Gothic (late 14th to mid-16th century), a simpler style marked by vertical window-tracery, depressed or four- center arch, fan-tracery vaulting and panelled walls

porticullis — a strong castle gate that can be raised and lowered

principium — the general's quarters in a Roman camp

Regency — the years 1810-20 when George IV, Prince of Wales, was named Prince Regent (acting King) because of the insanity of his father, George III

reredos — a wooden or stone screen usually set behind an altar

rood-screen — an ornamental wooden or stone screen separating the chancel from the nave of a church. This is usually found in cathedrals and very large churches of monastic origin. It was usually topped by a large crucifix and the figures of the Our Lady and St. John. These were demolished during the Reformation.

rose window — a circular Gothic church window with tracings resembling the petals of a rose

tessellated — a Roman wall or floor mosaic made up of tiny pieces of stone, tile or marble embedded in cement

THE UNITED KINGDOM
Regions—Counties—Islands

SCOTLAND
*Capital: Edinburgh
Island Councils
  1 Shetland Islands
  2 Orkney Islands
  3 Western Isles
Regions
  4 Highland
  5 Grampian
  6 Tayside
  7 Central
  8 Fife
  9 Lothian
  10 Strathclyde
  11 Borders
  12 Dumfries and Galloway
NORTHERN IRELAND
*Capital: Belfast
  13 Londonderry
  14 Antrim
  15 Tyrone
  16 Fermanagh
  17 Armagh
  18 Down
ENGLAND
*Capital: London
The North
  19 Northumberland
  20 Cumbria
  21 Tyne and Wear
  22 Durham
  23 Cleveland
  24 North Yorkshire
The North West
  25 Lancashire (Lancs)
  26 Merseyside
  27 Greater Manchester
  28 Cheshire
Yorkshire (Yorks) & Humberside
  29 West Yorkshire
  30 South Yorkshire
  31 Humberside
  32 Lincolnshire (Lincs)
East Midlands
  33 Derbyshire,
  34 Nottinghamshire (Notts)
  35 Leicestershire (Leics)
  36 Northamptonshire (Northants)
West Midlands
  37 Shropshire (Salop)
  38 Staffordshire (Staffs)
  39 West Midlands
  40 Hereford & Worcestershire (Worcs)
  41 Warwickshire
East Anglia
  42 Norfolk
  43 Suffolk
The South East
  44 Cambridgeshire (Cambs)
  45 Bedfordshire (Beds)
  46 Oxfordshire (Oxon)
  47 Buckinghamshire (Bucks)
  48 Hertfordshire (Herts)
  49 Essex
  50 Berkshire (Berks)
  51 Greater London
  52 Surrey
  53 Kent
  54 West Sussex
  55 East Sussex
The South West
  56 Gloucestershire (Glos)
  57 Avon
  58 Wiltshire (Wilts)
  59 Cornwall
  60 Devon
  61 Somersetshire
  62 Dorset
  63 Hampshire (Hants)
WALES
*Capital: Cardiff
  64 Gwynedd
  65 Clwyd
  66 Powys
  67 Dyfed
  68 West Glamorgan
  69 Mid Glamorgan
  70 South Glamorgan
  71 Gwent
ISLANDS
  72 Isle of Man
  73 Isles of Scilly
  74 Isle of Wight
  75 Channel Islands

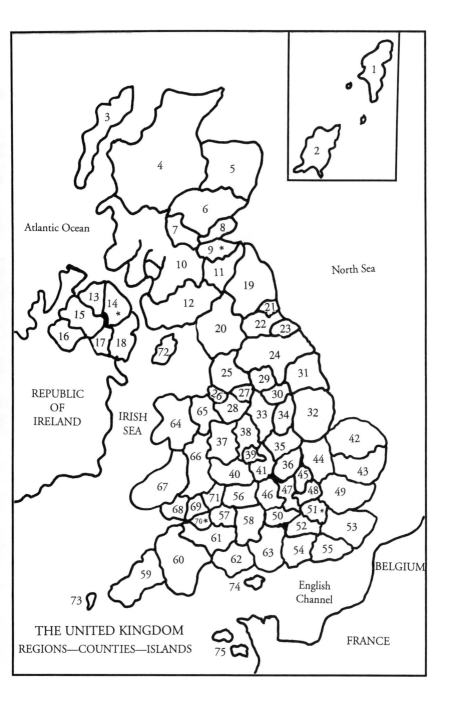

THE UNITED KINGDOM
REGIONS—COUNTIES—ISLANDS

tracery — ornamental openwork in Gothic windows

transcept — the part of the church which is at right angles to the nave

Tudor — period when the Welsh family of Tudor, 1485-1603, held the throne of England. Brick is the material most used.

Victorian — 1837 to 1901, mostly Gothic Revival and Greek Revival architecture

wattle-and-daub — interlaced flexible twigs plastered with a mixture of clay, chopped straw and horsehair which early man used for walls and fences

U.K. Regions, Counties, Islands and Capitals

The twelve areas of the United Kingdom are indicated in the key for the United Kingdom map. Their subdivisions are called **"regions"** in Scotland and **"counties"** in England, Ireland and Wales. **Abbreviations** of county names are included as many maps do not provide full names. The locations of **capitals** are indicated by asterisks. The black area in the center of Northern Ireland's counties is **Lough Neagh** (Lake Neagh).

Meanings of Suffixes on British Town Names

Suffixes on British town names are puzzling. When they end in **"gate"** (High**gate**), **"pool"** (Black**pool**), or **"bridge"** (Iron**bridge**), one can easily infer that the towns grew up near a gate, pool, port or bridge. But whatever is a **"by"** or a **"wick"**?

-**by** as in Der**by**, Kir**by**, Ten**by**, Nase**by** is from the Old English **"bu'y"** meaning **"to dwell,"** and it came to mean a habitation, village or town.

-**down** as in Ash**down** sounds as if it should be a low-lying area but instead it's the opposite. It's from the Old English **"du'n"** meaning a hill or expanse of high ground.

-**ford** as in Ox**ford** and Chelms**ford** is from Old French **"ford"** meaning a shallow place in a river where a man can cross by wading.

-**ham** as in Oak**ham** and Lewis**ham** is from Old English **"Ha'm"** meaning **"home"** which later changed to town or village.

-**heath** as in Black**heath**, is from Middle English meaning a piece of waste ground.

-**ley** as in Aud**ley** and Bever**ley** is from the Old French **"lai"** meaning a lake or a pool.

-**moor** as in Dart**moor** is from the Old English **"mo'r"** meaning an enclosed tract of waste ground.

-**stead** as in Hamp**stead** and New**stead** is Middle High German **"stede"** meaning place or town.

-**ton** as in Pres**ton**, Plymp**ton** and Knigh**ton** is another surprise as it sounds like "town." Instead, it's from the Middle English **"tunne"** meaning cask or liquid measure.

-**wick** as in Ha**wick** and War**wick** is Old English **"wic"** meaning dwelling place.

-**wood** as in Sher**wood** and Brant**wood** is the British word for woods.

Very old market towns have **"Market"** as a first name: **Market Bosworth, Market Drayton** and **Market Harborough;** and many situated near rivers take on the river name: Stoke-on-**Trent**, Hay-on-**Wye**, Hurworth-on- **Tees** and Kingston-upon-**Thames**.

Barton-in-the Beans! What's That? A: A British Village

British place names are fascinating. Dr. P.H. Reaney has delved deeply into the subject and the result is an intriguing book, *The Origin of English Place Names*. Barton-in-the-Beans is a Leicestershire village and name has a perfectly plausible etymology. **Barton** is an Old English name for a **farmstead** or **farmyard** and it being **"in-the-beans"** means it's in bean country and was named in 1659 when Leicestershire was blessed with a great abundance of peas and beans. Other odd names with interesting histories are:

Great Barr (Staffordshire) from the **Welsh "barr,"** a summit.

Horseington (Somerset) from Old English **"hor-spegna- tun,"** a village of horsekeepers or grooms.

Orchard (Dorsetshire) from the **Welsh "Argoed,"** a shelter of wood.

Plaxtol (Kent) from Old English **"pleg-stall,"** a play place.

Purps (Devonshire) from Old French **pourprise**, an enclosure.

Sapperton (Sussex) from Old English **"saperetun,"** a village of soap makers.

Sawrey (Lancashire) from Old Norse **"saurr,"** a muddy place.

Wookey Hole (Somerset) from Old English **"wocig,"** a snare)

Dr. Reaney explains how many names have not only lost their original meanings by attempts to give them "some semblance of sense" but in the process have an entirely different meaning. **Battersea** is an example. It sounds as if it were a place where heavy seas batter the land; instead, it was originally **"Beaduric's marshy island,"** then shortened to **Batrices-ege (693. A.D.), Batricheseye (1200), Batriseye (1366), Batersey (1408)** and finally **Battersea.** The name problems have been compounded, explains Dr. Reaney, by the means of similar sounds as interpreted by the numerous succeeding inhabitants of Britain: Celts, English, Scandinavians, Romans and French.

Many place names are derived from Celtic names for hills or mountains, **meneth, minid, mynydd and mynd—Longmynd** (Shropshire) and **Mynde** (Hertfortshire); and woods, **caito, cet, ciet, cit, cyt —Chittoe** (Wiltshire) and **Chithurst** (Sussex).

Some names came from rivers such as the river **Colne** (Essex) which has nearby villages called **Colne Engaine, Earls Colne, Wakes Colne** and **White Colne.** Scotland has towns called **Axe, Exe, Esk, Usk, Wiske**...all derived from **"Isca,"** meaning **"water."**

Many towns were named after people. **Wootton Wawen** (Warwickshire) is a corruption of the name of a Scandinavian, **Wagene de Wotton.** Some corruptions of French names are **Beer Hackett** (Devonshire) from **Haket de Bera; Papworth Everard** (Cambridgeshire) from **Everard de Beche; Poor Park** (Essex) from **William Lepuier;** and **Layer de la Haye** (Essex) from **Maurice de Haia.**

A Scandinavian nickname for a round-headed man—"kettle" (meaning "cauldron")—is remembered .in the names of many villages and towns such as **Ab Kettleby** and **Eye Kettleby** (Leicestershire) and **Ketsby, Kettleby** and **Kettlethorpe** (Lincolnshire).

Large and small towns can be followed by the Latin **"Magna"** or **"Parva"** as in **Ashby Magna** and **Ashby Parva** (Leicestershire); or preceded by **"Great," "Little"** and **"Much"** as in **Great Torrington** (Devonshire), **Little Gransden** (Cambridgeshire), and **Much Dewchurch** (Hertfordshire).

Some are combination towns using **"cum"** meaning "with:" as **Stone cum Ebony** (Kent). Others indicate position such as **Rinkinghall Superior** (Upper) and **Rinkinghall Inferior** (Lower or Nether) (Suffolk). **Aston Subedge** (Gloucestershire) is at the **"foot of the ridge." Thorpe sub Montem** (West Riding of Yorkshire) is at the **"foot of a mountain." Bradwell juxta Mare** (Essex) is **"next to the sea,"** and **Weston Super Mare** (Somerset) is **"on the sea."**

Welsh Names and Their Meanings

Many efforts have been made to preserve the Welsh language. The Welsh Language Society, founded in 1962, was especially militant in this respect, pushing for the teaching of Welsh in the schools. In 1981, this became a fact. Welsh is now part of the education curriculum.

Americans seeking "something different" will be charmed by the odd and hard to pronounce names as seen on shops and bilingual road signs. There should be no worry about language difficulties, however, as nearly everyone speaks English. Following are the meanings of some Welsh place names and some greetings.

PREFIX	PLACE NAME	MEANING
aber (mouth)	Abercraf	mouth of the river Craf
coed (wood)	Coed-y-Brenin	King's wood
eglys (a church)	Eglys y Drindod	Trinity Church
gelli (a grove)	Gelli-aur	golden grove
moel (a bare hill)	Moel Sych	dry, bare hill
nant (a stream)	Nantglyn	stream of the glen
pentre (a village)	Pentre Bont	village of the bridge
rhos (moorland)	Rhos-goch	red moorland
Ty (a house)	Ty-newydd	new house
ystrad (a valley)	Ystradowen	Owen's valley

SOME WELSH GREETINGS

Bore da — Good morning
Dydd da — Good day
Prynhawn da — Good afternoon
Nos da — Good night
Sut mac? — How are you?
Diolch — Thanks
Croeso — Welcome
Lechyd da! — Good health!

Heraldic Badges and Their Associations

Heraldic badges are emblems, which existed before heraldic shields came into use but are sometimes found on them with a motto, see Illustration I. They were used on **pennons** (flags) and seals and were used to designate a person or family. They were considered very important during dynastic wars, such as the War of the Roses. Herewith, the heraldic badges of England, Ireland, Scotland and Wales.

HERALDIC BADGES

SCOTLAND
The Thistle

ENGLAND
Yorkist White Rose
with
Lancastrian Red Rose

IRELAND
The Shamrock

The Daffodil

The Leek

WALES
The Red Dragon

ROSES A red and white rose combination is the badge of England, which dates from the marriage of Henry VII of the House of Lancaster to Elizabeth, daughter of Edward IV of the House of York, thus ending the War of the Roses. The Lancaster emblem was the red rose and that of York, was white.

SHAMROCKS Ireland's emblem is the shamrock. This dates from St. Patrick's crusade to explain the Christian Doctrine of the Holy Trinity to the pagans of Ireland and Britain. He picked up a shamrock to show that there were three leaves united on one stem: just as there were the Father, the Son and the Holy Spirit which made Christianity.

PURPLE THISTLE Scotland has revered purple thistles from when they saved Scotland from the Danes in the 11th Century. The legend is that Danes were about to capture a fortress by surprise by swimming shoeless across a moat, but the thistles there made them cry out in pain, thus warning the garrison.

THE LEEK, THE DAFFODIL AND THE RED DRAGON are Wales' three national symbols:

THE LEEK because legend has it that on **St. David's Day**, March 1, 640, the Welsh were victorious in repelling the Angles and Saxons who were trying to invade their land. To distinguish themselves from the enemy, they had placed leeks in their caps. Today, the leek is worn as a badge-cap by the Welsh Regiment in London.

THE DAFFODIL because it is one of the most common flowers of spring in Wales. It is worn and displayed on St. David's Day.

THE RED DRAGON Legend tells of the struggle between the **Red Dragon** (representing Wales) and the **White Dragon** (England) with the Red Dragon winning foretelling the victory of Wales made true by **Henry Tudor's** ascent to the throne as **Henry VII**. Henry VII was of Welsh descent and delighted the Welsh by incorporating the Welsh Red Dragon in the Royal arms. Later James I replaced it with the Scottish unicorn. The red dragon was placed on a flag again in 1959, when Queen Elizabeth commanded that the red dragon on a green and white field should be the Welsh flag. The words **"Y DDRAIC GOCH DDYRY CYCHWYN"** mean **"THE RED DRAGON LEADS THE WAY."**

Britain's Tradition of Labor and Invention

During Queen Victoria's reign (1819-1901), mainly because of its financial stability and Parliament's **laissez faire** doctrine (not intruding in the world of business), Britain was able to make advances in industry mainly because British manufacturers were quick to utilize inventions such as the steam engine and railroad, the Bessemer process which converted raw iron into steel, the power loom, the iron ship, steamships and underseas cables. Productivity climbed spectacularly. The products made possible by these inventions were exported to all parts of the world and Britain became so prosperous that by 1850, it was called **"the workshop of the world."** This was the Industrial Revolution and it eventually spread to Europe and the U.S.

The following are some of these inventions and where they can be seen:

FIRST IRON BRIDGE IN ENGLAND, 1777: Ironbridge (Shropshire) It spans the Severn River's great gorge.

FIRST SUCCESSFUL SMELTING OF IRON FROM COKE: In 1709, Abraham Derby invented the technique of smelting iron ore with coke at a Coalbrookdale suburb of Ironbridge Gorge (Shropshire). This is considered to be **the birthplace of the Industrial Revolution.**

WORLD'S FIRST PASSENGER TRAIN: Darlington (Durham) On September 27, 1825, George Stephenson drove the first fare-paying passenger steam train from Darlington to Stockton-on-Tees. It followed a man on a horse who carried a flag with a Latin inscription, **"Periculum privatum utilitas publica"** (The private danger is the public good). The train was named **"Locomotion No. 1"** and can be seen at the Railway Centre and Museum at the North Road station.

CROMPTON'S SPINNING MULE, Bolton, Cheshire, Greater Manchester. This invention revolutionized the cotton industry. At the Tonge Moor Textile Museum, one can also see **Arkwright's Water Frame** and **Hargreaves' Spinning Jenny**.

CARTWRIGHT'S POWER LOOM: Bradford (Yorkshire) has a memorial to Edmund Cartwright, in Cartwright Hall,

Lister Park. He was a clergyman with a bent for inventions. He also invented a wool-combing machine and helped Robert Fulton work out problems on the building the steamboat.

PORTLAND CEMENT: The Romans made Pozzuolanic cement from powdered limestone and volcanic ash in ancient England, but the English eventually lost the talent. In the early 1800's, Joseph Aspdin, a British bricklayer mixed together lime and clay and put this mixture through a number of other processes and got something he called Portland Cement because it looked to him like the fine stone quarried on the Isle of Portland.

How the U.S. Acquired the Potato, the Sandwich, the Apple, the Christmas Card

THE POTATO In the early 1500's, the Spanish conquerors who reached the Peruvian/Bolivian Andes found the Incas growing potatoes which they called **"papa."** The Spaniards called them **"patata"** and that has become **"potato."** When they took them back to Spain, they were first grown as an interesting plant; but by the end of the 17th century, they had spread throughout Europe and were a major food crop in Ireland. In 1613, some were shipped from England to Bermuda and from there to Virginia in 1621. Another source reports that potatoes were first grown at Londonderry, New Hampshire in 1719 from stock brought from Ireland and may be why they've been known as **"Irish potatoes."**

THE SANDWICH We owe the invention of the sandwich to the 4th Earl of Sandwich (1718-92) who would not leave the gaming tables for meals. When he got hungry, he would just order someone to bring him some food between two slices of bread.

THE APPLE OUR "AMERICAN AS APPLE PIE" APPLES? Yes, the Puritan Governor, John Endicott of the Massachusetts Bay Colony, brought over the first apple seeds in 1629. Later, the seeds a British ship captain had saved from an apple he was eating as his ship left London started the Pacific Northwest's apple empire. His name was Aemilius Simpson.

THE FIRST CHRISTMAS CARD. See Chapter Fifteen.

"Oranges and lemons," say the bells of St Clement's,
"You owe me five farthings," say the bells of St. Martin's,
"When will you pay me?" say the bells of Old Bailey,
"When I am rich," say the bells of Shoreditch."
—"London Bells," a child's nursery rhyme

CHAPTER FIVE

LONDON AND ENVIRONS

Londinium

London's history began in 43A.D. when the Roman Emperor Claudius swept across southeast Britain with his army to the Thames River. Sixty miles above the mouth of the Thames, there was a small village on firm ground called **Lud Hill** which the Romans took over. They renamed the area **"Londinium"** and protected it with massive walls going down to the river where they built **the first London Bridge.** The names of the Roman city gates still survive: Ludgate, Newgate, Aldgate, Cripplegate, and Billingsgate. This area is now the **City of London**, which is also called **"The City"** and **"the square mile."** It has streets named Cornhill, Poultry, Lombard and Jewry and is a business and financial quarter. In its midst are the remains of **Cripplegate Roman Fort** and the **Roman Temple of Mithras.** Mithras was the ancient **Persian God of Light,** whose worship was popular in the Roman Empire.

"London Bridge Is Falling Down"

This rhyme is said to date back to 1014 when King Olaf of Norway and his Vikings attacked London and pulled down the bridge that existed at that time.

The changing of the Guards.

London Bridge in the U.S.A.

Another London Bridge that was "falling down," that is, sinking into the Thames, was the one built in 1824 which could no longer handle city traffic. It was put up for sale so another could be built and was bought by Robert P. McCulloch, a California chain-saw magnate in 1968 as an attraction for Lake Havasu City, a community he was developing in the Arizona desert.

The Sacking, the Plague, the Great Fire, the Blitz

London has had a number of great disasters. Seventeen years after the Romans built Londinium, **Queen Boadicea** and her army sacked and burned a large area (See Chapter Eight). The Romans rebuilt the town and 6 roads radiating from it to what are today Chester, Colchester, Exeter, York, Bath and Canterbury. Around 410 A.D., when the Roman occupiers were recalled to Rome, London declined (See Chapter Eight). It recovered under leaders of succeeding invasions and later suffered and recovered from three great disasters: **The Great Plague of 1665, the Great Fire of 1666 and The Blitz** (the bombings during WWII). As England's capital city grew, it swallowed up a great many counties. These are called the **Home Counties**: Hertfordshire, Middlesex, Essex, Kent and Surrey. Today, the area of London encompasses 600 square miles.

London, as Home Base

London is like a candy box of favorite chocolates. There's so much to see and do that one can be hard put to decide what to pick first, especially if it's a first trip. Many **trippers** (tourists) make London their **"home base."** This allows them to see the sights of London and occasionally go off on day trips to outlying regions.

Transportation

It's easy to get around London. There's the **charabanc** or **tourist coach** (tour bus), and the **tube** or **underground** (subway). London's underground is the world's longest, in miles of track, and oldest. It was 100-years-old in 1963 and was an underground shelter during WWII. The major subway routes are displayed in tube stations, trains and most guide books; and the trains are noted for being very fast and efficient. London **hackney carriages** (taxicabs), the **famous black taxis**, have very courteous and informed drivers. Each driver and each taxi is licensed by the Public Carriage Office which has strict regulations to ensure the safety of passengers.

The Usual Sights

The usual sights one sees on a first trip are: **Westminster Abbey**, the **Tower Bridge**, the **Tower of London**, **Big Ben**, **St. Paul's Cathedral** with its American Chapel, **Westminster Abbey** where Britain's monarchs are crowned, **Buck House** (Buckingham Palace) with the **Changing of the Guard**, the **White Tower** with the **Crown Jewels**, Traff Square (Trafalgar Square)

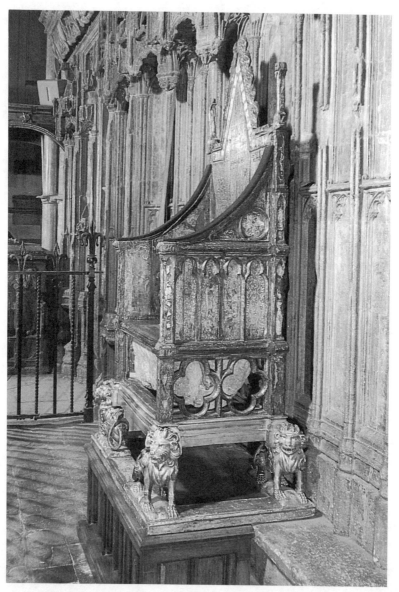

Coronation chair, Westminster Abbey, London (© Woodmansterne).

with **Nelson's Column** commemorating his victory over the French in 1805, **the V. and A.** (Victoria and Albert Museum), the **National Gallery, Madame Tussaud's Waxworks** and the **Tate Gallery**. (See Chapter Twenty.)

Some Unusual Sights

THE BRITISH MUSEUM LIBRARY Most people get a quick look at the **Assyrian bulls and lions, The Magna Charta** and **Egyptian mummies,** the **Rosetta Stone** and the **Elgin Marbles;** but they should also see the **library** which is considered one of the world's most beautiful rooms. **Karl Marx** and **Metternich** both **read** (studied) here. A must, is seeing the **Sutton Hoo Treasure,** 41 items of solid gold and a quantity of silverware found in the remains of a ship used to bury an Anglo-Saxon king on the grounds of the Sutton Hoo estate near Woodbridge, Suffolk.

THE BANK OF ENGLAND, Threadneedle St, EC2 is called **"The Old Lady of Threadneedle Street."** It's the central bank of England and has a museum with exhibits illustrating the history of the bank and a video explaining the role of the bank today. The same regiments that guard Buckingham Palace take turns guarding the bank at night: the five regiments of the Guards Brigade (Grenadier, Coldstream, Scots, Welsh, Irish), and other selected regiments, including Royal Artillery.

LORD'S CRICKET GROUND, St. John's Wood, is the home of cricket. It has a museum which houses the actual Ashes fought for by Britain and Australia (See Chapter Sixteen).

APSLEY HOUSE, Piccadilly, WI, near Hyde Park. Home of the Duke of Wellington and numbered **"No. 1 London"** in his **honour** (honor). It has a huge nude statue of Napoleon.

HIGHGATE CEMETERY, Swains Lane, has daily tours. Since it's opening in 1839 many of the famous were buried here: George Eliot, John Galsworthy, Michael Faraday, and Karl Marx.

DICKENS' HOUSE, 48 Doughty St is where he wrote *The*

Pickwick Papers, Oliver Twist, Nicholas Nickleby and *Barnaby Rudge.*

DR. JOHNSON'S HOUSE, 17 Gough Square is where Dr. Samuel Johnson compiled his famous **Dictionary**.

COVENT GARDEN, way back in time, was a **convent** area but the letter **"n"** somehow disappeared from the name. It was also for centuries, London's principal market for fruits, vegetables and flowers. In 1974, the market moved to Nine Elms, the south bank of the Thames; the old market buildings were transformed into shopping areas with bars and restaurants. Besides these attractions, Covent Garden has street entertainment and **public footpaths** for walking or picnicking. Some of the streets are even lit with 19th century gaslights.

THE HOUSES OF PARLIAMENT with the famous clock tower housing Big Ben, the 13 1/2 ton bell. The building covers eight acres. Underneath is St. Stephen's Hall, an ancient chapel where people can be married or have their children baptized. From the Stranger's Gallery, people can watch the Parliamentarians at work.

THE PUBLIC RECORD OFFICE, Chancery Lane. It's the home of the **Domesday (or Doomsday) Book**, the meticulous record ordered by William the Conqueror of all the holdings of all the inhabitants in 1086. His agents visited every manor and noted its owner, the people on the property and according to one account "there was not a single rood of land, nor an ox, or a cow, or a pig passed by, and that was not set down in the accounts." The agent also wrote down what each feudal lord ought to pay in taxes and feudal service. There is also **Shakespeare's Will** and the **Log of the Victory at the Battle of Trafalgar**.

CLEOPATRA'S NEEDLE, a pink granite obelisk (1500 BC) presented in 1819 to the British government by the Viceroy of Egypt. It wasn't erected until 1877.

LONDON CANAL MUSEUM, King's Cross, has a museum of the London canals and the canal peoples way of life. Two of the surviving canals, the Regent's Canal and the Grand Union

Canal, are accessible for pleasure trips today. "Little Venice," the canal area, is just north of Paddington railway station. There are lunch and dinner cruises.

Interesting Places and Activities

"SPEAKERS' CORNER" Sunday mornings, many go to hear the speakers at "Speaker's Corner," Hyde Park. This was the ancient site of the Tyburn Gallows where the condemned men were given a chance to speak before being hanged. Soap-box orators today discuss anything and everything.

THE PROMS are popular concerts at Royal Albert Hall where people can move about while hearing the music.

BRASS RUBBINGS Many cathedral visitors do their kneelings while making brass rubbings of memorial brasses (brass figures of Kings, Queens and Knights) to take home as wall decorations. It has become so popular that, to preserve the priceless brasses, exact replicas have been made for visitors to use. Brass-rubbing centers provide sheets of black or white paper and a gold, white or black heelball (a hard, waxy kind of crayon).

SHOPPING London is noted for shopping, so much so, that plane loads of Americans arrive daily just for the shopping. Young shoppers go to Carnaby Street, a pedestrian shopping street with black, yellow, white and orange tiles down its middle. Lovers of antiques go to Portobello Road. These are but a few of the many other London shopping centers: Oxford Street has big department stores among which are Selfridges and Marks & Sparks (Marks & Spencer); Regent Street for fine fashions and jewelry; Bond Street for fashions, leather products and jewelry; and Knightsbridge and Brompton Road with the luxurious Harvey Nichols Department Store for fashions and household goods and the world-famous Harrods, the largest department store in Europe. For more on shopping, see Chapter Nine.

THEATRES (THEATERS) London is called the theater capital of the world. There are 37 alone in the West End, the area around Leicester (pronounced Lester) Square. Others are on the South Bank near Waterloo and still others in the heart of the City. Half price tickets can be bought at the **half-price ticket office** in Leicester Square for that day only. One can book a seat in the "**Stalls**" or "**Pit**" of a theater. The stalls are the front and back sections of the ground floor. **Orchestra Stalls** are the first two or three rows. Seats can also be booked for **the dress circle** (mezzanine), **the upper circle** (the first balcony) and the **gallery** (the second balcony) from a **booking clerk** (ticket agent) at a ɔooking office or **kiosk** (ticket office). The **counter foil** is the ticket stub. **Candy butchers** (sellers) will go about the **gangways** (theater aisles) selling boxes of candy, ice cream and cartons of orange squash (orange soda). During **intervals** (intermissions) there are **stall's bars** (refreshment stands). Larger theaters have **crush bars** (buffets). (See Chapter Twenty.)

MORE THEATRE (THEATER) WORDS

the boards — the stage
a bomb — a hit (a bomb is a failure in the U.S.)
a comic turn or **a comedy chat** — a comedy routine
the cruncher — the punchline
the principal boy — usually a well-endowed girl playing Prince Charming in the Pantos (Pantomimes)
a star turn — the star
a straight play — a play sans music
a top-liner — a headliner
the try it on the dog audience — the preview audience
a turn—a performer

RESTAURANTS Foods from everywhere in the world can be sampled in London restaurants. It's easy to know if one can afford to eat in a restaurant of one's choice because restaurants are obligated to display their menus and prices on the outsides of their establishments, however, one must ask if the price includes a service charge and cover charge. Many offer fixed-price menus (see Chapter Eleven).

TEA Traditional afternoon teas are served in many of the top hotels. (Chapter Eleven tells all about tea.)

Day Trips from London
When leaving London on an excursion, one is said to be **going down**. When one returns, it is called **going up**. This expression came into use when trains first came into existence. The **railway companies** (railroad companies) called their trains to London **"Up-Line/trains"** and those leaving London, **"Down-Line/trains."** This use of **"up"** and **"down"** became a part of the everyday language of the inhabitants. The British always **go up to town** and **go down from town**; and **up from the country** and **down into the country**. (For more on trains, see Chapter Seven.)

Day trips can easily be taken from London. These are but a few of the many interesting sites in England that are within a day's reach of London. On the way to and from these sites there are magnificent views of the enchanting English countryside.

ARUNDEL CASTLE, Sussex, is a mecca for artists because it's so beautiful. It has a great art collection; and during the last week of August each year, the castle hosts the **Arundel Festival** which attracts artists from all over the world.

BATH, Avon The remains of the Roman Baths are a great attraction and should not be missed.

BRIGHTON, Sussex. Most people head for the Royal Pavilion in this famous resort town. It's an incredible Hindu-Gothic-Chinese building built by King George IV when he was Prince of Wales. There he lived with his morganatic wife, Mrs. Fitzherbert. Antique hunters will love **The Lanes**, winding narrow streets filled with tiny shops jam-packed with antiques.

HAMPTON COURT PALACE, Middlesex. The unfortunate Cardinal Wolsey built this palace in 1514 and it was so grand it put Henry the VIII's palaces to shame. Realizing his mistake, Wolsey presented the palace to the King but it didn't save him from Henry's wrath. Henry was enraged that the Cardinal was

The early home of Anne Hathaway is near Stratford-upon-Avon.

not able to get him an annulment of his marriage to Catherine of Aragon.

OXFORD UNIVERSITY, Oxfordshire is composed of 30 or more colleges. Students first came here in the 12th century. The beautiful buildings of the **Bodleian Library** should be seen as they are masterpieces of late Medieval and Stuart architecture.

STRATFORD-UPON-AVON, Warwickshire, has Shakespeare's birthplace; and just outside Stratford, in **Shottery,** is **Anne Hathaway's (his wife's) early home,** a charming Tudor-style thatched farmhouse.

ROYAL TUNBRIDGE WELLS, Kent is an attractive inland resort with the Chalybeate Spring, the "wells," of medicinal waters which attracted Lord North, one of King James I's courtiers in 1606. The town is situated 400 feet above sea level in one of the loveliest parts of Britain.

WINDSOR CASTLE, Berkshire, built by William the Conqueror, is the largest inhabited castle in the world and Queen Elizabeth's **favourite** (favorite) home. Queen Mary's Doll house is one of the attractions. It was presented in 1920 to King George V's wife as a token of national affection. It's a faithful replica of a 20th-century house, 1/12th normal size. The tiny books in the library were written by famous authors especially for this doll house.

Strong and content,
I travel the open road.
     —Whitman

CHAPTER SIX

WATCH FOR ZEBRA CROSSINGS

Left Is Right

The word **"wrong"** should be removed from one's vocabulary while driving in Britain. The British do not drive on the wrong side of the road; for them, driving on the right is wrong. **"When in Rome..."** should be kept firmly in mind while enjoying a new experience in driving. Having the steering wheel on the right-hand side of the car will take getting used to; as well as seeing what appears to be children or dogs driving cars because they are sitting in what to an American seems to be the driver's side. This will pass. Also, one may think that there's an antique car show going on somewhere by the large number of old cars on the road. Britain is a nation of individualists who don't go in for "keeping up with the Joneses." I doubt if they know the expression. If a car gives good service, it's not discarded...an admirable trait.

Old Is Good

It's lucky for the world that the British don't go about chucking out the old and replacing it with the new, otherwise, there'd be no Stonehenge or any of the other **henges** (stone circles) to fill us with wonder and conjecture as to how the **blue stones** were moved from what is now Wales without modern equipment. The blue stones are the blue-gray sandstones found in the Stonehenge grouping of stones that are not indigenous to the area. It has been determined that they came from Wales, 150 miles away, and only recently archaeologists have theorized that perhaps they were transported by sea to an area nearby and then moved overland. By what method, no one knows.

Thatched houses would only be seen in books. **"Cut-and-laid hedges"** would be replaced with wire fences, see Chapter Seven. **Barrister's wigs** would be passe'. **Hadrian's Wall** would be leveled as an obstruction. A new reigning sovereign would simply come into power by placing his/her left hand on the Bible and raising the right hand and solemnly swearing fealty to the nation. It would be just like home, so why go there?

Enjoy the "differentness," the old and new, side by side, the enchanting landscapes with ancient trees, the ancient castles and battle sites, the picture book villages, the "olde" ceremonies. Let's give a **three-times-three** for the British (a time-honored British cheer consisting of three Hip, Hip, Hoorays repeated three times...).

Self-Drive Hire Cars (Rental Cars)

Trains and buses with guides can take one anywhere in Britain but if there's a desire for getting off the beaten path, a **self-drive hire car** (rental car) can be rented at any **hire car firm** (rental car company). A car with an **automatic steerer** (automatic transmission) is easier to drive than one with shifts which requires learning to shift with a different hand. To be able to react swiftly in emergencies, it's best to keep the learning of new driving habits down to the minimum.

Ask the agent about becoming a temporary member of Britain's **AA** (Automobile Association) because it has a reciprocal arrangement with the American AAA (American Automobile Association). Also ask for instructions on how to use the **emergency telephone boxes** (telephone booths).

Car Parts

It's interesting to note that not one name for a British car part is the same as that in the U.S., not even the name for automobile. In Britain, it is known as a **motor car** but most times it's called **"the motor."** Not to worry, the names are close enough in meaning; besides, they won't be needed unless one experiences **motor trouble.**

Beginning with the front of the car and travelling to the back are: **headlamps** or **driving lamps** (headlights), **number plate** (license plate) and **bonnet** (hood). The dashboard is the **fascia board**, the windshield is a **windscreen** making windshield wipers...**windscreen wipers**. The rearview mirror is **the rear mirror** or **the driving mirror**, the turn signal is the **trafficator** (a blending of **"traffic"** and **"indicator"**), the parking brake is the **handbrake**, the defroster is the **demister**, the dome light is the **roof lamp** and the glove compartment is the **car locker** or **glove box**. The car is fitted with seatbelts front and back. These are mandatory for driver and passengers. Also, children under eight must not sit in the front seats. At the rear of the car, the trunk is the **boot** (a holdover from coaching days) and it holds a wrench **(spanner)** and an extra tire. Aha, the same name! Yes, but with a **"y,"** ergo **tyre**. Americans call tire patterns, treads; the British call them **tracks**. To remove a tyre, there's a jack (exactly the same name, but not a car part) which lifts the wheel so the tyre can be levered off with a **tyre lever**, a foot-long curved piece of steel. Finally, spark plugs are **sparking plugs** and the muffler is an **exhaust silencer**.

Petrol (Gas)

Petrol is graded by one to four stars. **Four star petrol** would be equivalent to American high-test gasoline. It is leaded and 97 octane. Unleaded petrol comes in two grades: Premium 95 octane and Super 98 octane. Petrol is sold by the **imperial gallon, 4.55 litres (liters)** or **1.2 gallons.** While the petrol is being pumped, the attendant will **do the windscreen** (clean the windshield) and then replace the **filler cap** (gas cap). It would be wise to get the gas tank filled on Saturdays because many gas stations are closed Sundays.

On the Road

While driving, repeating **"I must stay on the left side of the road"** to oneself can be a great help, especially when rounding a corner. It overcomes the overpowering urge one gets to swing to the right side of the street.

Speed Limits

Britain's roads are **properly sign-posted** (have road signs), and tourist attractions are indicated by **white-on-brown** sign-posts. Speed limits are also properly posted. The national speed limits are: **97 kph** (60 mph) for **single carriageways** (two-lane roads), **113 kph** (70 mph) for **motorways** (expressways or thru-ways) and **dual carriageways** (four-lane highways) and **48 kph** (30 miles per hour) for **built-up areas** (town and residential areas).

Road Warnings

It's important to know when to **stop**. Yes, there are traffic lights and red means STOP and green means GO as in the U.S.; but there are also some operated by pedestrians known as **Pelican Crossings**. This is an acronym for **pe**destrian **li**ght **c**ontrolled crossing. Since "pelicon" sounds much like "pelican," the more familiar name is used. When a button is pressed on a pole, a red light stops vehicles and a little green man appears indicating to the pedestrian that it is safe to cross the street. For the driver, there is a flashing amber light while the pedestrian crosses until a little red man appears. Should the pedestrian be **short-sighted** (near-sighted) or **colour blind** (color blind), the apparatus, at the same time, beeps continuously to indicate it's safe to cross the street until the beeping stops.

One should also keep an eye out for **Zebra Crossings**. These are slanted black-and-white stripes across the road and zig-zag lines along the side of the road indicating pedestrian crossings. They are further identified by a **beacon** (a large round orange marker on a black and white pole) at each side of the street. Pedestrians stepping off the **kerb** (curb) onto the striped pathways have absolute priority.

There are also **Bicycle Crossings** on certain routes. These have lights that are activated by the weight of the bike and rider and cause a **stop (red) light** to appear for vehicles and a **(green) go bikes** light for bikes.

All cars must yield at **round-abouts** (traffic circles) as priority is given to cars already in the circle. There, it's ok to yell **"quiet!"** to one's passengers and say a little prayer that one will enter the correct left lane and leave by the correct left lane. If rattled while in the round-about, just go around again.

Painted lines on roads also indicate STOP. A **white line across a road** means priority is given to cars on the major road ahead. **Single yellow lines along kerbs** (curbs) mean **no parking** except at night and on Sundays. **Double yellow lines** mean **no waiting**. One risks "clamping" by parking in these areas. Clamping means the car is rendered completely immobile until one pays to have it released.

Road Sign Meanings

There are a number of signs that are a bit difficult to interpret. **Clearway**, for instance, does not mean the way is clear for parking; rather, it means no parking along highway. **Flyover** (overpass) makes one think an airfield is in the vicinity. **Carriageway** (highway) is just another holdover name from the days of carriages and coaches. **Keep to the near side except for passing** simply means keep to the left. Other signs to watch for are **Deviation** or **Diversion** as both mean detour. **Give way** means (yield), **Double Bend** means there's an S curve ahead, and **Filter Left-No Signal** means one must gradually bear to the left as there's no traffic light.

MORE ROAD SIGNS

Airport Park — airport parking lot

Belisha Beacon — black-and-white poles topped with orange globes. Some have flashing caution lights; named for Leslie Hore-Belisha, a Minister of Transport.

Bypass — Detour

Caravan — trailer (family)

Car Park — Parking Lot

Careful—Loose Chippings — Careful—Fresh Gravel

Driftway — a road over which cattle are driven

Fell Road — a road going through an upland piece of waste pasture or wasteland

Four-Lane Carriageway — eight-lane highway, four lanes on each side

Footway — path

Give way — Yield

Hairpin Bend — Hairpin Turn

High Road — highway or main road

High Street — Main Street

lamp standard — street lamp post

lamp post — Victorian type used at house entrances

Level Crossing — RR crossing

Long-Stay Car Park — Long Term Parking

Main Carriageway — main highway

Metaled Road — macadamized road

No Entry — Do Not Enter

No Overtaking — No Passing

No Through Road — Dead End

Omnibus Terminus — Bus Terminal

Overbridge — railroad bridge

pavement or **footway** — sidewalk

police trap — speed trap

Pull-In — Drive-In

roadlamp — street light

Roadworks — Construction Zone

roundabout — traffic circle or rotary
Side Turning — side road
T-junction — road ends at a T
Three-Way — a meeting of three roads
tolsel, tolzey or **tolsey** — colloquial names for toll-
  booths
traffic block — traffic jam
traffic signal — traffic light
Trunk Road — Main Road
unmade road — dirt road
Unsuitable for Motor Traffic — a warning that the
  owner is not liable if one bogs down or gets stuck

Rest Stops

Seeing the sights from the car will be difficult until one
develops the feel for left-side-of-the-road driving. Viewings can
be handled by stopping at **Outlooks** (Overlooks). Rest stops
can also be made at **Lay-By Verges** (roadside parking areas). (A
Verge or **Grass Verge** is a road shoulder.) Lunch stops can be
made at **Roadside Pull-Ups** (diners).

Warning Hoots (Horn Honking)

A warning hoot means the car behind is about to **overtake**
(pass).

Car Trouble

If the car receives a bump, or a tire goes flat or the engine is
not ticking over well or **playing up** (giving trouble), it will
need **tending**. A **breakdown van** (tow truck) will take the car
to a **breakdown service garage** (auto repair shop). There, **panel
beating** will remove the dents, the **burst tyre's puncture** will
be **mended** (fixed) and the engine checked. **Men's and
Women's Open Toilets** are available for calls of nature. It is not
necessary to buy petrol to use the **loos** (toilets).

In case of a **car crash**, have someone **dial 999**. The police will
rope off the **scene of the smash** (accident scene) to keep the

kerb-watchers (rubber-neckers) at a distance. A **car tender** (emergency truck) will take over.

Roadside Advertisements

Driving along, there will be many interesting signs near churches, on **hoardings** (billboards), shop windows, and offices. **Take Courage** is not meant to buck one up, rather it's an advertisement for a popular ale. Mr. Courage was an 18th century brewer whose name lives on. Other frequently seen billboard signs are **Bovril**, a nourishing meat extract; and Heinz Beans shown as spread on toast. **Beans on Toast** is a popular snack in Britain. **Surgery** signs on houses or offices bring up the image of operating rooms but a "Surgery" is simply a doctor's or dentist's office. **Bring and Buy** and **Jumble Sale** signs will be seen near churches. The first is a sale where one donates something and buys something; the latter is a rummage sale. **Good As New** shops sell used clothing for the benefit of a charity.

MORE INTERESTING SIGNS

CHEMIST — Druggist
COMMISSIONER FOR OATHS — Notary Public
DOMESTIC REFUSE COMPOUND or **RUBBISH TIP** — garbage dump
ESTATE AGENT — real estate co.
NEWSAGENT CUM GPO — a newsdealer/postmaster
PERMANENT BUILDING SAVINGS — Savings and Loan
RIDING — Horse-Back Riding
TOOLSHED CUM GARAGE — toolshed/garage
TRANSPORT CAFE — Truck Stop
WIRELESS — radio

VEHICLE NAMES

articulated lorry — trailer truck

articulated truck cab or **prime mover** — truck tractor

banger or **old banger** (slang) — clunker or heap

breakdown van — tow truck...British soldiers call it "Recovery Joe."

caravan — RV or trailer

car transporter — car carrier

charabanc or **tourist coach** — tour bus

costermonger's cart — fruit peddler's cart

driving cabin — truck cab

dust lorry or **dust cart** — garbage truck

estate car or **shooting brake** — station wagon...shooting brake comes from when it carried a shooting party, guns and **gun dogs** (retrievers, pointers and setters).

family saloon or **saloon car** — family car

fishmonger's van — fish truck

hire car — rental car

lorry or **motor lorry** — truck

low loaders — lowboy trailers

milk float — milk delivery truck

motor or **motor car** — car

Pantechnicon van, removal van, furniture van or **carrier van** — originally a van for a London art store which became a furniture store and kept the name. **"Techne"** is Greek for **"art."**

petrol tanker — gas truck

public transport — public transportation

road haulier — truck

security van — armored car

the grabs (slang) — clam shell digger (shell-shaped to grasp large amounts of dirt)

trolley bus — trolley

VEHICLE DRIVERS

bus men — bus drivers

lorry drivers — truckers

BRITAIN

refuse men or **dust men** — garbage truck drivers
trolley men — conductors
van men — moving men

Down to Gehenna or up to the Throne,
He travels fastest who travels alone.
        —Rudyard Kipling, *The Winners*

CHAPTER SEVEN

ON YOUR OWN
Travel Options

Bargain cards or passes purchased in the U.S. simplify travel in Britain as one need not wait in queues to purchase tickets. They can be used for London buses, the Underground or for train travel throughout England, Scotland and Wales. Air-conditioned intercity buses link London with all parts of England, Scotland and Wales. There is also is a network of local and cross-country routes with scenic attractions.

Other travel options are by car, see Chapter Six, RVs and by air. There are **passenger** and **drive-on car ferries** to Ireland and the **continent** (mainland Europe) that are served by connecting trains and buses. To avoid the possibility of a rough English Channel crossing, there's the **Chunnel** (Channel Tunnel) which provides **passenger- and vehicle-carrying shuttle trains** between Folkestone and Calais.

The Gridiron or Tea Kettle (Train)

If the train is one's travel choice, it's advisable to **book** (reserve) a seat well in advance. It's most essential for sleeping car arrangements.

There are eight main train terminals in central London, each dealing with a specific region. Check ahead for the one needed. Tickets are purchased at a **railway booking hall** (railroad ticket office). Most long distance trains have both **standard** (tourist class) and **first class** carriages and one can choose a **coupé** (a half compartment) or a **cross-sill** (full compartment for sleeping accommodations). First class tickets cost about 50% more than standard class and usually include a restaurant and/or buffet car. Restaurant cars have two sittings. Ask the train steward for a **mealtime card**.

Available are: **single tickets** (one-way tickets), **return tickets** (round-trip tickets) or a **cheap day returns** (going and coming the same day). Tickets should be held as the **ticket collecter** will take them on the train or at the **barrier** (train gate) when one leaves the train. **Luggage trolleys** (luggage carts) are available for **cases** (suitcases). Baggage can be checked at the **left luggage office** (baggage room). Lost property is held at the **lost property office** (lost and found). Railway stations have **conveniences** (rest rooms) and **refreshment rooms** (snack bars).

MORE TRAIN WORDS

Bradshaw — a noted railway-guide, first issued by George Bradshaw in 1830

breakdown train — work train

B.S.T. British Summer Time — Daylight Savings Time

cattle truck — cattle train

Check Room — Baggage Room

cloakroom ticket — baggage check

engine driver, train driver or **railway engineer** — railroad engineer

fogger or **fogman** — one who sets up fog signals

footplate — platform for foot-platemen

foot-platemen — the engineer and his assistant; on steam trains, they are stokers

four-foot way — the standard space, between rails, 4 feet 8 1/2 inches

Goods Station — Freight Station

goods train — freight train

goods waggons, railway waggons or **goods trucks** — freight cars

a halt — a train stop
leading coach — first car
metal — ballast
Rack Railway — Cog Railroad
railway — railroad
railway carriage — railroad car
railway crossing — railroad crossing
railway cutting — railroad cut
railway engineer — designer/builder of railroads
railway man — railroad man
railway police constable — railroad detective
railway warrant — railroad pass
Refreshment Room — Snack Bar
retarded — delayed
Time Bill or **Time Table** — Time Table
truck — flat car
Up-Express — towards London
washaway or **washout** — washout (flooded line)

Where to Go?

Britain may be small but it has such a large selection of incredibly interesting places that are mostly tied to historic events, and it's chock full of artifacts **"from the year dot"** (from the year one), that one is hard put to decide what to see first. It's compactness is an added advantage because, being only 650 miles from top to toe, it's easy to get to where one wants to go; and with an amazing diversity of landscapes, it's a continual delight. There's something there for everyone as can be seen in this short review of the U.K's different areas:

ENGLAND'S NORTH COUNTRY is famous for industry and has many **major industrial towns** such as Manchester and Liverpool, wonderful countryside, a marvelous network of **canals, Neolithic monuments,** the **Bronte sister's Haworth,** a **Viking center** in York, the famous walled city of **Chester, five national parks,** the **Isle of Man** and the **Holy Island (Lindis-**

farne), where St. Aidan began to Christianize Britain in the 7th Century.

CENTRAL ENGLAND covers the area from Wales to Norwich and has seen many tragic events connected with its Royals **(Market Bosworth** and **Fotheringhay)** and has many of their beautiful homes **(Sandringham** and **Hatfield House)**. Besides its famous cities and towns **(London** and **Birmingham)**; it has a literary history **(Shakespeare's Stratford-upon-Avon** and **Robin Hood's Nottingham)**. It is also the home of **Oxford** and **Cambridge;** and holds a unique place in history as the **birthplace of the Industrial Revolution,** when in 1709, Abraham Derby invented the technique of smelting iron ore with coke near Ironbridge Gorge (Shropshire).

SOUTHERN ENGLAND extends from Land's End to the River Thames. It also has reminders of: prehistory with **Stonehenge** and **Avebury;** Roman history with the ruins of **Roman baths in Bath;** America's beginnings with **Plymouth,** the port from which the **Pilgrim fathers** set sail; and present history with **Windsor,** Queen Elizabeth II's favorite home.

WALES, though small, has a diversity of landscapes from the rugged mountain peaks and lakes of **Snowdonia** to the beautiful bays and inlets of the coast. It's from the hills of Wales that **Stonehenge's famous blue stones** were taken. **Caernarfon Castle** is where the Princes of Wales are invested.

SCOTLAND, the word alone is enough to evoke images of **tartans, bagpipes,** and delicious **scones and oatmeal.** Scotland's areas have familiar names: **Loch Lomand, Edinburgh, Balmoral, John o'Groat's, St. Andrews,** and the **Shetland Islands.**

NORTHERN IRELAND has a wealth of **Stone Age tombs, Celtic crosses, early Irish monasteries, Norman castles** and late **18th century houses. Armagh** is the spiritual capital of Ireland and **Downpatrick** has the **grave of St. Patrick,** Ireland's patron saint. The **Giant's Causeway,** a spectacular volcanic formation, attracts thousands of visitors each year.

Coventry was heavily bombed during WWII.

Travel Your Way/Trips Tailored to One's Own Interests

Organized bus trips are fine for one's first trip to the U.K. and for people who only want to see the most talked about sites; but if there's a preference for a trip tailored to one's particular interests, here are some suggestions with locations indicated as follows: **(E) for England, (W) Wales, (S) Scotland** and **(NI) North Ireland.** Each letter will be followed by the county in which the attraction is found and where needed, the nearest town:

Finding King Arthur

The legendary King Arthur has always stirred the imagination. Who is it that does not know about **Camelot,** the fair **Guinevere,** the brave **Lancelot,** the wise **Merlin,** the evil **Mordred** and the search for the **Holy Grail?** Whether King Arthur was a real person or not is not considered important. What is important is that he is a part of the legends of Britain and there are many places where he is reported to have been:

TINTAGEL, (E) Cornwall, a ruin of a Norman castle where it is thought he was born.

CADBURY CASTLE, (E) Somersetshire, North Cadbury, is thought to be Arthur's **Camelot.**

GLASTONBURY, (E) Somersetshire is where legend says Joseph of Arimathe'a came to bury **the chalice** from the Last Supper (The Holy Grail) and to convert the country's first Christians. Joseph is the rich Israelite who gave up his sepulcher to Jesus. It is also said that Arthur and Guinevere are buried beneath the altar in the ruined Abbey Church.

BRADBURY RINGS, (E) Dorsetshire, near Wimborne has a huge Iron Age fortification where King Arthur is supposed to have received his mortal wound fighting off the Saxons.

MARLBOROUGH, (E) Wiltshire, is famous for its **public** (private) school which has a great mound on its grounds. This was the site of a Norman castle under which, according to legend, Merlin was buried.

WINCHESTER CASTLE, (E) Hampshire, Winchester. Little remains but the 13th Century Great Hall which has, hanging on its west wall, what is thought to be Arthur's famous **"Round Table."**

CARMARTHEN, (W) Dyfed. Sometimes called "Merlin's City." Tradition says that Merlin was born here of a princess and a spirit. He prophesied **"When Merlin's Oak shall tumble down, Then shall fall Carmarthen Town."** The oak was wrapped in iron bands, embedded in concrete to keep it safe and placed in the Abergwile Museum. Nearby is what is thought to be **Merlin's Cave.**

STRATA FLORIDA ABBEY, (W) Dyfed. When Henry VIII dissolved the Abbey, legend says the monks took with them an olive wood cup they thought was **The Holy Grail.**

ARTHUR'S STONE (W) West Glamorgan is a millstone which is reputed to have split when pierced with King Arthur's sword. It's the 25-ton capstone of a 4,500 year-old burial chamber.

KNIGHTON, (W) Powys. Knucklas Castle where King Arthur married **Guinevere,** daughter of the giant Cogfran.

Magna Carta

The places associated with the foundation of the U.S Constitution are of great interest to people with an history bent.

ST. EDMUND'S BAY (E) Lincolnshire is where, in 1214, the English nobles drew the **"Petition of the Barons"** which is the basis of the Magna Carta.

KING JOHN'S CASTLE (E) Hampshire, Odiham. The castle from which it is thought King John set out to sign the Magna Carta.

RUNNYMEDE (E) Surrey. The fields of Runnymede are where King John reluctantly signed the Magna Carta on June 15, 1215. In 1957, a memorial was set up at the approximate spot inscribed **"To commemorate Magna Carta, symbol of freedom**

under law." On a hill above is a memorial to **President John Kennedy**.

BRITISH MUSEUM (E) London has two copies of the original Magna Carta. There are two more, one in Lincoln Cathedral and one in Salisbury Cathedral.

Favorite Authors

The place where one's **favorite authors** lived and worked might be fascinating to some people.

SAMUEL TAYLOR COLERIDGE Cottage, (E) Somersetshire, near Bridgewater was **Coleridge's** home from 1797-1800 and where he wrote *The Rhyme of the Ancient Mariner* and *Kubla Khan*.

THOMAS HARDY Cottage, (E) Dorsetshire, Higher Buckhampton near Dorchester is where he was born in 1840. Dorchester became Casterbridge in his **"The Mayor of Casterbridge."** The County Museum has a reconstruction of Hardy's study. Hardy went from architect to poet to famous author.

CHARLES DICKENS Birthplace Museum, (E) Hampshire, Portsmouth has many rare editions of his books plus memorabilia. **Rochester, (E)** Kent, was where he spent his boyhood. **Broadstairs, (E)** Kent was Dickens'summer retreat. It inspired *Bleak House* and *David Copperfield*. Across the bay is the **Dickens House Museum. Dickens' House** (48 Doughty St.) London, is where he wrote **Oliver Twist** and **Nicholas Nickleby**.

JOHN MILTON Chalfont St. Giles, (E) Buckinghamshire has **Milton's** cottage where he wrote *Paradise Lost* and began *Paradise Regained*. It is now a Milton museum. **Petty France** is a street in London where he lived for a time.

ALFRED LORD TENNYSON Somersby, (E) Lincolnshire **Somersby Rectory** is where **Alfred Lord Tennyson** was born in 1808. **Faringdon, (E)** The Isle of Wight, Freshwater is where Tennyson lived for 40 years.

GEORGE BERNARD SHAW Ayot St. Lawrence, (E) Hertfordshire. **Shaw's Corner** was the home of **George Bernard Shaw** for 46 years.

RUDYARD KIPLING Bateman's, (E) Sussex, near Burwash is a 17th century ironmaster's house that was the home of **Kipling** after his years in India, 1902 to 1936. It is now a **Kipling Museum.**

DYLAN THOMAS Laugharne, (W) Dyfed has the **Boat House,** home of **Dylan Thomas** for many years. **Brown's Hotel** was his favorite pub; and he's buried in the nearby churchyard.

WILLIAM WORDSWORTH Grasmere,(E) Cumbria **Dove Cottage was the home of William Wordsworth** and his sister **Dorothy** from 1799 until their death. The **Wordsworth Museum** is nearby. They are buried in the village churchyard.

SIR WALTER SCOTT Melrose, (S) Borders **Abbotsford House** was built by Sir Walter Scott from 1817 to 1822 at great expense.

SAMUEL JOHNSON Lichfield, (E) Staffordshire, is the birthplace of Samuel Johnson. It has a **Johnsonian Museum.** At **Stourbridge, (E)** West Midlands is **King Edward's School,** his school as a boy.

LORD BYRON Newstead Abbey, (E) Nottinghamshire was **Lord Byron's** estate. Originally, it was a priory founded by Henry II to atone for the murder of Thomas à Becket.

CHARLOTTE AND EMILY BRONTË Haworth, (E) Yorkshire has **Brontë Parsonage,** the home of the **Brontë sisters.** Charlotte's *Jane Eyre* and Emily's *Wuthering Heights* were written here. The parsonage is now a memorial to both sisters, furnished as it was in their day and with displays of their books.

ROBERT BURNS Ayr, (S) Strathclyde. **Robert Burns** was born in the suburb of Alloway. The **Burns Cottage** is furnished as when he lived in it and next door is a museum containing his manuscripts and letters.

Capital Cities
LONDON, (E) Greater London, **Capital of the United Kingdom.** See Chapter Five.

EDINBURGH, (S) Lothian, **Capital of Scotland** Edinburgh (pronounced Edin-borough) was originally Edwinesburg after King Edwin of Northumbria, who, in the seventh century, rebuilt an Iron Age Fort on the site where **Edinburgh Castle** stands today. **St. Margaret's Chapel** (1076) is the oldest part of the castle. One can wander through **Mary, Queen of Scots'** apartments and see the small room where her son, **James VI** was born. This much photographed castle dominates the city which is divided into Old Town and New Town.

Old Town has **Gladstone's Land** (a restored 17th century merchant's house); **John Knox's House**, (leader of the Protestant Reformation who established Presbyterianism as Scotland's national church); and **The People's Story** (a 16th century prison with a reconstruction of the ordinary life of Edinburgh from the 18th century to today).

New Town has the **National Gallery of Scotland**, the **Royal Botanic Garden** (famous for its rhododendrons) and the **Sir Walter Scott Memorial**. Scott was a famous poet and the father of the historical novel...*Ivanhoe* being the most famous.

CARDIFF (W) South Glamorgan, **Capital of Wales** Wales is known as the **"Land of Castles"** because it has over 400, one of which is **Cardiff Castle**, originally a Roman fort. The Normans built a castle on the site and later the castle was lavishly restored in Victorian style. Cardiff's position on the River Taff made it an important shipping port for coal and iron, during and since the Industrial Revolution.

The Welsh Industrial and Maritime Museum has a four acre exhibition area with displays of Cardiff's important past.

The National Museum of Wales in Cathays Park has a large collection of paintings by Welsh artists and French Impressionists.

The Welsh Folk Museum at St. Fagans, on the outskirts of the city, is an open-air museum with re-erected Celtic round houses which were excavated in various parts of Wales.

BELFAST (NI), Antrim, **Capital of Northern Ireland** Belfast is located on a bay of the Irish Sea and is noted for its large shipbuilding industry and for the manufacture of Ireland's famous linens. Belfast has many beautiful 18th and 19th century buildings such as the **City Hall** (Edwardian Baroque with a copper-covered dome); and the **Grand Opera House.** Of interest are the **Botanic Gardens,** the **Belfast Zoological Gardens** and a **castle** which was built above the city in 1870 for the Earl of Belfast.

OTHER PLACES OF INTEREST for visitors are the royal homes that housed **Mary, Queen of Scots** while Queen Elizabeth was deciding what to do about her, **famous British battle sites, Henry VIII's homes,** the **homes of famous inventors** and **British gardens.**

Unstructured Holidays

Many visitors are in the U.K. for a complete rest. An unstructured holiday would suit them fine. There are facilities for **canal boating, camping** and **hiking.** For those who would find these to be a bit strenuous, here are some restful ideas:

Farm Holidays Those with children might find staying at a working farm to be a unique experience. The children would love being with the animals and all would enjoy the home grown food and the sights and sounds of the countryside.

B&B's (Bed and Breakfast Homes) Since they don't have to be booked in advance, these allow one to roam freely by day with the assurance that a comfortable room will be available for the night in a family-run home and there will be a great British breakfast the next morning.

Self-Catering Homes or City Flats (Apartments) If a holiday free of "must sees" is desired, renting a **self-catering city flat** (furnished apartment), **house** or a **chalet** may be the answer. Self-catering means all the amenities are provided, except food. This allows for complete freedom to go about as one wishes. It can be a home base from which to go to any nearby sites; or just a place where one could get to know the people by joining in their activities such as Bring and Buys and Jumble Sales. And

Stone walls, flowering trees and thatched roofs are part of the scene outside Leicester.

there would be the **opportunity to learn how cricket is played by watching the long cricket matches**.

For a really relaxing time, there's that great British diversion, **a day in the country**. Most towns and cities in the U.K., even London, are ringed by countryside. On good days with the promise of "outbreaks of sunshine," lunches and tea things are packed and off the British go by bike, motor, caravan, bus or on foot for a relaxing day in the country.

Leicester—An Unstructured Holiday Suggestion

Leicester (Leicestershire) is an example of a good base because it has many advantages. It's a market town in the very heart of England and is a unique combination of old and new.

Today, it's the center of hosiery and **boot**(shoe) manufacturing but was once a Bronze Age settlement. When the Romans took over they called it **Ratae**. There are many Roman remains: a **Roman Forum**; the **Jewry Wall** composed of stones and

The Jewry Wall and Roman baths are just a few of the ruins in the Leicester area.

bricks; **mosaic pavements,** some being the cellar floors of some of Leicester's Victorian red-brick homes. Saxons, Danes and Normans followed. The **Church of St. Mary de Castro** was built by a Norman, the Earl of Leicester, to serve as the castle church. **Cardinal Wolsey's grave** is in the ruins of **Leicester Abbey.** After losing favor with Henry VIII because he couldn't arrange a divorce from Catherine of Aragon, Wolsey gave his possessions to the king and retired to York but this didn't save him from Henry's wrath. He was summoned to be tried for treason. Being old and ill, he stopped at Leicester Abbey for a rest, but while there, died.

The Abbey became the private home of the Cavindish family, the Dukes of Devonshire, and was burned down during the Civil War, see Chapter Eight. The ruins and grounds are now a lovely green, flowery public park in downtown Leicester.

Also of interest is the bustling **town market place,** the **Medieval Guild Hall,** and the **Leicester Castle** ruin where, it is

Hedgers are still constructing cut-and-laid hedges.

said, the Barons plotted to get **King John** to sign the **Magna Carta**.

The surrounding countryside has many **thatched roof houses** and farms bordered by **cut-and-laid hedges**. These are woven prickly hawthorn hedges that farmers use to keep animals from getting out of their fields. Hedgers wear heavy hedging gloves and use **bill-hooks** (thick knives with hooked points) to remove chips from behind the trees, which helps them to bend so they can be tied to stakes with hazel binders. The stems and branches are then woven together in the hedger's own design to make a tight fence. A true hedger is an artist and no two work alike.

OF EASY ACCESS FROM LEICESTER:

The famous Quorn and Fernie Hunts (See Chapter Sixteen.)

Bradgate Park, home of the nine-day Queen, Lady Jane Grey.

Belvoir Castle (pronounced Beever) has the famous Holbein portrait of Henry VIII. It is set in beautiful parkland with peacocks roaming freely.

Ancestors of Benjamin Franklin are buried in Ecton.

Belvoir Castle has a famous portrait of Henry VIII.

Sulgrave Manor (Northampton), home of one of George Washington's ancestors, Lawrence Washington, who was twice mayor of Northampton. The garden has some American soil on which is an elm grown from a shoot of the Cambridge, Massachusetts tree under which Washington became commander of the American soldiers in 1775.

Ecton, home of Benjamin Franklin's ancestors, many of whom were blacksmiths. The church has an American-donated bronze tablet with a bust in relief of Franklin, and in the churchyard are the burial plots of his aunt and uncle.

Hail, happy Britain! highly favoured isle,
And Heaven's peculiar care!
—William Somerville, The Chase, bk. i, I. 84

CHAPTER EIGHT

GOING BACK IN TIME/A BRITISH HISTORIC CHRONOLOGY

To really appreciate the U.K.'s great storehouse of artifacts, it would be helpful to know the meanings of the terms your guides will use: **cromlechs, dolmens, barrows, Papists, Dissolution, Roundheads, Restoration, Baron's War, Rump Parliament, Glorious Revolution, etc.** A condensed history of the United Kingdom of Great Britain follows revealing the meanings of all these terms and many others and placing them in their proper historical context. It will also show how long it took for representative government to become a reality; show how the language evolved; give the contributions of the invaders; and explain why the British went to France and Germany for some of their monarchs.

Important words and phrases are in bold face as well as the steps in the development of the language and parliamentary law. Rulers are in italics.

AROUND 6000 to 3000 B.C., THE NEOLITHIC PERIOD OR NEW STONE AGE One of the greatest revolutions in history begins in Britain. **Pastoralists**, thought to have come from western and northwestern Europe, begin farming, animal taming, building permanent homes. The development of religious concepts and social interaction matures. They also fashion **paleoliths** (stone tools) and build huge stone monuments:

Hadrian's Wall, Northumberland (courtesy of the British Tourist Authority).

menhirs (single massive stones); **dolmens** (two upright stones capped by a third); long and round burial chambers called **barrows,** and **cromlechs** (circles and squares of huge stones believed to be temples) such as **Stonehenge** in Salisbury, England.

AROUND 3000 to 1500 B.C., THE BRONZE AGE The arrival of peoples from the Low Countries and the Rhine who discover a method to alloy copper and tin to make bronze tools and spears. These are the **Beaker folk,** so called because they usually buried their dead with a drinking cup. **They may have introduced the Indo-European language.**

AROUND 1500 B.C. to 43 A.D., THE IRON AGE More invaders arrive who are attracted by Britain's iron and tin mines, its many harbors, its small size—no place more than 85 miles from the sea—and its Gulf Stream-tempered climate which allows some areas to stay green all year round. **Around 55 B.C. Julius Caesar arrives** on an exploratory expedition and

Cerne Abbas Giant, Dorset (courtesy of the British Tourist Authority).

he and succeeding Roman generals defeat some of the existing tribes.

Around 400 B.C., the Celts arrive in two waves The first, called **Gaels**, settle in the areas of Ireland and Scotland. The second, called **Brythons or Britons**, settle in Wales and Cornwall. Some attribute the name Britain to these people; others give Phoenicians the credit as their name for Britain was **Baratanic** (country of tin). The Celts contribute iron smelting, curing of hams, beekeeping, and a form of religion led by **Druids** who are priests, teachers and judges. **Celtic culture, folklore and language still live on in Ireland, Scotland, Wales, the Isle of Man and to some extent in Cornwall.**

43 to 400 A.D., THE ROMANS The Emperor Claudius sends legions to conquer the whole of **"Britannia,"** (their name) and to seek out peoples difficult to control. **Boadicea,** a Celtic queen, leading a great army, wreaks havoc on many Roman settlements. Defeated, she takes poison. (Her statue is on London's Westminster bridge.) The **Picts or Caledonians** of what is now

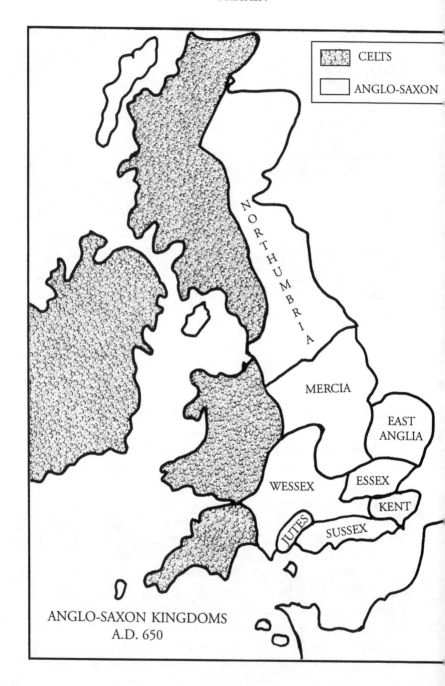

CELTS

ANGLO-SAXON

NORTHUMBRIA

MERCIA

EAST ANGLIA

ESSEX

WESSEX

KENT

JUTES

SUSSEX

ANGLO-SAXON KINGDOMS
A.D. 650

Offa's Dyke Path, Wales (courtesy of the British Tourist Authority).

Scotland constantly harry the Roman **castras** (forts) so Emperor Hadrian seals them off with a 100-mile stretch of wall, **Hadrian's Wall**. These forts eventually become cities with some form of **"castra"** in their names: Lan**caster**, Man**chester** and Glou**cester**. **The Romans contribute the Latin language, a system of laws**, baths, stadiums, customs and religion (when they become Christian); and straight-as-an-arrow military roads that became templets for many of Britain's modern roads, especially **Watling Street** and **The Fosse Way** which still have **Roman kerb-stones** (curbstones) and **drainage culverts** (drainage ditches). The people now speak both Celtic and Latin; and by the late first century, local self-goverment is granted to the **peregrini**, the Roman name for their subjects. Some are granted Roman citizenship.

AROUND 410 A.D., ROME IS OVERRUN BY GOTHS and no longer sends legions to Britannia. Roman power begins to dwindle.

432 A.D., PATRICK ARRIVES IN IRELAND and converts first the chiefs and then the people to Christianity.

450 to 871, LEFT TO THEMSELVES, THE BRITONS MAKE SOME EFFORTS TO REPEL INVADERS King Offa of Wales builds a Dike **(Offa's Dike)** to separate England from Wales. Mostly, the tribes fight each other. Some of these early kings invite mercenaries from the coastlands of eastern Germany to help them. **These are Teutons: Angles, Saxons and Jutes.**

871 to 850, THE TEUTONS (ANGLES, SAXONS AND JUTES) REBEL AGAINST THEIR EMPLOYERS AND DRIVE THE BRITONS TO THE WEST The **Anglo-Saxons** form seven kingdoms: **Kent, Sussex, Essex, Wessex, East Anglia, Northumbria and Mercia**; and the Jutes settle in what is now the Isle of Wight and some land to its north, see map, page 114, **A.D. 650 Anglo-Saxon Kingdoms.** Their rulers are given the title **"Cyng"** (father of a people), later **"King."** The wives are **"Cwen"** (wife of a Cyng), later **"Queen."** The Celts are pushed west to what is now Wales and Cornwall and almost all that is Roman is stamped out. Farms are established and **Angle-land** (the new name for Britain, later **England**) is divided into **shires** (counties), a system which still exist today. The seven kingdoms continually war with each other.

Around 775 **King Egbert of Wessex gains a measure of control over all the kingdoms.**

Around 501 to 542 Legend says **King Arthur**, a Celt, lived during this period.

In 597 A.D. **Augustine**, an Italian monk, **later St. Augustine**, is sent by **Pope Gregory I** to convert them to Christianity. **King Ethelbert of Kent** is baptized and Christianity spreads rapidly. **Augustine reintroduces the Latin language**, rebuilds the Roman church at Canterbury, establishes a Benedictine monastery and becomes the **First Archbishop of Canterbury**. More monks follow and establish many monasteries.

850 to 1066, THE NORTHMEN (DANES FROM NORWAY AND DENMARK) INVADE THE COASTS OF ENGLAND,

IRELAND AND FRANCE in several waves. They first build fortified towns along the coasts. **In France, they establish the Duchy of Normandy.** Their leaders are **jarls** (earls).

In 878, they invade Wessex but are defeated by Alfred, the Great, King Egbert's grandson, Alfred is called "the Great" because he is a **wise ruler, translates Latin texts into Anglo-Saxon, organizes laws and has them written down,** builds schools and has the history of England written, **"The Anglo-Saxon Chronicle."** This record of the principal events that occurred each year was written by learned men. It continued for 250 years after Alfred's death. Then there was a succession of rulers: **Athelstan,** Alfred's grandson, **Ethelred II,** King Sweyn of Denmark, **Canute** (Sweyn's son), and **Edward** (Ethelred's son).

Edward, the Confessor dies childless and **Harold, Earl of Wessex,** who is declared king by the **Witan** (the King's Council) clashes with **William, Duke of Normandy** who claims the title King, and is supported by the Pope. It's the famous **Battle of Hastings (1066),** which is immortalized in the **Bayeaux Tapestry.** Harold is killed, and **William the Conqueror** becomes king.

1066 to 1154, THE NORMANS (WILLIAM THE CONQUEROR) give the country an efficient system of government. For taxation purposes, he has all the land surveyed and recorded in **The Domesday Book,** or **Day of Doom Book,** as it is called because no one can escape having his property recorded. He builds stone churches and monasteries which become centers of learning; and **deprives the Witan of their power to elect a king. The French language is blended with the Anglo-Saxon.**

William II, his second son, succeeds him because his first son is ruler of Normandy. William II, the only bachelor king of England, is succeeded by his younger brother.

Henry I, who promptly wars with his oldest brother, wins and becomes **King of England and Normandy.** He wants his daughter **Matilda** to succeed him but she is married to a French Count and the English do not want to be ruled by the French.

BRITAIN

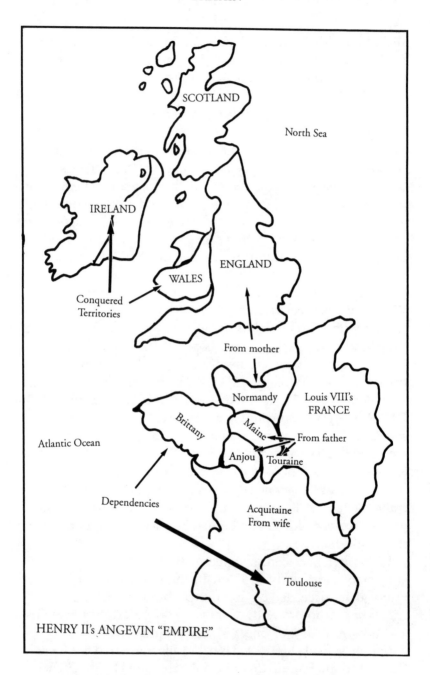

SCOTLAND

North Sea

IRELAND

Conquered
Territories

WALES

ENGLAND

From mother

Normandy

Louis VIII's
FRANCE

Brittany

Maine

Atlantic Ocean

From father

Anjou

Touraine

Dependencies

Acquitaine
From wife

Toulouse

HENRY II's ANGEVIN "EMPIRE"

Stephen, William I's grandson, is elected king by the barons.

Henry II, an Angevin and Matilda's son, is the next inheritor of England's crown.

1154 to 1399, THE ANGEVINS (PLANTAGANETS) **"Planta genesta"** is the broom plant and the name is given to the family because Henry's father always wore a sprig of it in his cap, see map on page 118, **Henry II's Angevin "Empire."** It was not strictly an **"empire"** but so called because of the many territories under Henry's rule making him the most powerful king of his time. He had **England and Normandy** as heir of his mother; **France's Maine, Anjou and Touraine** as heir of his father; **France's Acquitaine** through his marriage to Eleanor of Acquitaine; **Brittany and Toulouse** as dependencies on the English crown and the **parts of Ireland and Wales** that he himself conquered. France's Louis VII, ruled less than half of his country. Henry goes to work with a will and history records him as an administrative genius. He makes the Irish Parliament dependent upon himself, **starts a system of taxation** by hiring soldiers and forcing the barons to pay them. He also taxes the clergy causing a protest from **Thomas á Becket, Archbishop of Canterbury.** Thomas is murdered by some knights to ingratiate themselves with Henry. **Henry sends trained justices** (judges) **on circuit to judge cases and establishes the jury system. Their recorded decisions are honoured** (honored) **by other justices and the Common Law grows case by case.**

Richard I, the Lionhearted, Henry's son, succeeds but goes off to the Crusades. Needing money, **he sells town charters, marking the beginnings of local self-government.**

John I, his brother, succeeds and manages to lose most of the French possessions, thus angering the Barons. **They force him to sign a paper which lists the rights of justice and property, and declares that the king must rule by law, The Magna Carta** (Great Charter). It can be seen in the British Museum. The Barons and important churchmen now assemble once a year to vent their opinions. **This is called the Great Council and since**

The Roman bath at Bath.

it is a place of speechifying, it becomes known as **Parliament**, from the French **"parler,"** (to speak).

Henry III, John's son, succeeds the throne and the **Baron's War** breaks out. The king is captured and **the barons, clergy and, for the first time, representatives of the towns (the common people) meet and Henry is forced to give Parliament some government control.**

Edward I, his son, succeeds and accepts Parliaments limitations and because representatives of the people are included in Parliament, it is called **the Model Parliament.** After a time the nobles and churchmen meet in one place **(House of Lords)** and the townspeople in another **(House of Commons).** Edward conquers Wales and to appease the people, names his son, who is born at Caernarvon, **Prince of Wales.**

Edward II, his son, succeeds, and like his father, tries to defeat Scotland and is defeated by **Robert Bruce** at **Bannock-burn** and deposed by Parliament in favor of his son, Edward III.

Saxon church at Breedon-on-the-Hill.

Edward III—Knighthood is now in flower (1327-77) and the **Hundred Year's War** with France begins (1337 to 1443) because France helps Scotland resist annexation by England, interferes with England's rich wool trade and resists Edward's claim to the French crown. **The Black Death** (1349) kills one-fourth of the people and few serfs are left to work the land. Those that survive demand more pay and release from being bound to manors; and they band together to form unions of a sort.

Richard II, Edward III's grandson, is now king and kills the leaders of the serfs. When Richard demands absolute rule, his cousin, **Henry of Lancaster**, leads a revolt against him. Richard is forced to abdicate and is imprisoned in the Tower of London **During this period, John Wyclif, a Master at Oxford, translates the Bible into English and writers, such as Chaucer, begin to use the common everyday language (Middle English) in their writings instead of Latin.**

1399 to 1461, HOUSE OF LANCASTER (HENRY IV) has an

insecure and trying fourteen-year reign even though he claims his right to the throne as being descended from Henry III.

Henry V, his son succeeds. He renews the Hundred Years' War by putting in a claim for the French throne. By his brilliant victory at Agincourt (1415), he conquers all of the northern half of France. He marries Princess Catherine of France and by a treaty, it is agreed that he should be King of France after the death of Catherine's father, the insane Charles VI; but all goes to naught when he dies of camp fever (typhoid fever) during a brilliant victory.

Henry VI, his son, is king at age 9 months so his uncles govern for him. Through the efforts of **Joan of Arc**, England loses its last political hold on France. Though Joan is captured and executed by the British, her example inspires the French and bit by bit they recapture all their lands except Calais and **the Hundred Years' War ends in 1453. Richard of York**, whose emblem is the **White Rose**, wants the English crown. Henry adopts the **Red Rose** as his emblem and another war begins, the **War of the Roses**. Richard's son, Edward, defeats Henry and places him in the Tower where he stays until he dies, and Edward becomes Edward IV.

1461 to 1485, HOUSE OF YORK (EDWARD IV) fights to keep his crown. His two sons are the princes who are sent to the Tower and never heard from again. When Edward dies, his brother, *Richard III*, succeeds and is opposed by **Henry Tudor**, a Lancastrian claimant to the throne. Their armies meet and Richard is killed at the **Battle of Bosworth Field**.

1485 to 1603, HOUSE OF TUDOR, HENRY TUDOR BE-COMES HENRY VII and ends the War of the Roses by marrying Edward IV's daughter, Elizabeth of York. The feudal system is on its last legs and **country squires** (landed gentry) appear. Henry promotes commerce and industry and England becomes the leading textile producing country of the world. **To show the barons he's in charge, he establishes a Star Chamber to try the accused without juries.**

Henry VIII, his son, succeeds and cuts ties with the Catholic

Church because the Pope won't annul his marriage to **Catherine of Aragon**. Catherine's baby sons had all died in infancy so he wants to marry **Anne Boleyn** to get an heir. He names **Thomas Cranmer** Archbishop of Canterbury, head of the new Anglican Church (Church of England) and has Cranmer annul his marriage. By an Act of Parliament, he has himself declared **"Supreme Head of the Church of England."** He breaks-up the monasteries in England and Ireland (this is known as **The Dissolution**), seizes their lands and wealth and uses them for his own purposes and for establishing England's first real navy. He calls himself **King of Ireland; and joins Wales to England by an Act of Union.** He tires of Anne and has her put to death and marries in succession: **Jane Seymour** (dies in childbirth giving him an heir), **Anne of Cleves** (divorced), **Catherine Howard** (beheaded) and **Catherine Parr** (who survives him to marry again, a fourth husband).

Edward VI, (his nine-year-old son by Jane Seymour) succeeds and his uncle, **Edward Seymour, Earl of Hertford** rules as Lord Protector. A palace revolution led by John Dudley, Duke of Northumberland deposes Seymour and he's eventually executed. As Edward is dying of consumption, Dudley devises a new order of succession in which the real heir, Mary, Catherine of Aragon's daughter, is declared illegitimate and the crown is given to Lady Jane Grey, granddaughter of Henry VIII's sister.

Lady Jane Grey, the nine-day Queen, is deposed because the people prefer a Tudor and make Mary the Queen.

Mary I sends Lady Jane and Dudley to the tower to be executed. She tries to reestablish Catholicism and executes many resistors giving her the name **Bloody Mary**.

Elizabeth I, daughter of Anne Boleyn, succeeds her sister. Regarding **Mary, Queen of Scots** as a threat to her crown, she imprisons her for 20 years, then puts her to death. She favors the Church of England which allows the clergy to marry and uses a Catholic ritual but rejects the Bible in favor of **Thomas Cranmer's English Prayer Book**. The **Papists** (Catholics) oppose this as do the Protestant **Puritans**, who want a purer, simpler service. This is the time of **Merrie England, and Shakespeare, the Renaissance, the conquering of Ireland with the suppression of Irish monasteries and churches, the defeat of the Spanish Armada, and the time of exploration.** Elizabeth names James VI, of Scotland, the Queen of Scots' son, as her successor. He becomes James I of England.

1603 to 1714, THE HOUSE OF STUART James I's succession **unites Scotland to England** but Scotland keeps its own Parliament. **James causes trouble by claiming the divine right of kings** and sends English and Scottish settlers into **Ulster,** Northern Ireland. **Guy Fawkes** and some Catholic extremists form **The Gunpowder Plot** and try to blow up king and Parliament. In **1607, Jamestown, Virginia** comes into being and in 1620, the **Pilgrims** land in New England.

Charles I, James' son, **succeeds and dissolves Parliament but calls it back when he needs money. Before complying, Parliament makes the king promise not to dissolve it again.** It's called the **Long Parliament** because it lasts for 19 years, from 1640 to 1659. Some **Puritans** leave for the New World; others called **Roundheads** because they wear their hair short, dominate the House of Commons and pass laws to curb the king's power. Charles, angry, raises an army of **Cavaliers,** so-called because they ride horses (from the French **"cheval"**) and declares war on Parliament. Parliament also raises an army and they battle. This is the **Civil War** and it lasts four years (1642-1646). **Oliver Cromwell** leads the Roundheads to victory at **Marston Moor** and **Naseby** and Charles seeks refuge with the Scottish army but they turn him over to Parliament.

In 1649, the Rump Parliament (the end part of the Long Parliament) sentences Charles to be beheaded and declares England to be a **Commonwealth** (a republic) without a king or House of Lords. It governs England and sends Cromwell to quash revolts in Ireland and Scotland. In 1653, he returns, dissolves Parliament and nominates one of his own, the **Barebones Parliament,** named after a member, Praise God Barebones. The Commonwealth is declared a **Protectorate.**

Statue of Oliver Cromwell, London

Cromwell, Lord Protector The Puritans close the theaters, suppress some sports and declare Sunday as strictly a day of worship. Cromwell is succeeded by his son, **Tumbledown Dick,** so-called because he can't control the army. He resigns after a year and **George Monk,** a Cromwell general, arrives with an army, recalls The Rump and has it dissolve itself so a new Parliament can be legally elected. This Parliament offers the crown to Charles I's son, who becomes Charles II. This is called **The Restoration,** the return of royalty.

Charles II **During his reign, the The Habeas Corpus Act is passed, giving a prisoner the right to be told by a judge, why he is arrested. If arrested wrongly, he is set free; if not, the judge must name a trial date.** There are many disasters, **The London Plague** which kills 100,000 (1665), the **Great Fire** (1666), and the burning of a large part of the English fleet by the Dutch (1667). Charles II clashes with Parliament who now fears his Catholic brother James might succeed and present an **Exclusion Bill** to bar him from the succession. **To prevent passage, Charles dissolves Parliament and the first political parties come into being: the Tories** (the aristocracy, who later become the **Conservatists**) oppose the bill and **the Whigs** (Roundhead descendants representing the commercial classes, later **Liberals**) favor the bill. **Charles dissolves a new Parliament when the same bill is introduced and rules without it.** *James II,* succeeds his brother but when he has a son, Parliament has had enough of Catholics and forces James to flee to France. James' daughter, Mary, by his first marriage is invited to be Queen together with her husband, the Dutch William of Orange.

William and Mary Parliament prepares a **Declaration of Rights** which includes a ban on Catholics ruling Britain and bars succession by inheritance. William and Mary accept and the Declaration becomes law as the famous **Bill of Rights.** This is called **the Glorious Revolution** because the law is enacted without bloodshed and **Parliament is finally in charge of the country.** When William dies, Louis XIV of France, wants James' son, James Stuart, to be king but Parliament gives the throne to his protestant sister Anne. (James Stuart, keeps up his claim for 65 years and is called **The Old Pretender.** In 1744 and 1745, his son, **Bonnie Prince Charlie, the Young Pretender,** makes several attempts to gain the throne and is defeated at **Colloden.**)

Queen Anne, James II's Protestant daughter by his first wife, succeeds. **England and Scotland unite under one Parliament in 1707 becoming "Great Britain" with the Union Jack as the national flag.** The flag is a union of the crosses of St. George, St. Andrew and St. Patrick. (**"Jack"** is another name for "flag.") When Anne dies, the nearest Protestant heir is **George,** a great-grandson of James I, a German prince of the House of Hanover. His mother, **Sophia of Hanover,** would have succeeded because as granddaughter of James I she was next in line but she had died a few weeks before Queen Anne.

1714 TO 1910, THE HANOVERIANS, GEORGE I only speaks German and is more interested in ruling Hanover so he leaves government affairs to **Robert Walpole.** During his reign, inventions of methods of using England's abundance of coal instead of charcoal in blast furnaces and forges lead to a great production of pig-iron. This begins the **Industrial Revolution** when society begins to transform itself from a farming and cottage-industry society to an industrial society with a growing middle class.

George II succeeds his father, and also has Walpole and later, William Pitt as Prime Ministers.

George III succeeds his grandfather and loses the American colonies. During his reign, in 1801, an **Act of Union joins Ireland to England and Britain becomes "The United Kingdom of Britain and Ireland."** Britain becomes the **"workshop of the world."** An important invention of the time was **James Watt's method of using steam power** which revolutionized many industries.

George IV succeeds his father and Parliament passes **The Catholic Emancipation Act** (1829) giving Catholics the right to sit in Parliament. **Daniel O'Connell, an Irish leader,** fights to repeal the Act of Union in favor of **Home Rule** for Ireland.

William IV succeeds his brother. **The Great Reform Bill of 1832 is passed providing for a more representative government.** William's niece, Victoria, succeeds.

Victoria is Queen at age 18. She marries her cousin **Prince Albert of Saxe-Coburg-Gotha** and they have nine children who marry members of the royal houses of Europe making her the "grandmother of Europe." During her relatively peaceful and prosperous reign, however, there are many conflicts: the **Crimean War, The Indian mutiny of 1857, the fight of Ireland for Home Rule and the conflict with the Boers of South Africa.**

Edward VII, her son succeeds and helps form the **Triple Entente of Great Britain, France and Russia.** His son, *George V,* succeeds in 1910 and marries, **Mary** of the house of Teck, a distant cousin of Hanoverian descent.

1910 TO PRESENT, HOUSE OF WINDSOR, GEORGE V cuts off all ties with Germany at the outbreak of World War I and calls his line the **House of Windsor,** taking the name from Windsor Castle. In 1920, **Lloyd George puts through Parliament the Government of Ireland Act,** which sets up separate parliaments for southern and northern Ireland. **In 1921, Northern Ireland accepts but southern Ireland insists on complete independence.**

Edward VIII, George V's son succeeds in 1936 but abdicates to marry **Mrs. Wallis Warfield Simpson.**

George VI, his brother, becomes king. When World War II breaks out, he and his queen bear the brunt of the bombings by remaining in London with their people. In 1948, Parliament passes the **Republic of Ireland Act separating Eire from the Commonwealth of Nations. The new Republic of Ireland is proclaimed on April 18, 1949.**

Elizabeth II, George VI's daughter, succeeds in 1952. She is **long-descended,** that is, she can trace her ancestry back to Britain's earliest kings. **She marries Prince Philip,** a son of

Prince Andrew of Greece, who like herself, is a great, great grandchild of Queen Victoria. They have four children: Charles, Prince of Wales, Princess Anne, Prince Andrew and Prince Edward.

Words Dealing with Royalty

Blues (Royal Horse Guards) and **Life Guards** are two regiments raised in 1661 to be the cavalry brigade of the British Household. Their headquarters are in Whitehall, London. The Blues were a very senior and superior regiment officially known as **The Horse Guards.** They've been amalgamated with the **Royals** (Royal Dragoons) and are known as the **Blues and Royals** and wear blue facings on their uniforms. They ride beside and before the royal carriage on state occasions. The Blues were and still are quite separate from the Life Guards, who consider themselves the slightly senior Regiment. The Life Guards wear red facings.

Buck House — slang name for Buckingham Palace

Cap of Maintenance — cap worn by or carried before a person of rank proclaiming his/her high office

Court Holy Water — obsolete term for empty complements, much like our "banana oil"

Gentlemen of the Privy Chamber — officials in the royal household in attendance at court

Goldstick — colonel of the Life Guards who carried a gilded wand before the Sovereign

H.M. — Her Majesty

H.R.H. — Her Royal Highness

King-of-Arms or **King-at-Arms** — herald who reads royal proclamations

Life Peer — peer whose title is not hereditary

Lords and Ladies of the Bedchamber — officers of the royal household who wait, in turn, upon King or Queen

Privy Purse — allowance for a sovereign's private expenses

Right Honourable — title given to peers below the rank of

Marquis, to privy-councellors, to present and past cabinet ministers and to certain Lord Mayors and Lord provosts

Silver Stick — palace officer who carries a silver wand

St. Edward's Crown — symbol of monarchy used for crowning all kings and queens since Charles II, except for Queen Victoria, for whom the Imperial State Crown was made

Stone of Scone, Stone of Destiny, or Coronation Stone — in 1296, Edward I, in one of his forays into Scotland to bring it into submission, captured the King, John de Baliol, and proclaimed himself King of Scotland; he took the ancient Stone of Scone, a 450-pound block of sandstone, on which Celtic kings had been crowned, and placed it in Westminster Abbey under the seat of the Coronation Chair which has been used for 700 years

The Hons — short for Honorables, the sons and daughters of peers

The Household — royal domestic establishment

Worthiest of Blood — refers to the fact that in a question of succession, male supercedes female.

Honours (Honors)

Honours are a listing of Britons judged to have served the community with distinction. This is compiled twice a year by a committee and the Queen gives final approval. These are called **Birthday Honours** because they are traditionally granted in June on the monarch's official birthday, not his/her real birthday. There are also New Year Honours. The recipients can receive Baronetcies, Earldoms or Knighthoods. Those that enter an **order of knighthood** are allowed initials after their names. There are seven knighthood orders:

THE BATH is named for the symbolic act of bathing that was taken before entrance into knighthood. Today, there's a civil division and a military division and each has three classes:

G.C.B. Knight Grand Cross of the Bath

K.C.B. Knight Commander of the Bath

C.B. Companion of the Bath

THE GARTER was established around 1838 by Edward III with the motto **"Honi Soit Qui Mal y Pense"** (Evil be to him who evil thinks.) **K.G.** after a person's name indicates membership.

ORDER OF THE BRITISH EMPIRE was created by George V in 1917 for those who give conspicuous service of national importance. It was founded to give recognition to a wider selection of people or social class, both men and women, than the Bath and Garter honors. It has a **"Military"** and **"Civil"** section.

G.B.E. Knights and Dames Grand Cross

K.B.E. Knights Commanders

D.B.E. Dames Commanders

C.B.E. Commanders

O.B.E. Officers

M.B.E. Members

ST. PATRICK is an Irish order established by George III in 1783. **K.P.** indicates membership.

ST. MICHAEL AND ST. GEORGE, the soldier saints, was founded by George III in 1818 and is for soldiers and diplomats for distinguished service in foreign affairs.

G.C.M.G. Knights Grand Cross

K.C.M.G. Knights Commanders

C.M.G. Companions

ROYAL VICTORIAN ORDER was founded by Queen Victoria in 1896 for important or personal services to the sovereign or the royal family.

G.C.V.O. Knights and Dames Grand Cross

K.C.V.O. Knights Commanders

D.C.V.O. Dames Commanders

C.V.O. Commanders

M.V.O. Members of this fifth class

THE THISTLE is an ancient Scottish order and allows **K.T.** after one's name.

...Nothing to wear but clothes
To keep one from going nude.
—Benjamin Franklin King, *The Pessimist*

CHAPTER NINE

THE SHOPPING PARADE, THE BESPOKE TAILOR AND BOOTS

For the visitor, almost every shop in the U.K. can be a tax free shop. This means that you can recover the **VAT** (Value Added Tax) that is imposed on most goods, minus a small administration fee. Ask the **sales assistant** (sales clerk) for a tax free form and mailing envelope. At the airport, get the form stamped at the Customs & Excise desk.

Shop Names

Before you go to the **shops** (stores), **enquire** (inquire) about half-day closings because some shops close at noon on certain days of the week. (**"Stores"** are "warehouses.") Also ask for directions to the nearest **shopping parade** (shopping center), where the shoe store is a **boot shop**, the linens store, a **linen draper**; and the novelties store, a **puzzle shop**. Should you want a **hand-cut suit** (custom-made suit), find a **bespoke tailor** shop. The name bespoke tailor goes back to times when one would reserve a tailor's services, that is, **bespeak a suit of clothing.**

Inexpensive items can be found at **redundant shops** (surplus outlets) or **cost-sale houses** (wholesale houses). **Slop shops** sell cheap inferior clothing. For **off-the-peg** or **off-the-hook clothes** (ready-made clothes), you'll want a department store. There, the **ground floor** would be our first floor and the **first floor**, our second, etc..The **lift** is the elevator.

SHOPPING WORDS

bumf — junk
cash and wrap or **cash and carry** — cash and carry
carriage free service — free delivery
cost price or **trade price** — at cost or wholesale
export rejects — seconds
fire clearance sale — fire sale
kick — fashion
on tick or **on the slate** — on credit
pricey, posh or **dear** — dear or expensive
purchase tax — sales tax
reduced to clear — clearance sale
shop soiled — shopworn
shop walker — floor walker
shutter drill — closing time
the latest shout — the latest fashion
the never-never — the installment plan
the try-on — the fitting
to attend to — to wait on
trendy — stylish or fashionable
window gazing — window shopping

Sizes

Britain's manufacturers, as in America, use different sizing systems. Most are given in inches but some can be in **cm's** (centimeters). The following is a general guide. Ask the clerk for help before trying on anything.

Women's Dresses, Blouses, Knitwear, Lingerie									
U.K.	8	10	12	14	16	18	20	22	24
U.S.	6	8	10	12	14	16	18	20	22
To fit bust (inches)	34	36	38	40	42	44	46	48	50

Men's Suits, Overcoats ,Sweaters, Shirts and Collars
The same as in the U.S.

Women's Shoe Sizes							
U.K.	3	4½	5	5½	6½	7	7½	8
U.S.	4½	6	6½	7	7½	8	8½	9

Men's Shoe Sizes						
U.K.	5	6	7	8	9	10	11
U.S.	5½	6½	7½	8½	9½	10½	11½

WEARING APPAREL WORDS

SHOES:
> **bootlaces** — shoe laces
> **court shoes** — pumps
> **dress wellingtons** — long-legged elegant boots for military evening dress
> **high-lows** — high shoes fastened in front
> **jackboots** — boots reaching above the knee
> **kidskin** — calfskin
> **mutton dummies** — white sneakers
> **plimsolls** — sneakers
> **slop ins** — scuffs
> **stilettos** — spike-heeled shoes
> **undress shoes, carpet slippers** — bedroom slippers or slippers
> **winkle pickers** — shoes with pointed toes

CHILDREN'S WEAR:
> **Alice band** — hair band
> **balaclava** — woolen hat covering the ears and back of the head
> **gaufer-stitched smock** — ruffled or fluted smock
> **kissing strings** — cap or bonnet strings

Harrods, known throughout the world as a place to shop.

WOMEN'S WEAR:
backless dress — halter dress
bedgown — long dressing gown or short bed-jacket worn over a nightie
briefs or knickers — panties (slang)
Cami-knickers — teddys or body briefers
dressing gown — robe
frock — dress
jumper — pullover sweater
mascot — charm for charm bracelet
minikinis — bikini panties
nightdress or **nightie** — nightgown
overall — smock
pinny or **pinafore** — jumper
smock frock — smock
towelling wrap — terry robe
tub frock, machine wash — washable dress
twinset — twin sweater set

victorine — fur cape with long ends
waist slip — half slip
washing silk dress — washable silk dress
woolies — jumpers, jerseys or warm undervests; the name is short for "Woolworths"
wrap-around — overall apron
wrapover frock — wraparound dress
WOMEN'S ACCESSORIES:
crocodile-skin handbag — alligator bag
dorothy bag — drawstring or tote
head hugger, head scarf, head square — kerchief
ladies' purse notecase — wallet
netherstocks — stockings
tights or **pantytights** — pantyhose
MEN'S WEAR:
cheese cutter — square peaked hat
camelcloth coat — camelhair coat
drape suit — long jacket and narrow pants
dressing gown — robe
gilets or waistcoats — vests
great coat — overcoat
guernsey or gansey — fisherman's sweater made of waterproof oiled wool in traditional Island of Guernsey designs
jemmy — coat
Newmarket — close-fitting coat, originally a riding coat; named after Newmarket, a racing town
jumper — pullover
plus-fours — baggy knickerbocker suit
polo neck sweater — turtleneck sweater
pyjamas or **sleeping suits** — pajamas
singlet — undershirt
slipover — sleeveless sweater
smalls, pants, small clothes, or **underneaths** — shorts (underwear)

Trews — trousers in a clan tartan when the kilt isn't worn

turnups — trouser cuffs

vests — undershirts

waistcoat — vest

MEN'S ACCESSORIES:

billycock — bowler-type hat

bootlace tie — string tie

braces — suspenders

buttonhole — boutonniere

chimney pot hat,plug hat, topper, or **silk hat** — top hat

chip hat — hat of palm strips

note case, notebook or **pocket bookman's** — wallet or billfold

quizzing glass — monacle on a stick

shaving tackle — shaving gear

string tie — narrow tie

suspenders — garters

trilby or **trilby hat** — fedora

upperstock — stiff band worn as a cravat with a buckle in the back

wideawake hat — low, wide-brimmed canvas hat or a soft felt hat

JEWELRY:

Bristol diamonds — quartz crystal found near Bristol

earbobs or **earrings** — earrings

identity bracelet — identification bracelet

mascot — charm

necklet — necklace

starstone — star sapphire

RAINWEAR:

brolly — umbrella or bumbershoot

derriboots or **half-wellingtons** — short rubber boots

India rubber boots or **gum boots** — rubber boots

mack, mackintosh or **waterproof** — raincoat

ulsters and toppers — overcoats and hats of rainproof tweed

wellingtons — generic name for rubber boots

SPORTS WEAR:

anorak — parka

games tunic — gym suit

hacking jacket — riding jacket

high low — high shoe tied in front

P.E. or **P.T. shorts** — athletic shorts

polo neck or **roll-neck pullover** — turtleneck sweater

shooting coat — hunting jacket

snow spectacles — snow goggles

tanga — string bikini

thrum cap — cap made of coarse, shaggy cloth

trainers — gym shoes/sneakers

windcheater — windbreaker

wooly — sweater

MATERIALS:

elastic knitted textile fabric — stockinet (fabric used for stockings and undies)

fancy goods — showy materials

skin wool — wool from a dead sheep

toilinet — woolen material for waistcoats

trevira, man-made or **polyester** — polyester

winceyettes — linsey-wolsey, a coarse cloth of linen and wool or cotton and wool

MISCELLANEOUS:

cracker or **curler** — curl paper or curl rag

fal-lals — doo-dads

foot muff — muff for keeping feet warm

gear or **togs** — clothes

hair slides — bobby pins or hair clips

japanned leather or **patent leather** — patent leather

key-fob or **key ring** — key ring

nail varnish — nail polish

nightdress case — nightgown holder

pudding sleeves or **bishop's sleeves** — similar to the loose sleeves on a bishop's robe

scent — perfume

smoothshod — shoes minus spikes

sniffers, wipes or **hankies** — handkerchiefs or hankies

spectacles, gig-lamps or **peepers** — glasses or cheaters

stocking ladders — runs

tooth comb — fine tooth comb

zip fastener — zipper

GETTING DRESSED TERMS:

an ug-out — an **ug**ly **out**fit

dressed up like the dog's dinner — looking like the the cat's meow

duds — poor ragged clothes

get into clobber — get dressed up

got up to kill or **was smarmed up, tarted up, togged up, in clobber** or **toiletted** — was gussied up

ruched up — frilled

toilet cloth — toilette shoulder cloth used to keep makeup from soiling clothing

Malt does more than Milton can,
To justify God's way to man.
—A.E. Housman, A Shropshire Lad, I, xii

CHAPTER TEN

A PINT OF MOTHER-IN-LAW OR PUBS

"The Local"

Most visitors to the U.K. want the experience of visiting a **public house**, affectionately known as the **"pub"** or **"the local."** Most pubs are very warm and inviting with fireplaces, wooden tables, beveled glass, and decorations that have stood the test of time. They are a traditional social meeting place. Some have family rooms where children of all ages can accompany their parents. Children aged 14 to 17 can be admitted alone to pubs to get non-alcoholic drinks but one must be 18 to be served alcohol. **"The Snug"** is a small room reserved for regulars and trespassing is strictly taboo.

Pub Names

Pub names are meaningful. Some glorify important people: **Victoria, Prince of Wales, Earl of March, Duke of Wellington.** Some allude to their shields: **The Bull** (Richard, Duke of York), **The Blue Boar** (Richard III), **The Red Dragon** (Henry VII), The White Hart (Richard II). Some have historic names: The **White Rose** (Yorkists), **The Red Rose** (Lancastrians). Others are corruptions of names: **The Cat and Wheel** (St. Catherine's Wheel), **The Bag of Nails** (Bacchanals), **The Queer Door** (Coeur Dore-Golden Heart).

"Tied" or "Free" Pubs

Pubs can be **"Tied"** or **"Free."** Tied pubs serve only beer from one brewery, they are "tied to it," so to speak; while free pubs can serve many brands of beer. The offerings of **"Off Licenses"** (liquor stores) must be consumed "off" their premises. They're also known as **"the Offy"** or **"the Beer-off."** Off-license pubs also sell liquor to be taken home. Other vendors of spirituous drinks are **"Cut-Price Wine Shops"** , **"Licensed Family Hotels"** and inns having **"licensed victuallers"** (licensed inn-keepers).

Popular Beers and Ales

"Take Courage" is on many **hoardings** (billboards) in the U.K. It's not a government program to buoy up the populace, it's an ale. **"Courage"** is the name of the brewer. Previously, ads referred to **Courage's Ale.** "Pimm's," is another well-advertised alcoholic beverage: **Pimm's No. 1** is gin-based; **No. 2** is whisky-based, **No. 3** is rum-based and **No. 4** is brandy-based. **"Pimm's Cup"** is a sort of alcoholic fruit salad containing **Pimm's No. 1,** fizzy lemonade, and lemon, orange and cucumber slices. **"Guinness"** is a popular beverage that's known to many Americans. It's much like a bock beer with a high hops content and is called a **"stout."** A **"pint of mother-in-law"** is half **stout** and half **bitter.** Beer is the main choice of Britons. It's called **bitter** and is served at room temperature as it cannot be chilled. Most drinks are served the same way but ice is available for the asking. House wines are called **"plonk,"** possibly a corruption of the French **"vin blanc."** See below for more drinks and ales.

Pub Manners

It's traditional for most habitues to stand. Drinks are paid for as they arrive and tipping is taboo but one can buy the **"barman"** or **"barmaid"** (bartender) a drink. Pubs have limited drinking hours. Five to ten minutes before closing time, the bartender or landlord will say, **"Your last orders please, ladies** and gentlemen" and there's a rush to drink up as everyone must leave when they hear, "Time, ladies and gentlemen, please."

PUB HOURS *

England and Wales:
Weekdays: 11:00 a.m. to 11:00 p.m.
Sundays: 11:30 a.m. to 3:00 p.m.
 7:00 p.m. to 10:30 p.m.
Scotland:
Weekdays: 11:00 a.m. to 11:00 p.m.
Sundays: 12:30 p.m. to 2:30 p.m.
 6:30 p.m. to 11:00 p.m.
Northern Ireland:
Weekdays: 11:30 a.m. to 11:00 p.m.
Sundays: 12:30 p.m. to 2:30 p.m.
 7:00 p.m. to 10:00 p.m.

* Some pubs are now open all day, following the practice of Continental establishments in the Common Market; that is, from 10:30/11:00 for 12 hours, without the afternoon break. To do so is the choice of the landlord or the barman's employer.

Teetotal Drinks

"T.T's." or "water drinkers" (teetotalers) can order **"Adam's Ale"** or **"Adam's Wine"** (what some Americans call "City Gin"); or you can order a **"Babycham"** (a sparkling, non-alcoholic drink), a **"squash"** (a fruit-flavored drink), a **"gingerade"** or **"ginger beer"** (much like ginger ale), or an **"appleade"** (apple juice, often carbonated). **"Tinned drinks"** (canned drinks such as Coke or Pepsi) are also available.

Have fun, try a pickled egg, and don't get **"tanked up,"** **"squiffy,"** **"bottled,"** or **"tiddley"** (tipsy).

PUB OFFERINGS

athole brose — a whisky and honey mixture

banana split — half bitter and half lager

barley wine — beer with a high alcohol content, rather sweet

bitter beer — pale ale

bitter top — a pint of bitter topped with an inch of 7 UP

black and tan — stout and bitter beer

black beer — black syrupy beer from Danzig

black eye — rum and brandy

black velvet — stout and champagne or half bitter and half cider

Bristol milk — sherry

British wines — wines made in Britain with home grown or imported grapes

brown beer — weak, sweet beer

bumbo — a mix of rum or gin with water, sugar and nutmeg

cape smoke — South African brandy

cider — hard cider or applejack

cider-cup — cider with spices, sugar and ice

cider and — cider and spirits

claret-cup — iced claret, brandy and sugar

cobbler's punch — warm beer with spirits, sugar and spice

cold without — brandy with cold water

dog's nose — gin and beer

egg-flip — ale, wine, spirits or milk with eggs, sugar and spices

G & T — gin and tonic

ginger beer — effervescent ginger drink

ginger-cordial — cordial of ginger, lemon peel, raisins, water and sometimes liquor

half — short for half a pint of beer

half and half — half porter, half ale

hot toddy — a shot of scotch, sugar, lemon juice and hot water

jorum — a stiff drink
log juice — bad port wine
mild beer — the weakest draft beer
Mother's ruin, blue ruin, or **What killed Auntie?** — gin
old Tom — gin
peg — brandy and soda
pint of mild and bitter — half mild, half bitter on tap
porter — bock beer
red biddy — red wine and methylated spirit
rum and black — rum and black currant juice
scrumpy or **rough cider** — very alcoholic, flat, non-fizzy cider served **"from the wood"** (a small wooden barrel)
shandy — half beer, half lemonade
snakebite — half pint of bitter and half alcoholic cider
snowball — a mix of advocat (egg yolks and brandy), lime juice and 7 UP
squash — fruit syrup and water
stout ale — dark beer made from hops and brown sugar
tipper — ale brewed by Thomas Tipper in Sussex
twist — mixed drink
whiskey — Irish whisky
whiskey-mack — whisky and ginger beer
whiskey and splash — whisky and soda or seltzer
whiskey toddy — toddy with whisky as the chief ingredient
white ale — ale brewed or mixed with ingredients such as flour, eggs, etc., which make it whitish

PUB JARGON

Aleconner or Aletaster — civic officer who tastes the quality of the ale
as she comes — straight
beer engine — beer pump

beer money — money given in lieu of beer and liquor
the boozer — the bar
bottle party — BYOB
bottle-slider — tray for passing a decanter around a table
cork drip mat — coaster
a double — double shot
drink license — liquor license
the drinks trolley — drinks cart
drunk as a piper — drunk as a lord
have been in the sunshine or **have the sun in my eyes** or **three sheets in the wind** — to be soused
ice pail — ice bucket
jorum — a stiff drink
knock back a drink — toss off a drink
knock back a couple — have a few
"Let's have a jar." — "Let's have a drink."
liquorish — sottish
medical comfort — having a drink
nipperkin — a nip
nose painting — coloring of the nose caused by drinking
potato spirit — potato alcohol
prop up the bar — hold up the bar
recharge — refill
rummer — large drinking glass
screwed — looped
a short — a shot
a soaker — a drunk
squiffed — potted
stewed as a newt — drunk as a fish
suck the monkey — drinking from a cask through a **"monkey pump"** (an inserted tube); or drinking rum from a coconut
a sup — a snort

three bottle — one who can drink three bottles at one
sitting

to be one over the eight — to have drunk nine pints
of beer, one pint over a gallon

to be in liquor — to be high

twist — mixed drink

water of life — whisky or brandy

whiskified or **whiskeyfied** — looped

Who doth ambition shun
And loves to live i' the sun,
Seeking the food he eats,
And pleased with what he gets.
　　　—Shakespeare, *As You Like It*, II, v, 38

CHAPTER ELEVEN

EATING OUT, EATING IN & TEA

Eating Out

BREAKFAST Somerset Maugham, the famous British novelist once said, the best way to eat well in Britain is to have breakfast three times a day. The British are famous for their **hearty brekkers** (breakfasts) which are enjoyed thoroughly by all visitors to the UK: bacon, sausages, **kippers** (dried and smoked herring), tomato, eggs, toast, **donkey food** (bran cereal), marmalade, **lemon curd** (jam made with lemon juice, lemon rind, egg yolks, butter), tea or coffee. One can also have a **plain breakfast**: coffee, rolls or toast and honey.

LUNCH Pubs are popular places for lunch. A favorite pub meal is the **plowman's lunch** which can either be a large chunk of French bread with a large piece of cheese, pickles, butter and tea; or French bread with slices of roast beef, tomato and lettuce. Another good choice is **shepherd's pie** made with **minced** beef (ground beef) topped with mashed potatoes.

DINNER The cuisines of many countries are available, but one should make an effort to sample some of the great variety of Britain's own delicious dishes. They vary according to region.

Area Specialties

LONDON: Chelsea buns (yeast buns made with dried fruit, brown sugar and allspice. The dough is rolled jellyroll fashion, sliced and baked); **steak and kidney pudding** (Don't be put off by the name. It's a pastry filled with pieces of steak, kidneys and mushrooms.).

SCOTLAND: Scotch broth (mutton or lamb, barley, split peas, carrots, turnips, leeks); **cock-a-leekie** (beef, chicken, leeks and prunes); **Scotch Eggs** (hard-boiled eggs rolled in a mixture of sausage meat, egg, and breadcrumbs and deep-fried); **haggis** (steamed pudding made from chopped cooked lamb's liver, sheep's heart, onion, oatmeal and suet boiled in a sheep's stomach); **bannock** (flat, round, unleavened oat biscuit made on a griddle); **scones** (very short self-rising flour breads made plain with butter or with cheese or chopped apples); **atholl brose** (pudding made from oatmeal, double cream, honey and whisky); **Scotch shortbread** (wheat flour, corn or rice flour, butter, sugar, slivered almonds and caraway seeds)

WALES: Welsh rabbit (Gloucester or Cheshire cheese, crumbs and onions); **Welsh currant bread** (yeast bread with currants and honey glazing)

THE WEST COUNTRY: Cock-a-leekie soup (chicken, onion, carrots, leeks); **Cornish pasty** (beef, onions, turnips, and potatoes in a flaky wrapper); **Devonshire scones** (small round patties filled with strawberry or raspberry jam topped with whipped cream); **John Dory,** (the name for a Cornish fish stuffed with sole and served with lobster sauce); **Devonshire steamed fish pudding** (filets of white fish, an egg yolk, potatoes, shrimp, grated cheese, parsley); **Cornish split** (cake halved and filled with preserves and cream)

THE SOUTHWEST: Cream teas (tea and scones served with preserves and clotted Cornish cream...yummy!); **Bath buns** (yeast buns topped by crushed sugar lumps)

THE SOUTH: Dover sole, steak and kidney pudding (in a suet crust); **maids of honour** (puff pastry cheese cakes with blanched, ground almonds); **Wiltshire lardy cake** (thin flat yeast cake made with lard, **sultanas** [raisins], spices and **golden syrup** [light molasses-type syrup])

THE MIDLANDS: Beef olives (beef strips lined with bacon and rolled around a breadcrumb stuffing); **shepherd's pie** (ground beef, lamb, veal or pork or a mix of two of these with spices and grated cheese topped with mashed potatoes); **gooseberry fool** (gooseberries mixed with sugar and cream)

THE NORTH-EAST: Toad-in-the-hole (Yorkshire pudding topped with sausages or pieces of steak and onion); **jam roly poly** (pie crust spread with jam, rolled up, steamed and sprinkled with sugar and baked)

THE NORTH-WEST: Hot pot (a layering of lamb chops, sheep kidneys, onions, potatoes, oysters and mushrooms); **simnel cake** (butter, eggs, golden raisins, currants and ground almonds); and **Cheshire cheese**

IRELAND: Irish stew (mutton or lamb, onions, carrots, potatoes, butter); **mutton pies** (mutton, onions, carrots cooked in pastry); **Irish soda bread**

APPROXIMATE U.K. MEAL TIMES

Breakfast — 9 A.M.
Lunch — Noon
Tea — between 4 and 5
High Tea — 6 P.M. (takes the place of dinner)
Dinner — 8:30 P.M.

Restaurant Words and Advice

cloakroom — either a check room or a rest room
afters — desserts
ask for the bill — ask for the check
sugar caster — sugar shaker
bread and butter — considered extras and must be ordered
chips — French fries

coffee with **kip** — coffee (with meal) has to be asked for; outside London, it's usually served in the lounge at an extra charge

estaminet — a restaurant which allows smoking

feeling peckish, sharpset or **ravening** — feeling hungry

hot and hot — foods cooked and served in hot dishes

plonk — house wine

pusher — bread used for pushing food onto a fork

"Restaurant Customers' Charter" — sign in restaurant windows which guarantees a fixed price menu and indicates whether or not service charge is included

starters — appetizers

gents' cloaks or **ladies' cloaks** — restrooms

to book a table — to make a reservation

to stand shot — to be left holding the bag or the bill

water — water can be requested when giving an order

RESTAURANT FOODS

ENTREES:

angels on horseback — skewered oysters wrapped in bacon

archangels on horseback — scallops wrapped in bacon and **grilled,** that is, broiled

bangers and mash — sausage and mashed potatoes

beef alamode — beef larded and stewed with vegetables

Bidlington rarebit — a very rich cheese sauce on very soft buttered toast flavored with nutmeg

bubble and squeak — slices of cold beef warmed and covered with a fried mixture of cabbage and onion

canape diane — chicken livers wrapped in bacon and served on toast

cider glazed gammon — mildly cured ham cooked with hard cider and served with spiced peaches

devils on horseback — kidneys wrapped in bacon

Exeter stew — chopped beef, onions, carrots and herbs

faggots — spiced meat balls containing pig's liver

guard of honour — roast lamb with the bones crossing each other like swords

jemmy — baked sheep's head

Kentish bacon roly-poly — chopped bacon, onion and spices spread out on dough and rolled jelly-roll fashion, wrapped in foil and steamed; then served with a vegetable mix

Lancashire hot pot — lamb and kidney pot pie covered with sliced potatoes and baked

potted chicken — creamed chicken mixed with lemon juice, parsley and salt and pepper and served in ramekins

potted shrimp — tiny shrimp from Morecambe Bay coated with clarified butter

sausage and mash — sausage and mashed potatoes

Scotch woodcock — scrambled eggs flavoured (flavored) with anchovy paste and served on toast

steak and kidney pudding — steak and kidney stew covered with pastry

savoury — a seasoned dish like welsh rarebit

toad-in-the-hole — Yorkshire pudding topped with sausages

VEGETABLES:

jacket potato — baked potato

swedes — rutabagas

Windsor beans — broad beans

BREADS:

barm brack — round loaf made with self-rising flour, tea, brown sugar and dried fruit

brown bread — wholewheat or rye bread

cobloaf — round loaf of bread

country baps — rolls resembling our hamburger rolls

French Sticks — French bread

Indian bread — chappati or noam

maize bread — corn bread

malt loaf — yeast bread made with malt extract and black treacle, a sort of molasses

torpedoes — frankfurter-like buns used as biscuits

DESSERTS:

These usually arrive at the table on a **dessert trolley** (dessert wagon); custards and whipped cream are usually available to embellish cake.

apple snow — apple puree mixed with beaten egg white and served with custard

bakewell tart — raspberry jam is spread on a pastry base and an almond mixture is spread over that; it may be topped with a **pastry-grid** (lattice-top) before baking.

Battenberg cake — vanilla-flavored and raspberry-flavored sponge cakes cut in cubes and joined together with jam in a four-square design

bilberry pie — blueberry pie

bramble pudding — blackberry compote with apple slices

brown pudding — boiled pudding with dried fruit, ground almonds and spices

butter sponge — sponge cake made with butter; some plain, some with lemon strawberries or chocolate

canary pudding — lemon pudding

castle puddings — individual **sponges** (sponge cakes) served with jam sauce

crumble — a fruit cobbler like apple crisp

cabinet pudding — custard, candied fruit preserves and delicate cookies like ladyfingers

Eve's pudding — baked apple slices topped with sponge cake batter

flummery — almond-flavored jelly that's delicious with strawberries

gooseberry pie

roly-poly pudding — rolled suet cake, steamed

rum nicky — sticky tart made of dates and ginger

summer pudding — bread mixed with fruit

sponge sandwich — jelly roll

syllabub — mixture of lemon, sweet sherry, brandy and sugar topped with whipped cream

treacle tart — much like pecan pie sans pecans

trifle — (sponge cake slices sandwiched together with raspberry or strawberry jam, doused with sherry and then covered with custard to an inch or two in depth and then topped with whipped cream; teetotalers may use orange or other fruit juice for sherry...but it's not the same

CHEESE is an alternative choice for **"dessert."** Britain is noted for its delicious cheeses. Americans are familiar with **Stilton blue** but there's also a delicious creamy **Stilton white** which is too delicate to export. Other cheeses to try are: **Leicester red** (yellow colored), **Welsh Caerphilly, Double Gloucester, Wenslydale, Derbyshire** and **Cheddar.**

SAVOURY is another dessert-time choice. It's a small portion of a seasoned dish like **Welsh Rabbit.**

FAST FOODS:

beans on toast — baked beans on toast

bread and dripping — fat is poured off a roast, allowed to cool and set before being spread on bread

breadberry — bread and hot milk

bangers and bittersloater — sausages and beer

cornet — ice cream cone

fish and chips bought at a **chippy** — fish and chips shop

fish fingers — fish sticks

fish cake — fish croquette

hot sausage sandwich

Melton Mowbray pie or pork pie — well-seasoned chopped pork in a pie shell, eaten cold

Typical sidewalk queue.

priddy-oggies — pastry turnovers filled with pork and cheddar

sausage rolls — sausages in pastry. They are made two ways: **"puff?"** and **"short?"** Puff pastry is oilier having a greater fat content; short pastry is more biscuit-like.

slide — ice cream sandwich

Eating In

A **self-catering flat** or **house** (furnished apartment or house) has everything except the groceries. An arrangement can be made for milk delivery. It will come on a **milk float** (milk truck) or can be purchased at a grocery store. It's sold in glass bottles and is not homogenized, that is, there's cream on top. There's a trick to removing the thin metal top covering. Press down on the center with a thumb and the edges will automatically lift up.

Supermarkets are everywhere and one can also go to the **greengrocer** (vegetable store), fish store and butcher shop. In addition, many towns have **market day** once a week, usually in the town center where parking is forbidden during market hours so the farmers and vendors of clothing, shoes, antiques and what-have-you can set up their **stalls** (stands). Food shoppers usually take along willow **market baskets** or **holdalls** (shopping bags). Supermarkets provide **supermarket trolleys** (shopping carts) and **carrier bags** (plastic bags) for **parcelling** (bagging) groceries.

MARKET DAY FOOD HAWKERS (PEDDLERS)

butter wife or butter woman — butter seller
cheese monger — cheese seller
fish wife, fish fag or fish woman — fish seller

SHOPPING WORDS

box boy — grocer's helper
long dozen or **devil's dozen** — baker's dozen (13)
out of a packet — store bought
packet — package
parcel up — tie up
tinned goods — canned goods

Food Shopping

AT THE FISHMONGER (fish store) Britain being an island country, it's natural that fish would be a preferred item of food and each area has its specialty: **Scotland** for its salmon, kippers and salted herrings, **Dover** for sole, **Whitstable and Colchester** for oysters, **Yorkshire** for shrimp, **Devon** for bass, and **Cornwall** for fresh crabs.

MORE FISH WORDS

bloater or **two-eyed steak** — smoked herring
char or **red belly** — small fish in the herring family

English market in Leicester.

cockles — edible European bivalves (double shelled fish)

doctor fish — sea-surgeon (Acanthurus)

dace or **graining** — small river fish

haddock — ocean fish of cod family, **finnie haddie** or **finnan haddie** is a kind of smoked haddock

kipper — salmon or herring, split open, seasoned and dried

ling — codfish

plaice — European flounder

periwinkle, pennywinkle or **pin-patch** — edible snail

prawn — large shrimp

round fish — any fish that's not flat

soused herring — marinated herring

sprat — a small herring-like fish

whitebait — fresh sardines

tuna steak — tuna fish

zander — pike or perch

Fruit market on Queens Road, Leicester.

AT THE GREENGROCER (VEGETABLE STORE):
aubergines, eggfruit, brinjal, brown jolly or **mad apple** — eggplant
beetroot — beets
bilberries — blueberries
Bramleys — green cooking apples
bullock's heart — pawpaw
courgettes or **marrow** — zucchini or squash
egg plums — yellowish egg-shaped plums
Kentish cobs — hazel nuts or filberts
maize — corn
red streak — apples with streaked skins
sweetings — sweet apples

AT THE BUTCHER SHOP:
bones — spare ribs
bull beef or **bull-beeves** — coarse beef from bulls
chine of beef — rib roast
chump chops — lamb leg meat
cumberland sausage — large pork sausage
fillet steak — filet mignon
gammon — **ham** in the Midlands, **bacon** in northern England
joint — roast
minced beef — hamburger but not ground as fine as American ground meat
salt horse or **salt junk** — sailor slang for salt beef
silverside — top round steak
snorkers — sausages
souse — pickled pig's feet or ears
trotters — pig's feet
veal cutlets — veal chops
veal fillets — veal cutlets

AT THE SUPERMARKET:
bloater paste or **gentleman's relish** — herring paste for tea sandwiches
bully beef — WWI soldier slang for canned beef

butterine — margarine partly made from milk
creme fraiche — like sour cream
curd cheese — like ricotta or cottage cheese
cooking chocolate — baking chocolate
cornflour — cornstarch
egg powder — powdered eggs
ginger pop — ginger ale
haricot beans — dried beans
hive honey — honey
hundreds and thousands — sprinkles (tiny colored
   candies to ornament cakes)
jelly — gelatin
kissing comfits — breath mints
lemon squash — lemonade
monkey nuts — peanuts
pickles — pickled vegetables
pick tooth — toothpick
pine kernels — indian nuts
Ribena — black currant syrup
salad cream — mayonnaise
soda scones — soda crackers
soup squares — bouillon cubes
sweet oil — olive or rape oil
treacle — like molasses
vanilla pods — vanilla beans

MORE SUPERMARKET OFFERINGS

Biscuits (cookies) There is a tremendous variety of delicious cookies: Butter Crumb, Rich Marie, Gypsy Cream, Chocolate Whole Meal, scotch shortbreads, ginger nuts, sweetmeal, digestive biscuits (like animal crackers), Kentucky Cookies, (chocolate chip with coconut), Maryland Cookies (chocolate chip with nuts), brandy snaps and Custard Creams.

Clotted Cream or Devonshire Cream is a delicious heavy cream with 55 % butterfat. It's spreadable and used on scones and ice cream.

Fanny Adams is **tinned** (canned) mutton. It's WWI soldier slang and named after a girl who was murdered and dismembered in 1912.

Flour: **strong plain flour** (white) and **wholemeal flour** (whole wheat) are bread flours, **plain flour** is cake flour, and **self-raising flour** is self-rising flour.

Golden syrup is a syrup of honey consistency made from refined cane sugar.

Jellies and jams: lime, lime and lemon, Seville orange, lemon jelly, marmalade, orange jelly marmalade, lemon chip, **bramble jam** (blackberry preserves), lemon cheese marmalade and lemon curd marmalade.

Milk comes in imperial pint bottles (one and one-quarter times American pints). **New milk** is fresh milk. It can also be **skimmed** (skim milk), **semi-skimmed** (1% or 2% milk) and pasteurized. Pasteurized milk has a different **coloured** (colored) top. Cream can be **single cream** (18 % butterfat like half and half) or **double cream** (richer than American heavy cream). **Channel Islands milk** comes topped with cream.

Standard eggs come in several sizes: small, medium, Size 1 and large, Size 2. Small eggs are usually only available when pullets begin to lay.

Sugar comes in many forms: white, soft brown, light brown, caster (extra-fine), icing sugar (like confectioners 3X), Demerara, (light brown crystals for coffee), and sugar crystals (rainbow colored rock candy crystals for coffee).

Sweets or candy, a big item in the U.K. This is but 1/8th the assortment of candies available in a tiny newsagent's (newsdealer's) shop: mint humbugs, Royal buttermints, acid drops (lemon drops), barley sugarthins, buttered ginger, cherry menthol thins, mentho-lyptus tablets, clear mints, dairy butter toffees, kreemy bonbons and butter mintoes. **Fruit pastilles** (gumdrops) and **Pontefract cakes** (liquorice drops, the originals came from an old Roman town, Pontefract, meaning broken bridge).

APPROXIMATE EQUIVALENT MEASUREMENTS

METRIC		U.S. MEASURES
Measuring spoons:		
1.2 ml*		1/4 tsp
2.5 ml		1/2 tsp
5 ml		1 tsp
7.5 ml		1/2 tbsp
15 ml		1 tbsp
Dry measure:		
60 g**	2 oz	1/4 cup
125 g	4 oz	1/2 cup
175 g	6 oz	3/4 cup
250 g	8 oz	1 cup
1/4 kg***		1/2 pound
1/2 kg		1 pound
Liquid measure:		
60 ml	2 oz	1/4 cup
125 ml	4 oz	1/2 cup
175 ml	6 oz	3/4 cup
250 ml	8 oz	1 cup
500 ml		1 pint
1 l****		1 quart

*	ml	milliliter
**	g	grams
***	kg	kilograms
****	l	litres (liters)

Tea

HISTORY: The gracious British institution of Afternoon Tea was not in existence in England until Queen Victoria's reign even though tea had been imported and used for over 200 years. England had been a coffee drinking country with coffee houses

Tea time can be anytime.

but then the **John Company** (East India Company) put on an effective campaign to promote the drinking of tea. It was so effective that it was instrumental in causing the enactment of the Tea Act of 1773 which led to the Boston Tea Party. It's ironic that a coffee drinking nation switched to tea and America, a tea drinking nation switched to coffee.

The drinking of afternoon tea was inadvertently started by Anna, the wife of the 7th Duke of Bedford, who feeling hungry in the afternoons, solaced herself with a cup of tea and cakes at 4 P.M. in the privacy of her bedroom. This practice became popular at first with the aristocracy and then spread to the whole country. Eventually people had tea in tea gardens and finally, the tea shops of today.

TEA TIMES

Tea time can be anytime of day but as a rule, many have tea instead of coffee for breakfast and **afternoon tea** between 4 and 5. **Scottish high tea** is at 5 p.m. Some take a **cuppa** (cup of tea) all day long. Samuel Johnson, the famous dictionary writer, was one of these. He confessed to being "a hardened and shameless tea-drinker, who has for 20 years diluted his meals with only the infusion of this fascinating plant; whose kettle has scarcely had time to cool; who with tea amuses the evening, with tea solaces the midnight, and with tea welcomes the morning." (Samuel Johnson's Review in the *Literary Magazine*, 1757)

BREWING A PERFECT POT OF TEA:

1. To bring out the **flavour** (flavor) of the tea, the kettle should be filled with fresh cold water to be sure the water is filled with oxygen.

2. While the kettle is heating, fill an earthenware, porcelain, glass or silver teapot (never aluminum) with hot water to warm it, then dump it out.

3. Add to the teapot one teaspoon of tea for each person plus one for the pot.

4. **Immediately**, when the tea water reaches a rolling boil, pour it over the tea and cover the pot. Cover the pot with a tea cosy and allow the tea to brew for 3 minutes for small leaf tea and 5 for large leaf tea. Using a strainer, pour into cups and serve with sugar, cream or cold milk. Lemon is not usual, but a slice of lemon may be used in the summer-time. (Coffee is served with hot milk.)

5. Tea shops usually provide a teapot full of hot water and 2 tea bags plus another pot of hot water to dilute the tea, if desired.

KINDS OF TEA:

1. **Simple teas** and **Cream Teas** consists of hot scones with butter, jam and Devonshire cream.

2. **High teas** have a mixture of foods: thin cucumber or watercress sandwiches, sardine and tomato sandwiches, creamed foods on toast, small pieces of cold meat or fish, egg dishes, salads, scones, small cakes, tarts, shortbreads, whipped cream, pudding, and jam.

TEA OFFERINGS:

Abernethy biscuits — caraway seed cookies

Alma tea cakes — cookies made on a griddle

Bakewell tarts — almond cakes with a filling of raspberry preserves

Banbury cakes — oval-shaped currant/spice tarts

bannock — flat, round, unleavened oat biscuits made on a griddle

Bath-buns — raisin buns

Bath Oliver — biscuits invented by Dr. W. Oliver of Bath

Chelsea buns — sticky buns with dried fruit and honey glaze

Dundee cake — cake made with almonds, cherries, dried fruit and lemon peel

Eccles cakes — like Banbury cakes but have an oval shape

fairy cakes or queen cakes — cupcakes topped with icing and a cherry

ginger nuts — ginger cookies

jam doughnut — jelly doughnut

Yorkshire parkin — oatmeal, ginger and treacle cake

rock cakes — dried fruit buns but not made with yeast; rather, they have shortening "rubbed in" (worked in) as when making shortbread

TEA WORDS

sugar basin — sugar bowl

tea board — tea tray

tea break — like a coffee break

tea cloth — towel used in washing-up (washing) the tea things

tea fight or **bun fight** — tea party

tea lady — woman who serves tea from a large trolley (cart) in factories; is gradually being replaced by vending machines

tea lead — lead mixed with some tin that was used to line tea chests

tea meeting — public social meeting at which tea is served

teapot set — tea set

tea poy — small table, supported by a tripod, holding a tea service

tea trolley — tea cart

to pour out — to serve a cup of tea

"The tea is mashed." — "The tea is ready."

The English have an extraordinary ability
for flying into a great calm.
—Alexander Woollcott

CHAPTER TWELVE

THE BRITISH PEOPLE: WHAT ARE THEY REALLY LIKE?

If one were asked to name one characteristic the peoples of the U.K. are famous for, it would be **politeness**. If there ever were a contest to find the politest people on earth, the British would win hands down. Just buying a paper at a **newsagent** (newsdealer) is a case in point. You get at least four **"thank yous:"** one for coming in, one for handing in a bill to be changed, one when you receive the change and one when you leave.

A thank you for receiving a bill to be changed can lead to confusion when paying a cab driver. American cab drivers say thank you when you've tipped them. Their cab drivers, like newsagents and others, thank you for handing them a bill to be changed making you think that they think that they get the whole amount. **Not to worry!** They won't let you get away without your change. Waiters can also **"thank you"** to death. **"Thank you, may I help you." "Thank you, what will you have this morning? Eggs, yes, N'kew."** Sometimes the phrase becomes abbreviated. **"Yes madam, toast, N'kew."** Some variations on our "Thank you very much" were bound to happen with so many thank you's floating about. Some of these are: **"Ta"**, **"Thank you ever so," "Thanks very much, I'm sure," "I'm no end obliged, I'm sure," "Thanks awfully," "Thanks** frightfully," and **"Thank you very much indeed."** When you thank them, they'll say: "Not at all." (Don't mention it), or **"Thank you all the same."**

How did they come to be so courteous? Sociologists must have been puzzling over this phenomenon for years when one considers their ancestral background is filled with mayhem of all kinds embodied in the many invasions, the royal fights for supremacy, the many wars, the naval battles, the empire build-ing, etc. One would think they'd be loud, impolite and aggres-sive; instead, they are, for the most part, quiet, courteous, and reserved. Their ancestral background, however, has toughened their spines making them substantial, solid, **tough as old boots** (tough as leather) and tenacious, as symbolized by **John Bull**; therefore, able, with dogged courage, to **grit their teeth and soldier on** (grin and bear it) through two World Wars.

Being reserved is sometimes equated with being unfriendly. The British are not unfriendly. It's just that they value their privacy and the privacy of others. For example, we think it's being friendly to ask, **"What kind of work do you do?"** on meeting someone new. The British would consider that **bad form, unsuitable** and **not proper** (bad manners). They possibly get visual clues from one's **school tie** and **school jacket** and audio clues from one's use of the language as certain words can label one a **"U"** (upper class) or **"non-U."** For example, **"U's"** have **lavs** or **loos** in their homes, never toilets. They use nap-kins, never **serviettes**. Other words they never use are sports jacket, sweater and wallet. Politicians are very cognizant of this class distinction and some are known to have **"poshed up"** (used "U" terms) in their speeches for Parliament. "U" and "non-U" are terms originated in **"Noblesse Oblige,"** a **jokey book** (parody) by Nancy Mitford, Evelyn Waugh, John Betje-men and friends.

There is one instance when the British do "lose their cool" and that is when someone tries to **"jump a queue"** (push ahead on line); then you'll be told politely by some and rudely by others to **"get to the end of the queue."** Using queues makes sure everyone is served in turn. This worked well during the wartime shortages and has become such an ingrained habit that there's even a joke about it: **"An Englishman, even if he is alone, forms an orderly queue of one."**

Some Americans resent being called **"Yanks,"** by the British. It may help to know where the name came from. "Yank" goes back to our Revolution when the song **"Yankee Doodle"** was played frequently by Washington's troops. It seemed to the British soldiers to be our national anthem and they took to calling the Americans **"Yankee Doodles," "Yankees"** or just plain **"Yanks"** and the name stuck. At the time, America was **"the colonies"** and that name, also, has yet to be erased from their vocabulary.

In the main, Americans will be able to **get on** (get along) easily with the British. They'll find Brits to be warm and hospitable even if we commit cultural no-nos. There seems to be a universal agreement to overlook anything they would consider **"forthcoming"** (brash) coming from a compatriot. An Italian scientist once explained this phenomenon. He said, "In Europe, we are born **"born old,"** by that I mean, we immediately have the weight of history on our shoulders; and that includes every dispute from the beginning of time. You in America, on the other hand, only go back 500 years. In comparison, you are still in your infancy." Perhaps their tolerance is a wish that they could be just as unemcumbered with the past.

There is also in the UK today, to a lesser extent than in former days, a **class system** in which titles are very important. Britain is chock full of **Lords, Dukes, Marquesses, Earls, Viscounts, Barons, Knights (called Sir)** and a myriad of the royally **honoured** (honored) with the **Order of the Bath** or **Companion of the Bath** and such. The two world wars **put paid** (ended) the rigid stratification of classes of Queen Victoria's day but the people still feel the class system shapes their lives. Distinctions notwithstanding, all would agree they are **true Britons to their boot soles** (as Americans are real to their fingertips).

To get to know them better, let us explore other facets of their character, that is, how they react with each other; and enjoy the rich mixture of colloquialisms and slang that they use in their everyday lives.

Greetings and Partings

Hello is not usually used as a greeting. **"Ah, there you are!"** would be more usual in the sense of "Glad to see you." **"Ah, well met"** and **"How are you keeping?"** mean "How are you?" or "How are you doing?" Good friends may greet each other as **"Hi old thing"** or **"I say, old bean," "Hi dear boy!"** or **"Hi old mate." "Hi old fruit"** was used at one time, but perhaps no longer. Besides **"Good evening"** you may get shortened collo- quial versions such as **"Good even"** or **"Good den."** Some goodbyes are **"Cheers", "Cheerio"** and **"See you then"** (See you later) and **"I must be toddling along."** Our infantile "Bye bye" can just be as bad there as **"Cheerybye" "Ta" "Tara"** or **"Tata."**

That's Flaming Good! (That's Great!)

The British are great at applauding one's efforts and put American to shame with their many variations of "That's great! and "Wonderful!" Some of these are: **"That's: champion, rip- ping, top hole, wizard, dashed clever, frightfully brilliant, genuine, rattling good, unco-quid** (Scots for uncommonly good), **topping, super, thundering good, thumping good, up to the knocker** and **spiffing!"** Others are: **"Well said!" "Smash- ing!" "Good-oh!"** Jolly good! **"Oh, I say!" "Well done!"** and **"Capital!"** In wishing you luck, they'll say: **"You'll put up a damned good show!"** ("You'll do well!") or **"The best of British luck!" "The best of British!"** (without "luck") is usually satirical.

By George! (Imagine That!)

"Hallo or Hullo" together with a bemused expression are employed when faced with a surprising event in place of "What's this?" or "Will you look at this!" Our "My goodness!"

and "Imagine that!" translate to **"By George!" "Blimey!** **"Gosh!" "My hat!"** and **"Cor!"** (abbreviation of **Corblimey**-a euphemism for **God Blind Me!**). "You catch on fast!" becomes **"You've got it in one!"**

Cock-a-hoop (Pleased as Punch)

When the British are excited they'll say they're **"fool happy,"** **"on the high ropes," "over the moon," "in high feather," "in no end of a fig"** (in a tizzy) or **"in a pin"** (in a merry mood). When reporting a special celebration, they'll say they **"enjoyed it frightfully,"** or they were **"mafficking."** (Celebrating exultingly as London did after the relief of **Mafeking**, South Africa, on May 17, 1900. This was during the Boer War when a pinned down British force received reinforcements from Canada, Australia and New Zealand.)

Being Matey (Being Friendly)

On meeting someone outdoors, you may hear **"I say"** (Hi!) **"It's a cracking fine day!"** (It's a perfect day!). If asked how they are, they may say, **"Everything's ticking over nicely."** (All's going well.) If you're told that someone will **"call round"** to see you, it means he/she will "stop over." They'll most likely **"give you a shout"** (phone you) first. When visiting, you may be invited to **"Take a pew."** or **"Have a chair."** (Have a seat.)

Feeling Like Tuppence Ha'penny (feeling Rotten)

When things are **"at two and six"** (at sixes and sevens), or **"all anyhow"** (gone haywire), it's natural to **"get the wind up"** (get all upset). Some **"can't stick it,"** or **"stand the gaff"** (take the heat). They may **"get a frightful twitch on"** or **"get the jim jams"** (get the heebie jeebies) and start **"feeling dicky"** (shaky), **"swimmy"** or **"fuzzle headed"** (woozy). Some can **"be acid"** (bitter); some can **"be in a great taking on"** (have a fit) about it; and others may not **"care a dash"** (give a darn) as it's no use **"binding over"** (stewing over) things.

Feeling Broody (Feeling Low)

When one is in a **"dark patch"** (dark period), one can have **"the horrors," "the hump," "the sulks," "the megrims,"** or **"be cast down"** (feel blue), **"be under the black dog"** (be in a dark mood), or be **"nohowish"** (feel blah). Some will **"eat worms"** (sulk), others will **"get soppy"** (weepy) and **"blub"** or **"tune one's pipes"** (cry); and still others will **"get the fantods"** (get the fidgets) and **"chew the carpet"** (climb the walls).

Feeling Nervy (Nervous)

It's very **"off-putting"** (upsetting) to **"have a nasty turn"** (a scare). One can **"get the wind up"** (get a fright), **"be in a flat spin"** or **"proper state"** (tailspin), feel **"dicky"** (nervous) and be in a **"muck sweat"** (scared silly). **"Nervestorms"** (nervous upsets) can **"make one have a frightful twitch on"** (be nervous as a cat), or give one a **"heart-quake"** (the shakes).

Commiserations

Commiserations, as with Americans, are full of slang and colloquialisms, as in the following fictitious conversation:

"How are you getting on?"

"Job's news, I've had a spot of trouble. What I sold was catchpenny. You know, brummagem. I have a chance to fix things but it's rum going. I'm down in the swamp and may have the key to the street." (The news is bad. I'm in a lot of trouble! I sold some shoddy materials, junk. I have a chance to straighten things out but it's tough going. I'm losing money and may be out on the street.)

"I'm genuinely sorry. I thought you looked very rum. Dash it all! Hard cheese, old boy! I'm extremely sorry you've had the black ox tread on your foot. Poor blighter! You're a good chap. I can help you." (I'm very sorry. I thought you were looking odd. Damn it all! Too bad, pal. I'm sorry you've had such a bad time of it. Poor stiff! You're a good fellow. I'll help you out.)

"That's awfully decent of you. You're a stout fellow, as solid

as they come." (That's awfully good of you. You're a good guy, as good as they come.)

"Not at all. It's a bit of a do if neighbours can't help each other." (Don't mention it. It's a sorry state of affairs if neighbors can't help each other out.)

"All the same, that's very handsome of you!" (Just the same, it's very good of you.)

Other words of commiseration are: "Pity!" "Hard luck!" "Midluck!" and "Bad luck!" (Too bad!); "Poor old blighter!" "Wretched fellow!" "Poor wight!" and "Poor beggar!" (Poor stiff!). "Poor little snipe!" or "Poor little toad!" (Poor little thing!) is said to a child.

Personal Descriptions

From the foregoing, one gets the impression they are a bunch of fuddy-duddies. Not at all! In the area of name calling, they can match us name for name, some high-toned and some with a theatrical flare. After all, it is the land of Shakespeare. The ensuing descriptions of a man and two women will dispel that fuddy-duddy notion:

"He has a clock like a fiddle (a long face), a copper nose (red nose), is gap-toothed (snaggle-toothed) and wears a charley (small triangular beard like that of Charles I). He's thick-witted (dull), doesn't have much in the upperworks (head or brain) but is a decent sort of fellow (a good fellow)."

"She's a poppet (doll) with forget-me-not blue eyes (light blue eyes), ginger hair (tawny hair) and a trim and taut (slim and firm) figure."

"She's ever so shy (very shy) unlike her sister who is positively through the looking glass (a weirdo) and too bright by half (too smart for her own good.)"

A Man: Descriptions

If dumb: a **mug** or **mugg** (a patsy), a **right Charlie**, a **B.F.** (Bloody Fool), a **boiler** (a failure), a **busted flush**, a **jack fool**, a juggin, a **noodle**, a **wet-eared** ninny or a **pudding-headed, wooly minded twit.**

If effeminate: a **jenny, Nancy boy, Nance, Miss Nancy, a bit of an old bessie,** an **after-guard,** a **betty** (a man who does women's work), **Peter pansy, softling** (weakling) or a **carpet knight** (a knight by court favor and not by exploits).

If funny: a **mopoke,** an **amusing cove,** a **card,** a **Tom Noddy,** a **wag,** a **jack pudding,** a **merry Andrew** or a **rowdy-dowdy.**

If lazy: a **lead slinger** (gold bricker), a **scrimshanker,** a **scruffy layabout** and a **shirker.** Lead slingers **"swing the lead"** (that is, malinger) **and are bone idle.**

If likeable: a **bloke,** a **dear old chap,** a **steady chap,** a **mate** (pal), a **quite respectable old boy,** a **real brick,** an **old lad,** a **hearty,** a **stout fellow,** a **trump** and **a toff** (Cockney for "a real gent"). He can also be a **mucker,** that is a **mate** (friend) as in **"my old mucker"** (my old pal). **"To muck in"** is to lend a hand.

If nosy: a **Paul Pry** and a **Nosey Parker.**

If old: **a bit of a crock,** an **elderly buffer,** a **funny old git** or a **silly old gaffer.**

If a pimp: **a fancy man** or **ponce.**

If quiet: a **sober-sides.**

If rascally: a **cove,** a **young dog,** or a **cheeky old B.** "B" takes the place of impolite words beginning with this letter.

If repugnant: a **rotter,** a **bit of a bounder** or sneak, an **appalling little tick,** a **bull calf,** a **cad,** a **city gent** (city slicker), **a clever Dick** (smart Alec), a **clot,** a **bull calf** (lout), **a downy bird** (wily), **a jerk-off** (slob), a **pinheaded poop,** a **poisonous bloater,** a **superfatted warthog,** a **no-man** (one who always says "No") and the worst of all...**the dog's dinner, the dog's meat, offscum** or **like dust** (garbage). "Dust" is a euphemism for **"garbage"** in Britain. **"Dustmen,"** for example, collect garbage. One can also be **smarmy** (oily) and **base minded** (dirty minded).

If rustic: a **bucolic,** a **chaw-bacon** or a **hodge.**

If a show-off: a **big pot** (big shot), **a bumble or bumbledom** (a blow-hard), **a cocky little ass, a dicky, a pompous prig, a** gab-man, a wiseling and a copper captain (one who styles himself as a captain without grounds).

If a tramp: a pie-powder.

A Woman: Descriptions

If a drudge: Mrs. Mop.

If easily frightened: a jelly baby (sugar baby).

If fussy: a busy and Miss Prunes and Prisms.

If a lady of the evening: a crumpet, a paid bint and an experienced little piece.

If messy: a Judy (a frump like Punch's wife) with a witch's tangle (messy hair).

If mysterious: older-than-the-rocks-among-which-she-sits.

If old: a gamp (hag) or an old trout.

If overweight: bonny is a kind appellation, two ton Tessie would be unkind.

If silly: scatty, a daisy (a dilly) a silly little scrap, silly old faggot; and to be really rude, a silly old moo cow.

A Man or Woman: Descriptions

If frosty: not forthcoming.

If neat: tidy, jemmy or gemmy.

If poor: footy, on strap or on the cheap. Whip-the-cat is to economize.

If smart: a brains trust, booksie, a dabster, knackish, clever as paint, Prof, Professor or a sly boots.

If a spendthrift: a squanderboats.

If square: dreary and suburban.

If stingy: fast-handed (close-fisted), mean, near the bone, a nip cheese, a pinch fist, pinch gut or pinch commons.

If unstable: a peg too low, around the twist, barmy, bonkers, a crack-brain, crackers, daft, dotty, going offside (going off the deep-end), mental, wonky, mildly potty, nutters, a nutcase, off one's tot (head), slightly mad or potty.

If a wet blanket: a damp squib, a dry file or a dry old stick.

For more, see Appendix, Chapter 12, under A Man or Woman: More Descriptions.

Very Personal Descriptions

Head: **bonce** or **loaf**

Hair: **black-polled** (dark hair), and **pollarded** (bald)

Face: **crab-faced**, (crabby looking), **pudding face** (homely), **dish-faced** (round, flat face) **mulberry-faced** (red with anger or the heat) or **the codfish type** (fish faced)

Facial hair: **dun-drearies** (long side whiskers as worn for the first time by a Mr. Dundreary), **newgate fringe** (a beard under the chin), **charley** (triangular beard) and **sideboards** (side-burns)

Eyes: **bird-eyed** or **hawk-eyed** (sharp-eyed), **sharp-sighted** (far-sighted), **short-sighted** (near- sighted), **boss-eyed** (cross-eyed) and **wonk-eyed** (bleary eyed)

Ears: **tabs** or **earlaps** (ear lobes) and **stick-out ears** (jug ears)

Nose: **boko**

Mouth: **pan mouthed** (big mouthed)

Tongue: **red rag**

Throat: **throttles**

Neck: **bull-necked**

Figure: **cobby** or **stuggy** (thick set), **lard fat** or **podge** (a fatso) and **sack-line figure** (boyish figure).

Shoulders: **bottle-shouldered** (round shouldered)

Breasts (women's): **knockers**

Belly: **tum** or **tumtum** (tummy), **bow window** (bay window) and **fish-bellied**

Hands: **mutton fisted** (coarse large fists), **hamfisted** (clumsy) and **cackhanded** (left-handed or clumsy)

Legs: **sparrow legged** (thin legs) and **duck-legged** (short-legged)

Lashing Out

The British can **make long noses** or **cock snooks** (thumb noses), call names and get just as **flipping mad** or **blood livid** (mad as all get out) as we do but use different expletives. Some examples:

They **got his monkey up** (got him mad). He **got purple** (black with fury) as he gave them a **dressing down** (scolded): "You're **bird witted** (dim-witted), **beefbrained** (dull), **beefwitted** and **a blithering idiot** (stupid)!" He **drummed the devil's tattoo** (drummed his fingers) on the table. **"You don't know B from Battledore"** ("You don't know your nose from your elbow."), he shouted. I'm **tired of your backing down·**(gold bricking). **"It just makes my blood boil!"** (It drives me bats!)

"Don't take umbrage." (Don't get on your high-horse.) **It's bumkum** (bunk), a **dough-baked idea** (half-baked idea), **deuced silly** (stupid) and **a lot of crafting dottle** (drivel). It won't work so **pull up your socks** (be sensible) and **give over** (stop it).

He was trying to do his accounts but the **kick-up** (ruckus) the children were making finally got to him. He shouted, **"Fire and brimstone!** (Hell and damnation!) **Stop that blasted row!** (Stop that racket!) **Have you got cloth ears?** (Are you deaf?) **Belt up!** (Shut up!)"

Blowing one's top is **getting one's wind up** or **going up in the air.** A scolding is **a wigging,** a **dress out,** a **come down upon** or **a dressing-down. Being carpeted and flogged** is being scolded and spanked.

"Confound it! (Damn it!). If you don't shut your **fly-trap** (mouth), **I'll shut it for you!** I'm going to **thump your nose** (punch your nose) and **dust your jacket** (beat you up). A **dust-up** (fight) is what you need to sort you out (teach you a lesson). It'll be a **ding-dong** (a hell of a fight)." Other names for a fight are: **a blinding row, an argy-bargy, a bit of a barge in, a bit of a dust up** and a **free fight** (free-for-all).

"That's bought it! (Damn it all, that does it.) **I've copped a basinful** (I've had it!) **You turn me up** (make me sick) **you double-tongued** (two-faced) **booby** (boob). **You're a ruddy liar** (You're a lying so-and-so), so **be off with you** (scram)!" Other ways of saying "Beat it!, or Get lost!" are: **"Beetle off!" "Be off**

with you!" "Stuff it!" "Get weaving!" "B—off!" "Clear off!", "Buzz off!" "Get knotted!" "Shift it!" "Get cracking!" and "Push off!"

There are More Angry Expressions under Chapter 12 in the Appendix.

Interesting Expressions

The British have many interesting expressions which are easy to understand such as **"living in a shop window"** (living in a goldfish bowl), **"in the fullness of time"** (in due time); but what could **"let's return to our muttons"** mean? It means **"let's get back to the subject."** It comes from an old French farce **"Maitre Pathelin"** in which the witnesses kept straying away from the matter in dispute—the sheep—until the judge in exasperation said, **"Ravenons a nos moutons!"** and that made such an impression that it found it's way into the English language, perhaps via the Normans.

Many expressions are like private jokes in the you-had-to-be-there category, those that are understood only by the few people who carry the wit of the ages. Often these sayings seem rather obscure and far-fetched today. One such is **"Oh Queen Anne's dead."** ("That's stale news!") Why? Who knows? The origin of **"Bob's your uncle"** is also very obscure but comparable to our "That's it," "It's finished," "Done," "Complete!" Another with an obscure beginning is: **"to be marked with a white stone"** (born with a silver spoon in one's mouth).

"Tight as Dick's hatband" and **"queer as Dick's hatband that went nine times round and wouldn't meet,"** have an explanation. They refer to **Richard Cromwell, son of Oliver Cromwell,** who inherited the Protectorship of England but was unequal to the job and gave up after a year, earning him the disparaging name of **Tumbledown Dick** or **King Dick.** The British Crown was called **"Dick's hatband,"** a crown that just wouldn't fit.

"Going to pigs and whistles" means "going to wrack and ruin," that is, **"being on Queer Street"** (having money troubles). Queer Street is an imaginary street where British people live when they have money troubles. **"To be in chancery"** means "to be in hot water," that is, involved in litigation. **Chancery** was formerly the highest court of justice next to the House of Lords. **"To hunt the gowk"** is "to go on a fool's errand." **Gowk** is Scottish for the cuckoo. **"To put on side"** is "to show off." **"A curate's egg"** means something is "half good and half bad." It got into the language from a Punch cartoon in which a curate was asked if his egg was bad. "Oh no," he said. "Parts of it are excellent." He was breakfasting with his Bishop and formidable Bishop's wife and had to be diplomatic.

"Jam tomorrow and jam yesterday, but never jam today" (something promised never comes) is from Lewis Carroll's "Through the Looking Glass."

"Quite!" is an expression Americans should adopt. It saves a lot of talk as it can mean: **"Oh absolutely!" "I'm counting on you" "You're hopeless!" "Exactly!"** and **"Indeed, yes!"**

"Bloody" can be used in both good and bad situations but is mostly attached to heated or extreme expressions. First the good: **"That's bloody marvelous!"** and **"He looks bloody cheerful."** And the bad: **"Bloody fool!" "I'm in a bloody awkward patch" "Bloody hell!" "You're bloody crackers!" "You're making a bloody hash of things" "I feel perfectly bloody" "As if I bloody well care"** and **"Stop being bloody-minded."** (Stop being awkward and uncooperative.) Women usually desist from using the whole word, substituting for it the letter **"B"** as in **"That's B-good!"** and **"Stop being B-minded."**

Another all-occasion word is **"jolly."** It's mostly used in good situations. But the bad: **"It was a jolly shambles!" "It's jolly rum! (odd)"** and **"Be jolly quiet!"** And the good: **"That's jolly good!" "It's a jolly good show!"** and **"It's a jolly jape! (joke)."**

Vivid Expressions

They were chattering away **"nineteen to the dozen"** (a mile a minute), and **"She can talk the hind leg off a donkey."** (She can talk one's head off.)

"I've had a basinful!" ("I've had it up to here!")

"Now you're talking in imperial measures." ("Now you're talking big money!")

"She dropped a brick or **dropped a clanger."** ("She made a blunder!")

"It's plain as a pikestaff." ("It's plain as the nose on your face.")

"He has a long arm." ("He has a boarding house reach.")

"She's straight out of the egg." ("She's unbelievably naive.")

"It's easy as shelling peas." ("It's easy as pie.")

"It's as near as damn it." is the preferred short version of "**It's as near as Damn it! is to swearing."** ("If it was any nearer, it would bite you.")

"I was turned down like a bedspread." ("I was turned down flat.")

"You've got him on a plate." ("You've got him where you want him.")

There are so many more, that to be better appreciated, they've been categorized according to meaning. As will be noticed, troubled times generate the most expressions. These can be found in the Appendix under Chapter Twelve, More Interesting Expressions.

Mid pleasures and palaces though we may roam,
Be it ever so humble, there's no place like home.
— John Howard Payne, *Clari, the Maid of Milan,* **Home Sweet Home**

CHAPTER THIRTEEN

THE BRITISH PEOPLE: HOME AND HEARTH

This chapter deals with the everyday lives of the British people: **religion, courtship, marriage, housing, children, health, family celebrations and death;** and will clearly demonstrate the amazing flexibility of the English language. It is incredible that of the myriad expressions that the British and Americans use in their daily lives that so few match.

Religion

The two established national churches are the **C. of E.** (Church of England) which is Anglican or Protestant Episcopal with the British monarch as its head; and the **Church of Scotland** (Presbyterian). There are also many other Protestants, Roman Catholics, Jews, Muslims, Hindus and Sikhs. The Church of England is governed by two archbishops, one in Canterbury and one in York. Each section has **bishoprics**, governed by bishops; and these in turn are divided into **parishes** whose churches are officiated by **vicars, rectors** and **curates.** There are two kinds of services: The **High Church** which follows much of the ritual of the Catholic Church; and the **Low Church** which has a much simpler ritual.

In many British novels, one reads that the rector is given **"the living"** of the parish, meaning he is allowed to be the vicar and receive an annual salary. Some of these are called **"rural pocket** livings" as they are given by local lords of the manor who have **"proprietary chapels"** (private chapels). The livings are **"in their pockets,"** so to speak, so they can appoint whom they like. When a vicar is on holiday, usually a **"locum"** takes his place. Locum is short for the Latin **"locum tenens"** meaning **"holding the place."** Physicians also use locums.

RELIGION WORDS AND TERMS

being Pi (Pious), churchy or **a ruddy saint** — being very religious

choir organ — choir organ

Chapel Master — music director or conductor

Chapel Royal — chapel in a royal palace

church parade — Easter parade

church rate — weekly offering

churchway — road leading to a church

D.V. Deo Volente — God willing

half-baptise — to baptize privately and hastily

hot-gospeller — a revivalist preacher

Last Unction — Extreme Unction

Old Ned, Old Nick, Old One, Old Poker or **Old Harry** — the Devil

roundheaded — puritanical

the last trump — doomsday

to be brought up chapel — to have a strict religious upbringing

to ring bells backward — to give sad tidings, beginning with the bass bell

warden — sexton

MORE RELIGIOUS TERMS

A **Breeches Bible** is so called because **"breeches"** was substituted for the word **"aprons"** in Genesis III 7.

Chapel is a dissenters' place of worship; also called **Low Church.**

THE BRITISH PEOPLE: HOME AND HEARTH

A Chapel of Ease is a chapel for those who live far from a parish church.

A devil dodger is a preacher who rants; or a person who attends all kinds of churches to be on the safe side.

A dry mass (from the Latin **"missa secca"**) meaning a mass without consecration or communion.

An Enclosed Order of Nuns is a cloistered order, that is, the nuns never leave the convent as nurses or teachers. It is a Contemplative Order for prayer.

A lichgate is a roofed churchyard gate to rest a bier under where the first part of the Burial Service used to be said. **"Lich"** is an obsolete name for **"body,"** living or dead.

Queen Anne's Bounty is a fund for augmenting the poorer livings of the Church of England.

A Sunday saint is one whose religion or morality is confined to Sundays.

Courtship and Marriage

When a young man gets **besotted about** or **mashed on** (crazy about) a **bird** (girl), he may describe her as **dishy**, a **raver**, an **absolute stunner**, or a **knocker** (raving beauty or knockout) and determine to **chat her up** (talk to her) and perhaps **have a walk out** (get a date). **Walking out** can also mean **"going steady."** If she has rather **a pash on** (a crush on) him, she will accept the date but there's always the chance that they **won't get on** (get along) with each other. She may decide that with him, it's **cupboard love** (he's after her money) so he'll **be dished** (dumped) for being **a line shooter** (giving her a line).

If the girl is **half knocked off her balance** (knocked for a loop) about him because he's **over head and ears** (head-over-heels) in love with her, they'll be **wallowing about in treacle** (getting lovey-dovey) and deciding that **two can live as cheap** (cheaply) as one. He'll **throw his cap over the windmill** (pop the question) and **touch wood and whistle** (knock wood) that all will turn out well. He'll have her meet his **mum** (mother), **governor** (dad) and **nan** (granny) and she'll do the same.

185

They'll be **bespoken** (engaged) and then it's **decision time**. Should they have a church wedding, a **hedge marriage** (secret marriage), or a **Registry Office marriage** (civil marriage)? Once that's settled, should it be a **penny wedding** (one in which the guests give money to set up the newlyweds) or not? The **groomsman** or best man will be chosen, the **bride cake** (wedding cake) ordered and the groom-to-be will buy a **favour** (a bunch of ribbons to wear as a boutonniere) and a **morning gift** (gift for the bride given the after-wedding morning) which she'll always keep in her **glory box** (box of mementos).

If all goes well, that is, she's **homely** (a homebody) and **keeps a good house** (has plenty of food on hand); and he's a **pattern husband** (ideal husband) and **called affectionately, "my old pot-and-pan"** (rhyming slang for "man"), and neither is **having it off** (having an affair); there's a good chance they'll reach their **silver wedding day** (silver anniversary) together.

Where to Live?

Finding a place to live involves checking the **estate adverts** (real estate ads) and going to a **house agency** (real estate office) to consult an **estate agent** (real estate agent). He may tell them of a **three-bedroomed** (three bedroom) house that's available in a **building estate** (housing development). The owners have a **genuine reason for sale** (must sell) so the house may not be **pricey** (expensive). He'll give them an **order to view** (permit to see the house) and if they like it, they can discuss **house purchase schemes** (methods of payment) and get an **undertaking** (have an understanding) about payment.

MORE REAL ESTATE LANGUAGE

bed-sitter or bed sit — one-room apartment
bedsitterland — a rooming house row
chummage apartment — shared by two or more
combined room — studio apartment
cottaged — area covered with cottages
council maisonette — small house or flat

detached house — one family house

dormitory town — bedroom community

first offer — first refusal

flat — apartment

full board — room and board

furnished show flat — model apartment

life renter — right to use for life

K. and B. — kitchen and bath

mews — name for all areas converted from stables. The first mews were at Charing Cross, London, where a king kept his hawks. "Muer" is French for "to molt." When the area became the Royal Stables the name stuck.

mod. con. — modern conveniences

moonlight flitting — rent dodging

one-room flat — no kitchen

open-plan flat — one-room apartment

peppercorn rent — nominal rent

ribbon building or **ribbon developments** — towns that grow in long strips along roads

single-storey building — one-story building

tenant at will or **tenantship** — tenant who can only stay as long as the owner wills

terrace house — one in a row of houses

third girl — a **flat mate** (roommate), term used in advertising for a third person to share an apartment

three-bed semi — semi-detached house, a mirror image of the adjoining house

tower block — high rise apartments

two-up, two-down — two rooms up and two down

vacant possession or vacant tenancy — empty house or flat

weekly property — rental property

British Homes (Outside)

Should they want to build, they'll need a **planning permission** (building permit) and then will be involved with choices of everything connected with building: **builder's timber** (lumber), **weather boarding** (clapboard), **waste pipes** or **foul water drains** (drain pipes), **up-and-over garage doors** (overhead doors), **Bath stone**, (building stone quarried at the town of Bath), **drive gates** (driveway gates), water supply pipes (water pipes), **dry-stone walls** (walls built without mortar), **French roofs** (mansard roofs), **ha-has** (sunk fence walls or ditches), **hoggin** or **hogging** (screened gravel), etc.

MORE BUILDING TERMS

alleyway — an alleyway is an **alley** in London, a **twitten** in Sussex, a **rennel** in Durham and a **jetty** (pronounced jitty) in Leicester

chimney stalk or **chimney stack** — smoke stack or tall chimney

close — the old word for the field of homes around a large church; today usually a cul-de-sac with a group of homes; in North Country and Scotland, it's a **"hus"**

cob — building material for walls made of mixed clay and straw

    conversion — rebuilding

    crazy paving — flagstone walk

    cross garnet — T-shaped hinge

    dead wall — blank wall

    extension — site annex

    Home-Farm — farm attached to or near a great house

    madge — lead hammer

    paling — picket fence

    party wall — wall shared in a double house

    planks — boards

    ring wall — enclosing wall

    Roman cement — hydraulic cement made from cal-
        careous nodules (chalky lumps from London clay)

    self-help — do-it-yourself

    slop-built or jerry-built — jerry-built

    snow-guard — board to keep snow from sliding from
        the roof

stair tower or **turret** — turret
to **smarm** — to plaster
tradesmen's entrance — where goods are delivered
waste ground — empty lot
water butt — rain barrel
wood-wool slabs — slabs made from long wood shavings (excelsior) with a cementing material used for lining partitions

Finishing Touches

Once the house shell is erected, there are many items to install: **louvre windows** (louvered windows), **double glazing** (storm windows), **building board** (plasterboard), **draught-board-tiled floors** (checkerboard-tiled floors), **French sashes** or **French windows** (French doors), **skirting boards** or **skirting** (base boards), **air extractors** (ventilators), **distributing boxes** (fuse boxes), **electric flex** and **power points** (electric cords and outlets), **light fittings** (light fixtures), **stairways** (staircases), **cockle** (slang for furnace or stove), **geyser** (gas water heater), **door furniture** (door hardware), **bell-push** (door bell button), **deadlatches** (deadbolts), etc.

Then it's time for **paint pots** or **paint tins** (paint cans), **emulsion paint** (latex paint), **colour washing** (water paint), **roller blinds** (window shades), **hat pegs** (coat hooks), **jardiniere curtains** (tiered curtains), etc.

Moving

When the house is **ready to take up residence** (ready for habitation), it's time to select a **haulage firm** (movers) from the **house removals ads** (moving & storage ads) in the phone book and start filling some **packing cases** (packing boxes).

British Homes (Inside)

First, **homekeeping** (housekeeping) items and then items used in specific rooms. Note: the **ground floor** corresponds to our first floor and the **first floor** would be our second.

HOMEKEEPING (HOUSEKEEPING) ITEMS

FOR CLEANING:
- **coom** — soot
- **duster** — dustcloth
- **dustette** or **hand hoover** — hand vacuum
- **hoover, cleaner** or **carpet sweeper** — carpet sweeper
- **J-cloths** — handi-wipes
- **sluts wool** — dust balls
- **smut** — dust
- **to bottom** — to clean floors and rugs
- **to bottom it** — to clean thoroughly
- **to hoover** — to vacuum

FOR HANDWORK:
- **cage work** — open work (hand work)
- **canvas work** — embroidery on canvas
- **cotton wool** — absorbent cotton
- **household pins** — straight pins
- **ladies' companion** — knitting bag
- **lump of cotton wool** — cotton ball
- **reels of cotton** — spools of thread
- **housewife** or **sewing outfit** — sewing kit

MISCELLANEOUS:
- **American cloth** or **oil cloth** — glazed tablecloth
- **burning glass** — magnifying glass
- **carriage clock** — travel clock
- **book matches** — matchbooks
- **book room** — small library in a private home
- **congreve match** and **safety match** — friction match invented by Sir William Congreve; a safety match will only ignite on the matchbox's chemical strip, not on any rough surface
- **drawing pins** — thumb tacks
- **dunlopillo** — Dunlopillo was originally a foam rubber pillow made at Fort Dunlop, Birmingham, but name has become generic for foam rubber
- **electric torch** — flashlight

glory hole — room for miscellaneous odds and ends
key fob — key holder
leadfoil wrapping — aluminum foil
lino — linoleum
lucifer — match
pencil torch — penlight
paraffin — wax
sellotape — scotch tape
thermos flask — thermos bottle
torch or **torchlight** — flashlight
torch batteries — flashlight batteries
FOR KITCHEN:
Domestic appliances:
cooker or **cooking range** — stove
cookery book — cookbook
fridge/freezer — refrigerator/freezer
grill — broiler
paraffin stove — kerosene stove
the deep freeze — freezer
Cooking and baking items:
baker's board or **moulding board** — bread board
baking sheet — cookie sheet
baking tin — baking pan
biscuit box — cookie tin
butter cloth, butter muslin or **sponge cloth** — cheese-cloth
cookery book — cookbook
chinois — conical sieve
fish-slice — fish knife
flacket —bottle or flask
flan tin — tart pan with removable bottom
kitchen paper — paper towels
larder — pantry
multicooker — electric frypan
oven gloves — oven mitts
palette knife — spatula

pinger — oven timer

plated biscuit barrels —silver cookie jars

porridge stick — wooden spoon

pressure pot — pressure cooker

pudding basin — small bowls used to boil or steam "puds" (puddings); they come in half-pint, pint and one and a half pint sizes

punnet — berry basket

signal bell — timer

slice — spatula

tin (of food) — can

tin opener — can opener

The washing-up: doing the dishes:

draining board — drain board

bristol-brick — earthy material for scouring silver

plate powder — silver polish

pedal bin — step-on garbage can

rubbish bag — garbage bag

slop basin or **bowl** — scraper bowl

washing-up bowl — dishwashing pan

washing-up machine — dishwasher

washing-up water — dishwater

FOR DINING ROOM:

British plate — German silver

butter boat — melted butter pot

butter cooler — dish for keeping butter in cold water at table

canteen cutlery or **tableware** — flatware or silver

canteen or **canteen of cutlery** — flatware chest

claret jug — red wine pitcher

crockery — table ware

doyley — doiley

egg cosy — egg cover

egg-spoon — specially shaped stainless spoon for eating boiled eggs

everymeal set of china — everyday set

ewer — pitcher or jug
fish carver, fish slice or **fish trowel** — fish server
lay the table — set the table
pepper pot — pepper cellar
standing bowl — footed bowl
standing cup — footed cup
sugar basin — sugar bowl
trolley or **dinner wagon** — serving cart

FOR BATHROOM:

ballcock — flush valve
bath — bathtub
bathroom and **lavatory** — usually two separate
  rooms; **bathroom** is for baths and has tub and **wash-hand** basin (wash basin); lavatory has a toilet
  known as **the loo** or the **W.C.** (Water Closet)
bathroom basin — bathroom sink
bath safety rail — bathtub security rail
bath-tap — bathtub faucet
cistern — toilet tank
cutthroat razor — straight razor
face flannel — face cloth
flesh brush — back scrubber
flush box or **cistern** — toilet tank
jack towel — roller towel
ladyshaver (for legs) — an electric razor or a shaver
  with a wind-up mechanism
lavatory or **loo paper** — toilet tissue
linen hamper or **linen bin** — clothes hamper
loo paper, toilet roll, or **lavatory paper** — toilet tissue
loofah, luffa or **loofa** — fibrous network in a gourd
  used as a flesh brush
puff-box — bath powder box
shaving tackle — shaving gear
surgical spirit — alcohol
tooth glass — toothbrush holder
wash ball — bar of soap

washhand basin — basin

FOR LOUNGE: LIVING ROOM

cushion underlay — rug cushions

domestic fender or **kerb** — hearth fender

draught screen — screen for drafts

fitted carpet — wall-to-wall carpet

fireside companion set — fireplace tools

inglenook — chimney corner

lounge suite — living room suite

moquette — upholstery fabric used for **lounge suites** (living room furniture)

pelmet — valance

pencil or **pinch-pencil** curtains — pinch-pleated curtains

radio valves — radio tubes

radiogram — victrola or record player

soft furnishings — store department that sells soft materials: rugs, carpets, curtains, cushions, etc.

spark guard — firescreen

standard lamp — floor lamp

tranny — transistor radio

FOR BEDROOM:

bed clothes — bed linen or bed covers

bedside light — bedside lamp

coffret — set of perfumes

duvet or **continental quilt** — eider-down or swans-down quilt

French bed — daybed

hair grips — bobby pins

hairdressing scissors — barber scissors

sliding box — drawer

spring bed — box spring mattress

tallboy — highboy

tidy bin — waste basket

looking glass — dressing table mirror

wardrobe — closet

wipes or **paper hankies** — kleenex

FOR LAUNDRY ROOM:

clothes peg — clothespin

indoor airers — indoor dryers

linen basket — laundry basket

wash-house — laundry

washing bags — laundry bags

washing board — washboard

washing line — clothesline

FOR GARDEN or YARD:

basket chairs — wicker chairs

clothes pegs — clothespins

dustbin — garbage can

outdoor rotary airer — outdoor rotary clothesline

punnet — originally a small squarish straw basket for berries; today they are made of plastic

rotary scythes — rotary mowers

rubbish tip — garbage dump

Ray Bans — sunglasses

sun loungers — lounge chairs

tree lopper — lopping shears

weather cloth — tarpaulin

FOR GARAGE, WORKSHOP or STORE (STOREROOM):

adjustable spanner — adjustable wrench

bottle jack — hydraulic jack

buttery — wine storeroom

buttery bar — ledge for liquors

crosshead screwdriver — phillips screwdriver

gum — rubber cement

hack log or **chopping block** — chopping block

lumber room or **store** — storeroom

paraffin — kerosene

petrol chainsaw — gasoline chainsaw

sawing jig — miter box

stocklock — lock with a wooden case

stone-oil — petroleum

stonecoal — hardcoal

DOMESTIC WORKERS

casual or **odd-man** — one who helps about the garden, does odd jobs

coal heaver, coalman and **coalie** — coalman

cook/general or **cook/housemaid** — cook/housekeeper

dustman or **dustie** — garbage man

fire brigade or **fire service** — fire department

fire office — fire insurance company

gasogene or **gazogene** — apparatus for making aerated water

gent's hairdresser — barber

free fitting — free installation

hobjobber — odd jobs man

house decorator/painter — interior decorator

housecraft — homemaking

milk roundsman or **milkie** — milk man

painting smock — paint smock

paper stainer — one who prepares wallpaper

resident homely woman — housekeeper/homemaker

resident lady companion — companion

The Char

A **char** is a cleaning woman. Char comes from the Old English **"cieran"** meaning "to turn" or do "turns of work." Other names for a cleaning woman are **daily, daily woman, Mrs. Thing** and **treasure,** that is, hard to find. She can be a woman who does **daily work** (comes in once a day), an **obliging lady** who obliges (that is, cleans), or a **scrubbing woman** (scrub woman). A maid comes under another category. She **does for someone** (works as a maid) and can be a **general** (maid-of-all-work), and is sometimes called the **slavey.** Homes for the wealthy can have a **parlour maid** (parlor maid), a

between-maid or **tweeney** (the maid who helps the cook and tablemaid).

Pregnancy

To be gone is a slang term for being pregnant. Other interesting expressions for the time a woman wears a **maternity smock** (maternity dress) are: **in pod, preggers, preggio, up the spout** and **in the club**.

Besides **love child**, an illegitimate child is called a **by blow**, a **come'-o'chance, come'-o'-will** or **side-slip**.

BABY WORDS AND TERMS

baby relax chair — baby stroller
bearing cloth — baby blanket
bring up the wind — burp
child minding — baby sitting
child transporter — baby carrier
cot — crib
disposable nappies — disposable diapers
Ducks — Darling
gee-gee — horsie
karri cot — carry cot
little beggars or **kids** — affectionate for "children"
long clothes — baby's first dress
moses basket — portable baby bed
peepbo or **peek-a-boo** — peek-a-boo
poppet — doll or child
pilch — flannel cloth for wrapping a baby
poppet — doll
puff puff (train name) — choo-choo
pullalong — pull toy
pram or **perambulator** — baby carriage
push chair — stroller
springer — slinky (toy)
stabilizers — training wheels for bikes
teats — baby bottle nipples

the mulligrubs — colic

Children's Games

Many of the games American children play such as **London Bridge** were brought over by the colonists. That has kept its original name but many others were changed, such as: **all hide and seek** (hide and seek), **clumps** (20 questions), **cross-and-pile** or **cross-or-pile** (heads or tails), **give-a-back** or **make-a-back** (leap frog), **hidy-hole** (cat's cradle), **draughts** (checkers), **glove puppet** (hand puppet), **naughts and crosses** (tick-tack-toe), **pitch and toss** (pitching pennies), playing **"shops"** (playing "store"), **ring-on-a-string** (button button), **ringtaw** (marbles), **tig** (tag) and **postman's knock** or **parlour game** (post-office or spin-the-bottle).

MORE CHILDREN'S GAMES

All Fives — domino game in which the **end pips** (end dots) **sum** (add up to) a multiple of five

alphabet bricks — alphabet blocks

Animal Snap —card game using animal sounds

bolt hole — child's hiding place

Catch-the-Ten — card game whose aim is to catch (obtain) the 10 of trumps known as the long ten

Cockalorum — boys' jumping game

Crambo, Cramboclink or **Crambojingle** — word rhyming

Dib — game played by throwing **dib stones** (small sheep bones) up in the air from the palm of the hand and then catching them on the back of the hand. A dib is one of the small bones in the leg of a sheep.

Egg Dance — dance performed blindfolded among eggs

Fox and Geese — board game wherein certain pieces called **"geese,"** try to corner a piece called the **"fox."**

glove puppet — hand puppet

Housey Housey or **Bingo** — Bingo

Hunt-the-Slipper — ring game in which the one in the middle tries to catch a shoe passed around by the others

india rubber ball — rubber ball

Jingo-Ring — ring game where children dance around one child singing, "**Here we go round the jingo ring.**"

Lucky Bag or **Lucky Dip** — grab bag

Muggins — a form of dominoes

Newmarket — card game in which, to win, one must match the cards on the table

Shovel-Board or **Shuffle-Board** — Shuffle-Board

Family Celebrations

BIRTHDAYS Adults are usually greeted with **"Many Happy Returns"** on a birthday. **"Happy Birthday"** is said to a child because of the birthday song, "Happy Birthday to you."

MOTHER'S DAY has three names: **Mothering Sunday, Refreshment Sunday** or **Mid-Lent Sunday.** It is celebrated on the fourth Sunday of Lent and used to be the day when servants and apprentices had the day off to visit **Mum** (Mom) and present her with violets and a **Simnel cake.** The cake's name comes from simila or semolina flour, a fine-grained flour used for cakes by the Romans. It's a rich spice cake spread with apricot jam and almond paste, also made for Christmas and Easter. This **Mothering Day** tradition was falling by the wayside; then during WWII, American servicemen stationed in the UK took Mothering Sunday to be Mother's Day and somehow, this was taken up by the British and became a general Mother's Day celebration.

FATHER'S DAY is also a relatively recent import from the United States and Germany. **Pa, Dad,** and **The Old Man** are the usual names for **Father. Bart** and **the governor** are names used by the children of Baronets.

For other celebrations, see Chapter 15, Customs.

Health

The National Health Service is administered by the Secretary for Health in England and the Secretaries of State for Scotland, Wales and Northern Ireland and provides comprehensive coverage for every resident. Doctors, dentists, pharmacists and opticians are independent contractors within the service. Over 80 percent of the U.K.'s health costs come from general taxation. The rest comes from National Health Service Insurance contributions paid for by workers, their employers and the self-employed; and from charges for drugs and such prescribed by family doctors and from general health treatment.

HEALTH WORDS

FEELING FINE: feeling fit, in fighting fit or **in the pink of health** (in the pink).

FEELING BAD:

Feeling bloated: **bilious**

Feeling wierd: **being a bit seedy, a bit off-colour, a bit peaky, a bit dicky**

Feeling weak as a kitten: **feeling weak as water**

Hacking cough: **sounding like a dying duck in a thunderstorm**

Heart condition: **developing a heart**

Heavy cold: **having a heavy chill**

Out of breath: **blown or puffed out**

Sudden illness: **coming over queer** or **coming over bad**

Throwing up: **upjacking** or **up-chucking**

Tired brain: **having a brain fag**

Worn out: **feeling rather brittle, fagged out, part worn, overspent, whacked, pegged out** or **not up to much**

Very pale: **looking smock-faced**

ILLNESSES: Derbyshire neck (a form of goiter), **gamey leg** (game leg), **green-stick fracture** (partially broken bone, usually in children), **megrim** or **migraine** (migraine), **rainbow** (discolored bruise), **soldier's pox** (venereal disease), **the pip** (syphilis),

typhus fever (typhoid fever) and **whisky-liver** (cirrhosis of the liver)

DOCTOR WORDS: B.M.A. (British Medical Association), **F.R.C.P.** (Fellow Royal College of Physicians), **Medical Council** (medical society), **Surgery** (doctor's or dentist's office), **mad doctor** (slang, one who treats people with mental diseases), and **locum** (doctor's sub)

NURSE WORDS: trained nurse (registered nurse), **Matron** (head of the hospital), **Sister** (head of a ward or department), **Staff Nurse** (Sister's Deputy), **SRN** (**State Registered Nurse**) and **SEN** (**State Enrolled Nurse**)

HOSPITAL WORDS: An urgency (an emergency), **blood wagon** (ambulance,) **ambulanceman** (ambulance attendant), **cottage hospital** (small hospital in a cottage), **Disabled Soldier's Institute** (Veteran's Hospital), **operating theatre** (operating room), **trolley** (gurney), the **sluice** (hospital cleaning department), **wheeled chair** or **invalid chair** (wheel chair), **blanket bath** (bed bath), **cast one's water** (urinalysis), **casualty** (accident), **close-stool** (commode), **roomridden** (roombound), **glucose drip** (I.V.), **walking frame** (walker) **halt on two sticks** (hop about on crutches), **Panic Stations** (Code Red or Emergency)

CHEMIST (DRUGSTORE) WORDS: Chemist/Pharmacist (Druggist), **aperient operatives** (laxative makers), **Committee on Safety of Medicines** (like the FDA), **deaf aid** (hearing aid), **doctor's stuff** (medicines), **cotton wool** (cotton), **elastoplast** (band-aid), **sticking plaster** (adhesive bandage), **eye bath** (eye cup or eye wash), **health lamp** (heat lamp), **hop pillow** (pillow containing dried hops as a sleeping aid), **sanitary towel** (sanitary pad), **thumb stall** (thumb cover)

MEDICINE WORDS: back-kick (side effects), **black drop** (mixture of opium, vinegar and sugar), **black-wash** (lotion of calomel and lime water), **cough sweets** or **throat pastilles** (cough drops), **devil's dung** (asafoetida-a smelly gum resin of some Oriental plants used as an antispasmodic), **Gregory's**

Mixture (rhubarb, magnesia and ginger), and **sleeping draught** (sleeping powder).

WEIGHT WORDS: slimming or banting (dieting), **keeping one ticking over** (staying in good shape). British scales give the weight in **"stones"** or **"kilos."** Each stone is equal to 14 pounds avoirdupois and is the standard for weighing men and animals. (For wool, each stone is 24 pounds; for hay, 22 pounds; and for cheese, 16 pounds.) Each kilo is approximately two and a quarter pounds.

HEALTH SAYINGS: There is nothing so good for the inside of a man as the outside of a horse. Horseriding (horseback riding) is good for your health.

A creaking gate hangs longest. This is said to comfort the infirm. It means, although you have a lot of discomforts, you'll be around a while.

Organizations

There are many organizations one can join. For boys, there's the **Boy's Brigade**, which promotes habits of obedience and the **Scouts Association** (Boy Scouts). Other groups are: **Evergreen Clubs** (Senior Citizen Clubs), and **Freefooders** (opponents of taxes on food).

Death

In the UK, as in the US, most people flinch from saying the word **"dead"** or **"died."** Both prefer to use euphemisms, colloquialisms or slang. For dead: **deadborn** or **stillborn, dead as mutton**; for died: **pegged out, pranged** and **"went for a Burton"** (RAF, Royal Air Force terms), **went west, crossed over** or **passed over, died with one's shoes** (died with one's boots on), **packed up** or **snuffed it** (kicked the bucket), **took the ferry, called it a day** or **went over the rainbow** (crossed over). Drowning is called **making a hole in the water.**

A board for measuring and lifting a corpse is a **dead-deal**, the **deadhouse** is a funeral parlor or mortuary, as here. When the **cortege** arrives at the graveyard, **the long box** (coffin) is placed in **the long home** (grave); then if one has not been **cut off without a shilling** (without a cent), it's time to pay **legacy duties** (death duties).

Obituary notices in the **press** (paper) may say, **"No flowers," Family flowers only,"** or **"Floral tributes to the Funeral Director's."** Many also include a very touching saying or poem.

Man goeth forth to his work,
and to his labour: until the evening.
—The Book of Common Prayer, *Psalms civ.* 17

CHAPTER FOURTEEN

THE BRITISH PEOPLE: THE WORLD OF WORK

Finding a Post (Job Hunting)

In seeking a post (job), as with us, one either goes to a **job centre** (employment office), consults the newspaper ads under **Situations Vacant** (Help Wanted) or puts an ad in under **Situations Wanted**. Farms and factories usually say **Hands Wanted**. One's first job is called a **first poster** and one should be prepared for a **training scheme** (try-out period) during which one is **vetted out** (checked out). An experienced person looks for a **top level** (administrative) position having **a salary with noughts on the end** (one in five figures) and **attendant perks** (perks).

UNUSUAL OCCUPATION NAMES

The out-of-the-ordinary names given to some jobs are mostly colloquial or slang as for example:

An **awakener** is a **knocker-up**. He has the job of getting workers up mornings.

A **bookie** is a **bookmaker** and a **punter** is his customer.

A **junk man** is a **scrap merchant, rag and bone man, old clothes man** or **breaker**...presumably because he breaks things up before selling them again.

A **landscape artist** is a **paysaygist,** derived from the old French word for country or landscape, "paysay."

An officer that guards a wood (woods) is a **wood-ward**. The **"ward"** part is understandable in the sense of **"to ward off trouble."** Another strange name is that given to a wood's overseer, **wood-reeve**. The origin of **"reeve"** is obscure but it has been in continuous use since the 700's and is a good example of how words, as well as artifacts, are kept long past the time they would be discarded in the U.S.

A **saddler** is a **whittaw** or **whittawer** from Old English meaning he **taws** (tans) leather. **Whit** is short for **"white,"** but why it is **white-tanning** is obscure. A **knacker** can also be a saddler but the name is now usually given to one who buys old, worn out horses and takes them to his **knackery,** (glue factory). **Knack** in this case is a **sharp knock or rap** and perhaps refers to how the horse is sent on to horse heaven.

A **scientist** is a **boffin**.

A **shill** is a **puffer** at a **knock-out auction** (auction with punters) to **puff up** (run up) bids.

A **traveling salesman**, besides being called a **travelling representative** is also called a **rep, travelling hawker, a bagman, a cheap jack** or a **cheap john** and his work is **flogging** (selling).

A **veterinarian** is a **cow leech**.

MORE OCCUPATION NAMES
WHITE COLLAR:
  book-canvasser — book salesman
  book-hunter/searcher — rare book finder
  C.A. or **Chartered Accountant** — C.P.A. Certified Public Accountant

dry salter — one who deals in gums and dyes
keeper of the museum — museum director
pavement artist — sidewalk artist
private inquiry agent — private eye
quantity surveyor — one who estimates and obtains materials needed for a job
wax chandler — candle maker
Office workers:
clerkling — young clerk
confidential secretary or **P.A.** — personal/private assistant
familiar — assistant
managing director — manager
minutes secretary — recording secretary
senior typist or **typing pool superintendent** — office manager
build-up trays — stacking trays
White collar work words:
the bumpf or **the griff** — office gossip
dog kennel — cubby hole office
a lickspittle or a **pushful peeler** — bootlicker or apple polisher
pen driver — pen pusher
ready reckoner — adding machine
saleroom — salesroom
trade cocktail party — office cocktail party
BLUE COLLAR:
Farm workers:
corn chandler or **corn factor** — grain merchant
feeder — dairyman
grainer — farmer
hayward — officer in charge of fences to keep out cattle
hog ringer — one who puts rings in pig's snouts
seedsman — nursery man selling seeds as well as plants

shoeing smith — blacksmith or farrier
tree feller — tree cutter
Local Council (Town or Village Board) workers:
  excisemen — revenuers
  flusher — sewer flusher
  sewermen — sewer workers
  trolley-man — trolley conductor
Water workers:
  bargee — bargeman
  coal whipper — one who unloads coal from ships to barges
  dragman — fisherman using a dragnet
  pond master — one in charge of a swimming bath (swimming pool)
  ship boy — young boy worker
  ship breaker — one who breaks up old ships
Other blue collar workers:
  chief storekeeper — warehouse manager
  clerk of works — construction foreman
  donkey man — one who runs a donkey engine
  dry waller — a builder of walls without mortar; in the U.S., a dry waller puts up plasterboard
  forester — forest ranger
  gaffer — foreman or boss
  joiner — one who works with wood
  key holder — building guard
  overlook — overseer
  piecener or **piecer** — one who pieces or patches
  silk thrower or **throwster** — one who makes raw silk into thread
  work girl — woman doing manual work
  works manager — supervisor
Blue collar work words:
  bricking — brickwork
  coal tip — coal dump
  danger money — hazard pay

donkey pump — steam pump
fire post — lookout tower
floatstone — bricklayer's smoothing tool
jointing rule — bricklayer's straight-edged ruler
lagging pipes — wrapping pipes
late turn — late shift
sawing jib — miter box
scent factory — perfume factory
working beam — walking beam

WORK WORDS IN GENERAL

beavering away — plugging hard
by work — moonlighting
clock-in (out) or **check-in (out)** — punch the clock
cooking the books — doctoring the books
daily breading — the old grind
day book — order book
elevation — promotion
extraordinary general meeting — special meeting
fortnightly pay parade — semi-monthly payroll
going counter to established rules — bucking the system
head office — main office
journey money — trip allowance
"Once more into breach!" — "Back to the old grind!"
pay list or pay roll — payroll
pay packet or **wage packet** — pay envelope
pay sheet or pay bill — pay list
proper day's work — good day's work
radio-pager — beeper
rare hard worker — steady worker
rise or rise in pay — raise
superannuation — retirement
teasy work — low pay job
wages — pay
wages office — pay window

working like stink — working like mad
work-mates — fellow workers
whip around — passing the hat

Industrial Actions (Strikes)

Strikes have interesting expressions. **Work to rule** is working according to the books, **a lightning strike** is a wildcat strike, **down-tools** needs no explanation and **a black leg** is a scab or strike breaker.

Getting the Elbow (Getting Fired)

Getting fired has engendered a great number of euphemisms: **cashiered, sacked, got a kick, got one's cards, got the books, got the bucket, got the push** and **got to the wall.**

It makes one depend on a **redundancy allowance** (severance pay), the **labour exchange** (unemployment office), **the dole** (welfare) and one hopes, not **the leaving shop** (pawn shop).

...young and old come forth to play
On a sunshine holiday.
　　　　　—John Milton, *L'Allegro*, I, 95

CHAPTER FIFTEEN

HOLIDAYS, CUSTOMS, PROVERBS AND SAYINGS

Bank Holidays

The legal holidays in Britain are called **bank holidays** because these are the days when the banks are closed by Act of Parliament. Bills falling on these days are payable the following day. Bank holidays are held on Mondays in the better weather part of the year to make for long weekends. The bank holidays for most of the U.K. are:

January 1 — New Year's Day

January 4 — Bank Holiday (Scotland only)

March 1 — St. David's Day (Wales only)

March 17 — St. Patrick's Day (Northern Ireland only)

Good Friday Bank Holiday

Easter Monday Bank Holiday (except Scotland) Easter is a moveable holiday as it is celebrated on the first Sunday after the full moon, between March 22nd and April 25th

May (first Mon) — May Day Bank Holiday

May (last Mon) — Spring Bank Holiday (formerly **Whitsun**)

July (2nd Mon) — Orangeman's Day (Northern Ireland only)

August (first Mon) — Summer Bank Holiday (Scotland only)

August (last Mon) — Summer Bank Holiday (except Scotland)

December 25 — Christmas Day Bank Holiday

Boxing Day Bank Holiday — day after Christmas except if it occurs on Saturday or Sunday, then the following Monday

SCOTLAND also has a number of national celebrations:

January 25 — Burns Night

October 30 — Hallowe'en

November 5 — Bonfire Night

November 29 — St. Andrew's Day

December 31 — Hogmanay

IRELAND also has a number of feast days:

December 28 — Day of the Holy Innocents or Children's Day

May 1 — May Day

June 24 — Feast of St. John

September 29 — Michaelmas

CYMRU (Welsh name for Wales) has:

March 1 — St. David's Day

In July — Royal National Eisteddfodau, a festival of music and song

There are hundreds of customs and festivals in Britain, some going back to pre-Christian days. Traditions are Druid, Viking, Roman, Celtic or Anglo-Saxon in origin. The first missionaries adapted many of the ancient pagan holidays to Holy Days. A number had been discontinued but with the realization that they were a wonderful part of the national culture, they've been revived, some with gusto.

Superstition and Folklore

Many customs are linked to superstition and folklore, the need to follow certain procedures to prevent disasters from happening. For example, in some villages, on **Plough Sunday** (the first Sunday after **Twelfth Night**), a plough is brought into the church to be blessed. Twelfth Night is January 6th, 12 days after Christmas. The next day, **Plough Monday**, is when the first furrow of the New Year is ploughed. The decorated plough is then dragged through the village by beribboned young men accompanied by fiddles, pipes and accordion. They stop at homes for alms for charity.

In a number of villages there's the burying of the **corn dolly**, a doll made from the last corn-stalks of the previous harvest. It is thought to be a pre-Christian fertility symbol to guarantee next year's crop. Corn dollies are sold at the **craft stalls** (craft stands) of fairs and charity bazaars and are hung up in barns to preside over **harvest suppers**.

Wassailing the apple trees is an old West Country custom. The villagers pass around a cup of **wassail** (a mixture of ale, chopped roasted apples, sugar, nutmeg and toast), sprinkle some liberally over the orchards and then build bonfires to protect the trees from frost.

Eat and drink good cake and hot ale,

Give earth a drink and she'll not fail.

—Old saying

Lighting bonfires at dusk on **Hallowe'en** is supposed to drive away evil spirits. As the fires die down, everyone hurries home, not to be the last one out before the fires go out as it was believed that the **Devil takes the hindmost**. Other customs are religious in nature and follow the rituals of the church: Christmas, Easter, Saint's Days etc., but even so, many superstitions are related to these...such as being sure to put away the Christmas decorations before Twelfth Night, as it's considered bad luck for them to be up after that date.

Yearly Festivals and Holidays

OLD YEAR'S NIGHT (NEW YEAR'S EVE) On New Year's Eve, in some British areas, some give **apple gifts**. These are apples mounted on tripods and decorated with nuts and **yew** (evergreens) to symbolize sweetness, fertility and immortality. And there are many ancient customs relating to the first new moon to ensure a prosperous new year.

Hogmanay is the name the Scots have given to this, their most important day of their year. It is thought the name either comes from a special cake baked for the occasion or from an ancient dialect. At midnight, families toast each other with a sort of local liquor called **uisgebeatha** (Gaelic for "water of life," whose pronunciation has become **"whiskey"**), link arms and sing **"Auld Lang Syne."** With drinks are traditional treats, shortbread and **black bun** or **Scotch bun**. Black bun is a very rich fruit and nut cake which is heavily spiced, laced with **whisky** (whiskey), brandy or rum, encased in pastry and baked for a very long time. Legend has it that it should be made in January to be eaten at Hogmanay. After the cake, younger members of the family leave to **first foot** their friends. A **"first foot"** is the first person to visit a house in the New Year. Preferably, he should be one with dark hair or a child to bring good luck, and must have with him a small piece of coal. As he puts it on the fire, he gives the wish **"Lang may your lum reek"** (Long may your chimney smoke). He also gives the housewife some cake and salt to **"handsel"** (bring luck to) the household.

At midnight, all over Britain, the merry ringing of church bells welcomes in the new year.

NEW YEAR'S DAY In London's Trafalgar Square, the British **bring in the New Year** by general high-jinks and dancing about. Years ago, New Year's Day was not a big holiday in England. It was a work day if it came on a week day. Today, many factories shut down from Christmas Eve to January 2nd.

TWELFTH DAY—Epiphany, January 6th This used to be a day for commemorating the gifts of the Magi by giving presents. A huge cake was baked containing a single bean and whoever got the bean became **"King of the Bean,"** and reigned over a 12-day-long festival. This is no longer done. In Ireland, **Twelfth Day** is called **Small Christmas** and the Christmas holly is taken down and burned. Shakespeare may have originated the name **Twelfth Night**.

ST. DAVID'S DAY—March 1 St. David is the patron saint of Wales and on his feast day, it is the custom for the Welsh to wear leek blossoms on their hats commemorating a victory over the Anglo-Saxons. The 12th century cathedral at St. David's, Wales, contains the bones of the saint.

ST. PATRICK'S DAY—March 17th, is Northern Ireland's greatest national holiday. It is the day their patron saint died in AD461. Attending church is required as it is a holy day of obligation. Later, there are parades with families participating.

LADY DAY (OUR LADY'S DAY), March 25th, is **Annunciation Day**, a religious holiday and one of the four **Quarter Days** of the year. Quarter Days were when servants were paid, daughters received allowances and when house and farm rents were paid. The other Quarter Days are **Midsummer Day** (June 21st), **Michaelmas Day** (Sept. 29) and **Christmas Day**. These are all connected with the Equinoxes and Solstices of the sun.

BORROWING DAYS, in Scotland, are the last three days of March, (OS) Old Style, that is, according to the Julian Calendar which was used in Britain until 1752. According to Scottish folklore, March borrowed these three especially stormy days from April.

FASTENS TUESDAY, Shrove Tuesday or **Pancake Tuesday** This is the day before Ash Wednesday when pancakes are served with **caster sugar** (a powdered sugar) and lemon juice. They are made from spoonfuls of batter, fried, flipped over in the pan and fried on the other side. The idea is to use up supplies before the Lenten season starts. In the town of Olney, Buckinghamshire, this holiday is celebrated by the well-known **Pancake Race** which traditionally is open only to local women aged 16 and over who must wear headscarves. A new wrinkle, lately added to the race, is a competition with the ladies of Liberal, Kansas, U.S.A.

THE PASSING BELL It used to be a custom in England to toll the church bell when a person died. It was thought that it drove away demons so as to protect the departing soul. **Nine tailors** were tolled for a man, six for a woman followed by one more for each year of life. (**"Tailors" was originally the word "tellers"** as the bells **"told"** everyone that someone was dead.) At Ayot St. Peter's, Hertfordshire, this tradition continues to-day, the **Nine Tailors and 33 strokes** are tolled every Good Friday for the passing of The Lord.

APRIL FOOL'S DAY, April 1, occasions the same joking that goes on in the U.S. except the person sent on a fool's errand is called an **April fish**. In Scotland, he/she is called **a gowk**. Mid-day traditionally ends the April-fooling.

EASTER, A Sunday between March 22nd and April 25th This is a **"holy day of obligation,"** when all Roman Catholic and Anglican Christians are obliged to go to church and receive Communion. Churches are lavishly decorated. A few still keeping the old tradition of using evergreens—symbolic of eternal life— and biblical texts embroidered in red and white; but most prefer displays of spring flowers with Easter lilies. Family graves are decorated with flowers, a Welsh custom denoting the Resurrection. It is also considered lucky for churchgoers to wear a bright new piece of clothing, an Easter bonnet or a complete new outfit. The Easter Parade is also traditional.

The name Easter comes from the pagan festival of the goddess **Eostra**; and the Easter bunny is derived from the Easter hare, supposed to be sacred to Eostra. Many ceremonies connected with Easter have disappeared, but that of the egg, the source of new life, continues. Eggs are hard-boiled, dyed and either concealed about the garden for an Egg Hunt or rolled down hills symbolizing the rolling away of the stone from Christ's tomb. This same symbolism is also carried on in Dunstable, Bedfordshire on **Good Friday**, however, instead of eggs, children scramble for oranges which are rolled down Dunstable

Downs. Good Friday is also considered a good day for planting potatoes. Other Easter customs that have survived are **Street Ball Games, Morris Dancing,** and the giving of money to charities.

Other traditional Easter foods are spring lamb and rhubarb (southern England); stuffed veal (northern and midland England); decorated chicken pies (Scotland); cheesecakes (west Midlands); custards (Yorkshire and East Anglia); and puddings flavored with tansy (Cumbria). Tansy is a bitter and aromatic plant used for both cooking and medicinal purposes.

On Easter, Whit Monday (6 weeks after Easter Monday) and August Mondays when a Fair is on with **roundabouts** (merry-go-rounds), **coconut shies**-pronounced "shys"—(booths with coconuts as targets or prizes), shooting galleries, **swing-boats** (boat-shaped swinging seats) and dodge-ems, etc., **Cockney peddlers** (known at times as **costers, costermongers** or **barrow-boys**) used to wear pearl button costumes (**pearlies**) and wore feather hats while they peddled fruits from **wheeled barrows** (wheelbarrows). (**Cockneys** are traditionally Londoners born at the East End of London within the sounds of the **Bow bells:** St. Mary-le-Bow Church.) Nowadays, they use these costumes for fancy dress affairs. Many districts, other than just London, have their **pearly kings and queens** who appear at charity shows. (**Coster** comes from the costard apple, a large-sized apple, and **monger** means dealer, hence, a **coster-monger** is an apple seller.)

BLUEBELL SUNDAY On a Sunday when the bluebells are in bloom in the Swithland Woods (Leicestershire), there's a church service led by the Vicar of Swithland followed by a Salvation Army band rendition of appropriate hymns.

MAY DAY (First Monday) There are many, many May Day events to celebrate the beginning of summer. In Padstow and Minehead (Cornwall and Devon), the **Old Oss**, a person covered with a hoop-shaped frame draped in black topped by a fearsome mask and a conical cap, prances through the streets chasing young girls to celebrate the coming of May. One called

Bluebells in bloom in Swithland Woods.

Hob-Nob sometimes appears in Salisbury. At Aston On Clum, (Central-Western England) there is the **arbor tree ceremony** on the 29th of May. A large black poplar tree is decked with flags on long poles and left in place until the next Arbor Day. It is thought this was done originally to keep witches away. At Wellow and Kingsteignton (Devon) **maypole dancing** has been revived. In Knutsford-once Cnutsford, Cheshire (Northern England) for the **Sand in May festival,** no vehicle is allowed on the streets where flowers and love knots are drawn in brown and white sand. This practice dates to the time **King Cnut** forded the river there. As he was shaking sand from his shoes a wedding party went by. He wished the couple as many descendants as there were grains of sand in his shoe. It was thought at that time that complicated patterns warded off evil spirits.

   OAK APPLE DAY—May 29th It commemorates the Restoration of Charles II in 1660. It refers to the time Charles hid in an oak tree after the battle of Worcester to elude the Roundheads who searched for him. At Castleton, Derbyshire, there's a procession and maypole dancing.

LADIES' WALKING DAY is celebrated on the first Thursday in June in Neston (Northern England). It's a procession of women of the Neston Female Friendly Society (founded 1717) who, according to tradition, must be dressed all in white and carry white garlands and walk through town to the parish church.

WELL DRESSING is done on Whitsuntide, the Saturday nearest to the 24th of June. It's an ancient tradition at Youlgreave, Derbyshire (Central England) and other Derbyshire towns. The wells and even pumps and taps are decorated. Springs and wells have been venerated from ancient times in the worship of well spirits. When Christianity came, the wells were dedicated to the Virgin Mary or one of the saints and continued to be decorated.

EISTEDDFODAU, Wales (pronounced Eye-sted-fah-dow, like "ow" in owl). It's Welsh meaning **"a sitting"** or **"a session"** and is applied especially to gatherings of bards and musicians at Cardigan, Dyfed. It's a popular annual festival dating back to 6th Century Druid conclaves. Contestants come from all over Wales to join in the competitions in vocal, choral and orchestral music, poetry and literature, drama, and arts and crafts. They compete for an **"eisteddfa"** (eye-sted-fah) or bardic chair (from bard, a minstrel). The main purpose of the festival is to maintain and strengthen the Welsh language and culture. Welsh is the only language used during this gathering. It's held alternatively in North and South Wales during the first week of August. There is also an **International Eisteddfodau** held annually the second week of July in Clywd, North Wales. Artists from over 30 countries compete in folk singing, choral work and folk dancing.

LITTLE EDITH'S TREAT is celebrated every July 19th in Puddinghoe, Sussex by a church service, a village fete and races. Over 100 years ago, little Edith Croft died at the age of three months and her grandmother left money in a will directing that 100 pounds should be spent every year on her birthday.

There are a number of other traditions linked to bequests such as the singing of the Easter hymn every Easter eve over the grave of William Hubbard of Market Harborough. When he died in 1786, he left a guinea a year forever to the choir of St. Mary's in Arden to pay for this. At St. Ives in Cornwall, John Knill asked that children dance at his mausoleum.

THE LANGLEY BREAD is a bequest by Robert Langley, who died in 1656, that bread should be provided for the town poor. Every January, groceries are given to the elderly in his name.

SWAN UPPING is held on the third week of July (Monday to Thursday) beginning at the London Temple, Embankment SW3 steps of the Thames River. The swans, by tradition, belong to the Queen and two London **livery companies** (City of London Guilds, the Dyers and Vintners). A colorful procession to the **6 rowing boats** (row boats) used in the upping is led by the **Royal Keeper of the Swans** with a banner. The Queen's rowers are in red livery, the Dyers in blue and the Vintners in green. The boatmen go as far upstream as Henley. On the way, the swans are **upped** (lifted) into boats, counted, **marked** with their owner's symbol and released.

AUGUST BANK HOLIDAY used to be on the first Monday in August and it was a day for picnicking in the country. Now it's the last Monday of August and most people go to the seashore.

HARVEST SUPPERS are held in church halls on **Harvest Festival Sunday** in the fall. Special thanksgiving hymns are sung such as the time **honoured** (honored):

> "We plough the fields and scatter
> The good seed on the ground"
> and
> "Come, ye thankful people, come
> Raise the song of Harvest Home."

There's a sale of vegetables, baked goods, homemade jams, jellies, tea and cakes. Bakeries sell bread in the shapes of fish and tied-up sheaves of grain at this time of year.

PUNKIE NIGHT is celebrated on the last Thursday in October at Hinton St. George, Somerset (Western England). **Punkie** is short for pumpkin and the children beg for candles to light their carved pumpkin and turnip lanterns. It is thought to be unlucky to refuse them as the lanterns represent the spirits of the dead that return on Hallowe'en. They sing: "Give us a candle, give us a light. If you don't, you'll get a fright."

RINGING FOR GOFER is a bell rung by bequest on six October and November nights at Newark-on-Trent to commemorate the safe return of a merchant who was lost in Sherwood Forest.

GUY FAWKES DAY—November 5 is a non-legal holiday, the anniversary of the Gunpowder Plot (1605) when Guy Fawkes tried to blow up King James I and Parliament. It is recalled in a rhyme:

Please to remember the fifth of November
Gunpowder, Treason and Plot.
We know no reason why gunpowder treason
Should ever be forgot.

A few days before the 5th, children carry stuffed grotesque figures called **"guys"** through the streets and ask passers-by to **"Spare a penny for the guy."** The money is used for fireworks which are stuck in the pockets, hand and hatbands of the "guys" and on the night of November 5th, huge bonfires are lit on village greens and the grotesque figures are tossed into the flames. There are fewer guys these days because people have been complaining about the begging, but there are lots of organized bonfires at schools, village greens and in private gardens.

VETERANS CAR RACE is on the 1st Sunday in November. Drivers and passengers in period costumes race from London to Brighton—60 miles—in vintage cars. They celebrate the raising of the speed limit from 12 miles an hour; and the abolition of the man who was required to walk with a red flag in front of a car.

REMEMBRANCE SUNDAY, Veteran's Day is celebrated on the nearest Sunday to November 11th.

CHRISTMAS EVE is a special time in many homes in Ireland. It is when a tall candle is placed in a window to light the path for the Holy Family. The youngest child has the honor of lighting the candle as he/she will live the longest and carry the custom on.

THE GLASTONBURY THORN is a tree believed to be a descendant of **St. Joseph of Arimathae'a**'s thorn staff. He planted it in Glastonbury, Somerset soon after the crucifixion when he arrived to bring Christianity to the people. Several days before Christmas, the Mayor and the Vicar of St. John the Baptist, cut sprays from the tree to send to the Queen.

THE YULE LOG is a contribution of the Scandinavians. The burning is symbolic of the burning up of feuds and disputes which are resolved by drinking **wassail** to the destruction of quarrels. Charred remnants of the log are kept to light the next year's log and the ashes are preserved to mix with earth in spring to assure a bountiful harvest.

CHRISTMAS Years ago, a special mass was celebrated on the day of Christ's birth. It was called **Christes Mass,** hence the name Christmas. Trees are decorated with **gauds** (tree ornaments) and **fairy lights** (tree lights). It used to be that no gifts were under the trees. They were given on **Boxing Day**, the day after Christmas. (See Boxing Day.) Today, children hang their stockings above the fireplaces or on the ends of their beds on Christmas Eve so that **Father Christmas** (Santa Claus) can fill them. On Christmas Day, gifts are under the trees in fancy wrapping. At dinner, paper hats are worn. These pop out with a bang from large tubular paper packages called **"Christmas Crackers."** Traditional entrees are turkey, goose or chicken with stuffing and roast potatoes; and for dessert, mince pies and plum pudding. Small silver trinkets such as thimbles, rings, etc. are put into the **Christmas pudding** to bring good luck to the finders. In late afternoon, there is **Christmas tea,** whose chief feature is a rich fruit cake with **thick marzipan** (almond paste icing) topped with white sugar frosting. During the holiday season, children are taken to see the **Christmas pantos** (Pantomimes): Cinderella, Babes in the Wood, Aladdin, Robinsoe Crusoe, etc. Children used to visit homes before Christmas to sing carols and receive a hot drink and some coins. They would say:

Knock, knock the napper,
Ring, ring the bell,
Please give us something
For singing so well.
If you haven't a penny
A ha'penny will do,
If you haven't a ha'penny
God bless you.

Today, not many go about because parents fear for their safety; however, organized groups from churches or other organizations do sing carols for various good causes. They carry a lantern on a pole and usually are accompanied by a musical instrument.

A Christmas tradition since the time of King George V, is the Christmas Message from the Queen, televised since 1960. Other ceremonies connected with the Queen are: **The Ceremony of the Keys** which is held daily at the Tower of London. At 9:40 p.m. the **Chief Warder** in Beefeater costume, and the **Key-Bearer** (an escort of the Brigade of Guards) are challenged with the words, **"Whose keys?"** and the traditional reply is, **"Queen Elizabeth's keys."** This precautionary ceremony is an outcome of **The Gunpowder Plot.** Parliament has a similar challenge but it's not as ceremonious. Other traditions include: the **Changing of the Guard** at Buckingham Palace; and the **Changing of the Horse Guards** at Whitehall.

A recent tradition is the erection of a huge **Christmas tree in Trafalgar Square.** It is presented annually by the City of Oslo to commemorate Anglo-Norwegian cooperation during WWII.

The custom of sending **Christmas cards** was started in Britain in 1843 when a businessman, Sir Henry Cole, asked an artist friend, J.C. Horsley, to design a card to send to friends and business acquaintances. The greeting Horsley wrote on the card is still used today, **"A Merry Christmas and a Happy New Year to You."**

The Irish call Christmas by the Gaelic name **Nollaig. Bringing home the Christmas** is how they describe all the goodies they've bought for the Christmas table. On Christmas night, all the members of the family gather to recite the **Family Rosary** and feast at a table presided over by the oldest members of the family.

BOXING DAY BANK HOLIDAY is celebrated on December 26th unless that is a Sunday, then Monday is a Bank Holiday and there are no newspapers. There is only one other **press holiday** (newspaper holiday)...Good Friday. Presents are given to servants, tradespeople and other service people such as the postman, **dustman** (garbage man) etc. the gifts are in **"boxes,"** hence, Boxing Day. The custom originated with the ancient Romans. Boxing Day is called **St. Stephen's Day** in Ireland and the custom there is to abstain from meat in honor of the saint who, it is thought, saved the Irish from the plague.

SOME PROVERBS AND SAYINGS

All is gas and gaiters! — All is well.

All is not beer and skittles! — It's not all fun and games!

In for a penny, in for a pound. — Go whole hog.

It is idle to swallow the cow and choke on the tail. — It's senseless to give up so near to success.

Ne'er cast a clout till May be out. — Warm clothes needed until the end of May or when the May flower blooms.

No names, no pack drill. (Pack drill is marching up and down in in full **kit**-back pack.) — No name, no blame.

To make a spoon or spoil a horn. — Give it the old college try.

Touch wood and whistle. — Knock wood

Where there's muck, there's brass (money). — Dirty work is profitable work.

Why keep a dog and bark yourself? — Why hire someone to do a job and then do it yourself?

ADVICE, SUPERSTITIONS, ETC.

Borrowing Days:

According to Scottish folklore, the last three days of March are supposed to have been borrowed from April and are supposed to be especially stormy.

On finding a pin:

See a pin and pick it up,
all the day you'll have good luck;
see a pin and let it lay,
bad luck you'll have all the day.

On lightning:

Beware of an oak, it draws the stroke;
avoid an ash, it counts the flash;
creep under the thorn,
it can save you from harm.

On May dew:

The dew of May 1st is reputed to beautify faces and whiten linen.

On rain:

If it rains on St. Swithin's Day (July 15), it will rain for forty days.

On seeing a number of magpies:

One for sorrow, two for mirth;
three for a wedding, four for birth.

For when the One Great Scorer comes
To write against your name,
He marks—not that you won or lost—
But how you played the game.
  —Grantland Rice, *Alumnus Football*

CHAPTER SIXTEEN

RECREATION

The British enjoy many of the same forms of recreation that American enjoy, but some are very different, as for example: **cricket, going to pubs** (See Chapter Ten), and **the hunt**. A description of each of these follows; later there will be words associated with other forms of recreation such as gardening, fishing, etc.

Cricket

Cricket is as close to the British psyche as baseball is to Americans. It's puzzling to Americans that cricket should be so popular because it seems to be such a complicated and slow game. Imagine a game going on for three to four days! And the scoring! 300 to 400 runs! Also, since its inception circa 1300, it has accumulated many odd-sounding names: **popping crease, maiden over, googly, leg before wicket**, etc. that are difficult to understand. The only cricket expressions that Americans understand and use—but not very often—are **"That's not cricket!"** meaning "Standards of fair play have not been maintained." and **"It's a sticky wicket."** meaning "It's a difficult situation."

HISTORY Depending on which authority is consulted, the name came either from the French **"criquet"** meaning **"a stick used in a game"** or from the Old English **"cryce"** meaning **"stick."** The game evolved over the centuries and when it

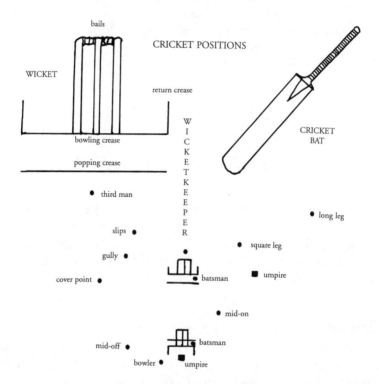

became very popular, clubs were formed. The most famous is **M.C.C.**, the **Marlybone Cricket Club**, which was initiated by **Thomas Lord** in 1787; and so the ground they play on is called **"Lord's."** It became such hallowed ground to cricketers and cricket fans that when the club made two moves through the years to other locations, the original turf was dug up and reinstalled. (See Chapter Five.) It's a matter of such prestige to belong to the M.C.C. that at times it has a waiting list of over 10,000, all wanting to wear its famous egg and bacon (red and yellow) tie.

UNIFORM Cricketers wear long white trousers, white **boots** (shoes), white shirts and when needed, white sweaters. Club badges are on cricketer's caps and blazer pockets. **Batsmen's**

(batter's) legs are protected by heavy pads of leather and canvas and their hands by padded gloves. The **wicketkeeper** (catcher) wears heavier pads and heavier gloves. The others players have no protection.

THE PITCH (CRICKET GROUND) is usually slightly larger than a baseball field, see Illustration II—Cricket Positions. Two wickets stand about 22 yards apart in the center of the field. A **wicket** is an upright arrangement (22 inches high) of **three sticks** called **"stumps"** in a row, with two **bails** on top which the batsman is supposed to defend against a **bowled ball**. **Bails** are two 4-inch-long wooden cross pieces set loosely in grooves on top of each wicket and are what the bowler and fielders want to dislodge as that would put a batsman out and give them extra runs. **Bail** comes from Old French **"baille"** meaning a barrier or palisade.

The pitch has lines called **creases** drawn in whitewash on the ground (see illustration). There are two at each wicket. The **bowling-crease** is in line with each wicket, extending four feet four inches on each side of the central stump. At the ends of this line and at right angles to it, are two four foot arms extending behind the wicket called **return creases.** These creases mark the area in which the bowler's (**pitcher's**) rear foot must remain when he releases the ball. It's comparable to a pitcher's mound. The **popping crease** is four feet in front of the bowling crease and is parallel to it. Two batsmen stand, one at each wicket, between the bowling and popping creases.

THE BALL is a hard ball, smaller than a baseball, and slightly heavier. It has a core of cork, around which are wound layers of twine and thin cork shavings and is covered with heavy red leather with 6 parallel seams.

THE BAT looks a little like a flattened baseball bat. It is made of willow and must be less than 38 inches long. The blade is four and a half inches wide (see illustration). A batsman can hit the ball to anywhere on the field as there are no foul areas.

THE PLAYERS There are two teams of 11 men, and one player on each team acts as **captain**. At the start of the match, two umpires take their positions and the captains toss a coin. The winner can decide whether his team plays or takes the field. If he decides they should play, he sends out the first pair of batsmen in their protective gear. The other captain sends his players to any of the special fielding positions indicated in the illustration: **bowler, wicketkeeper, slips, gully, third man, cover, mid-off, mid-on, square leg** and **long leg**. Mid-off and Mid-on are sometimes called **silly mid-off** and **silly mid-on**. There are a number of other positions where the captain can place these players depending on the techniques of the particular batsman, the skills of the bowler, and the conditions of the ground. See "Other positions for players" in More Cricket Definitions below.

THE MATCH As in baseball, the object of the game is for one team to make more runs than the other; but unlike baseball, cricket uses two batters at a time, one near each wicket. The batter that is **up** is called the **striker** and his partner, the **non-striker**. The batter must be careful to keep one foot behind his popping crease when batting and his partner must remain entirely behind his popping crease. The bowler takes a position near the non-striker and **bowls** (pitches) the ball with his arm kept straight when it's above his shoulder. His objective is to **break the wicket** (displace the bails) as this **retires** (puts out) the batter. The striker's job is to defend the bails by hitting the ball out of the way far enough so he and the other batsman can run and exchange sides. They run with their bats in hand as the bats must touch the ground beyond the popping crease at the opposite end for the runs to be counted. If the ball has been hit far enough, the batters can exchange places up to a limit of 6 times before the ball is returned. These are called **runs** provided the bails remain intact because the fielders, on recovering the ball, can also try to hit them off. A batsman continues defending the bails until he's put out, either by having the bails knocked off the wicket, by having a hit ball caught or until he breaks one of the batsmen's rules.

When a bowler has bowled six perfect balls, he has completed an **over**. This means that bowling is resumed at the other wicket by a different bowler and all the fielders move to corresponding positions on the other end of the pitch. When this second bowler achieves an over, the bowling reverts to the original end with the original bowler unless the captain decides he's **"too expensive,"** that is, too many runs are being scored off the balls he's **delivering** (aiming at the wicket). The captain may then **"change the bowling"** (have someone else bowl). The only players who stay put are the batsmen who maintain their positions until they are counted **"out."** **"Out"** batsmen are replaced until 10 have had a chance at bat. A complete cycle, where each team has had its turn at bat and the starting team is up again, is called an **innings** (the word "innings" is always plural).There are only **two innings** to a match, but if the batsmen are good, matches can continue for up to four days...with breaks for four o'clock tea.

Today, attempts are being made to speed up the game by having a set number of 40 or 50 overs bowled by each side instead of bowling until each side has had all its 11 players at bat.

COMPETITIONS There are **county matches** within the U.K. and **test matches**, series of games with other cricketing countries: Australia, New Zealand, South Africa, India, Sri Lanka, Pakistan and the West Indies.

THE ASHES Winning the Ashes (winning the yearly cricket match with Australia) is the dream of British cricketers. The Ashes themselves are really the ashes of a bail which are kept in a small wooden urn in a museum of cricket at Lord's. It all began as a joke. On August 29, 1882, Britain was defeated for the first time by Australia on its home grounds. The next day, the Sporting Times carried an obituary:

"In affectionate remembrance of English Cricket. Deeply lamented by a large circle of sorrowing friends and acquaintances. R.I.P. N.B. The body will be cremated and the ashes taken to Australia."

The next year, when Ivo Bligh, later Lord Darnley, took the

British team to Australia, Punch magazine published some verses about the coming match which contained the line **"When Ivo comes back with the Ashes."** Britain won the match and according to one account, Lady Clarke, in whose home the visiting team stayed, took a **bail**, burned it, put the ashes into a small wooden urn and gave it to Ivo Bligh as a joke. Since then, it became traditional for each team to try to win **"The Ashes"** even though they never move from Lord's where they have reposed since Lord Darnley's death.

MORE CRICKET DEFINITIONS

bowled for duck is to be dismissed without scoring.

a break is a deviation (veering) of a ball on hitting the **pitch** (the ground).

to break one's duck is to make one's first run.

a bumper is a ball that rises sharply from the field.

capped is being accepted by a cricket club and being given the club cap and badge.

a catch out is to put someone out by catching the ball before it touches the ground (like a fly ball).

century means one batter has scored 100 runs in an innings.

close field is the field near the batsman.

a daisy cutter is a ball that skims along the ground.

deep field is the outfield behind the bowler.

a dolly catch is an easy catch.

a donkey drop is an overhand ball thrown right on the wicket.

to draw stumps is to end the game by withdrawing the stumps.

a duck or duck's egg is a zero run on the scoring sheet...a goose egg.

a googly is a ball that swerves one way and and then breaks the other way.

a grub is a ball bowled along the ground.

an appeal is saying **"How's that?"** to the umpire; it means the fielder wants a decision.

long hop is a ball pitched so that it bounces making it easy to hit.

long stop is the player who stands well behind the wicket to stop missed balls.

maiden over is an over in which no runs are made. (See over.)

out of ground means a batsman has gotten out of his permitted or safe area.

a poke is batting gently and cautiously.

a rubber is a series of test matches.

a scorer is one who keeps the record of runs.

a stonewaller is a batsman who aims only to protect the wicket rather than making runs.

Wisden is the bible of cricket fans; it is published annually with all the matches and results (stats); a person who "eats and sleeps cricket" is jokingly called a **"Walking Wisden."**

OTHER POSITIONS FOR PLAYERS: long leg, deep fine leg, short square leg, short fine leg, extra cover, mid wicket, long slip, short slip, long field, long off, long on, silly point, backward point, fly slip, deep mid off, short leg, and leg slip. The **deep** positions are a distance from the wickets and the **long** positions are far off near the boundaries of the cricket field.

Football (Soccer)

FOOTBALL (soccer) is known as **Association Football** and is regulated by the Football Association. All use of arms and hands is prohibited except by the goalie. It's the most popular sport in the U.K. and is said to "produce more **fervour** (fervor) and fanaticism than any other pastime in the world." Thousands jam the stadiums every Saturday during the football season. Some fans can become so impassioned at a team loss that they quite forget they're a very polite people and **hooli-**

A rugby scrum in Leicester.

ganism (violence) breaks out, usually on the way home, in the form of fights, breaking windows, etc.

RUGBY FOOTBALL is a variant form of Association Football which permits carrying the ball and is the forerunner of American football, the latter being first introduced at Yale University in the middle of the 19th century. This form of football originated at Rugby School in 1823 when the score was tied in a battle between two class teams when suddenly, a boy picked up the ball and ran with it across the goal line. This is commemorated by a placque at the school. The point was not allowed but it so took the imagination of the school that they allowed their teams to carry the ball and also permitted tackling and kicking.

Fox Hunting

HISTORY It is thought that the sport of fox hunting began in England in the 15th century. The modern version began in the 19th century and became a national upper-class sport.

The hunt at Drayton.

The hunt at Drayton.

UNIFORM Hunting **kit** (uniform) is usually a **pink coat** with a **white stock** (cravat) and silk **topper** (top hat) for senior or important Hunt Members/subscribers. The **"pink" coats** are really red. They're called **"pinks"** after **Mr. Pink**, a celebrated Hunt tailor who was said to **"cut a very smart coat."** Black coats and **black velvet caps** are worn by members more junior in length of membership or importance; and by farmers over whose land the Hunt rides and by others who are allowed to join the Hunt. Green, yellow or gray uniforms are worn by members of noble families.

OTHER PARTICIPANTS IN THE HUNT The Hunt is conducted by the **Master of the Hounds** (leader) who controls the hounds, usually 15 to 20 couple (matched pairs). **There are also paid employees, a Field Master (a huntsman, the Master's deputy), whippers-in** (hunt employees who keep the foxhounds from wandering), **grooms, second horsemen** (who provide relief horses) and **earth stoppers** (those who stop up all the **earths** (fox holes).

THE HOUNDS There are about 25,000 hounds used by 48,000 people who ride to hounds in 195 hunts throughout Britain. The most famous are the Quorn and Fernie in the Leicestershire hunting season.

THE MEET Hunts are conducted at **Hunting-tide** (the non-growing season as the hunt can range far and wide over farmer's fields). Hunting people consult the **Hunting Fixtures** column in their newspapers for place and time of the meets. A hunt begins with a **Meet** at the home of one of the members. **Stirrup cups** (glasses of port or sherry) are passed to the hunting people while they are on horseback. At a signal from the field master (the master of hounds' deputy when actually hunting) the foxhounds move off to **draw** (search) the **covert** (a thicket where it is thought the fox may be). The master or his deputy controls the hound by **cheers** (calls by voice) and by sounding his copper **hunting** horn. When the hounds make a racket indicating they've found the scent of fox, the hunting horn is sounded, all shout **Tally-ho** and the chase begins. If a fox is killed, it is an **honour** (honor) to be given the **brush** (tail), **pads** (feet), **mask** (head) of the fox or a **smear of foxblood**. At the end of a meet, the foxhounds **"walk"** off briskly. They do not run as they would risk having a whip around their **sterns** (tails).

ARGUMENTS FOR AND AGAINST THE SPORT It's an expensive sport and is surviving in spite of much controversy. **"Antis,"** as those against the sport are called, use many means to stop hunts such as blocking the entrances to kennels and have even resorted to violence. In 1992, Parliament had a five-hour debate about giving foxes the same legal protection against cruelty as has been awarded to cats and dogs but the foxes lost by a vote of 187 to 175. Parliament has also debated recently on the abolition of fox hunting but no decision has been reached as many members join in the sport. An argument to keep the sport is that in places where fox hunting has been banned, the foxes have flourished and ventured into residential areas after ducks, chickens and even cats. Also, should Hunts be banned, thousands of foxhounds would have to be destroyed as they are not good as house dogs or pets.

HUNT WORDS

the field —the actual hunt

to hunt counter — following the scent backwards

hunters — special horses bred for fox hunting

hunting mass — a hurried abridged mass for impatient hunters

hunting people or **hunting men/women** — participants in an actual hunt

pilch — a light saddle

rat catcher — unconventional hunting outfit

riding waistcoats — riding jackets

skirter — a hunter who avoids the jumps

twenty-couple — 40 foxhounds

upping-stone, mounting stone or **upping block** — block of stone used as aid for mounting a horse

to whip off — stopping the hounds from going after rabbits when they should be going after foxes

Other Forms of Recreation

GARDENING Britain is a nation of garden lovers. Flowers are everywhere. It's not unusual to see men and women alike, with sprays of flowers in their shopping baskets or **bicycle bins** (bike baskets). Small **glass houses** (green houses) are an ordinary sight in many gardens, some free-standing, others attached to homes. Glass houses provide cherry tomatoes (a good Vitamin C source) all year long as the growing season required for tomatoes is too long for many parts of Britain. Britain is renowned for its formal gardens, many of which were created by **"Capability" Brown** (Lancelot, real given name), gardens that emphasized **"the natural look."** His nickname came from his saying that a site had **"capabilities."** Maps are available giving driving directions to all the famous gardens.

GARDENING EQUIPMENT

backacting trencher —backhoe
cold house, cold frame or **forcing pit** — cold frame
duster — sprinkler
glasshouse, forcing house, hothouse or **greenhouse**
— greenhouse
garden glass — bell jars for covering plants
hessian sacking or **crocus sacks** — burlap bags
notched shears — hedge clippers
rotovator — rotary cultivator
swing anvil pruner — pruning shears
tattie-bogle or **bird scarer** — scare crow
tree lopper — lopping shears

FLOWERS, PLANTS AND TREES

Beauty of Bath — apple variety
bird cherry — wild cherry
campion — pinks
capsicum — peppers
casual or **wilding** — volunteer (plant that comes up
by itself)
catcher or **catchfly** — sticky campion
charlock — wild mustard
corn — any grain, wheat in England, oats in Ireland
and Scotland
corn flag — gladiolas
dead men's bells — foxglove
devil's snuff box — puff ball
dog daisy or **ox-eye daisy** — ox-eye daisy
gardener's garters — variegated ribbon grass
the gold — marigold

MISCELLANEOUS GARDENING WORDS

after crop — second crop
aftermath — grass that springs up after mowing

allotment — a piece of public land let out for individual use
American blight — plant-louse, apple tree pests
coppice — small grove of woods
coverts — thickets
earthing up — spading
grass mowings — grass clippings
green fingers — green thumb
hosepipe — garden hose
ivy — English ivy
lad's love — wormwood used in beer
long purples — purple loosestrife
may-white hedge — hawthorne hedge in bloom
North American pines — jack pines
osiers — willows
plane tree — sycamore
queen apple — quince
rick — haystack
rockery — rock garden
seed packets — seed packages
side-saddle flower — pitcher plant
sparrow grass — another name for asparagus
spinneys — small clumps of trees
stone crop — sedum
sunk garden — sunken garden
sweet bay — laurel
the May — hawthorne
to spike a lawn — aerate it
toothache tree — prickly ash
wild carrot — Queen Anne's lace

WORDS ASSOCIATED WITH VARIOUS FORMS OF RECREATION

GENERAL
caravan — travel trailer
playpark — playground

W/E — Weekend

BIKING

    bicycle bin — bicycle basket

    cycle — bike

    gent's cycle — man's bike

    ladies' cycle — girl's bike

    penny farthing — old-fashioned bike with a large and small wheel

BOATING

    rowing boat — row boat

CARD GAMES, ADULT

    blind hookey — a gambling card game

    brag — a variation of Poker

    Devil's books — playing cards

    I'm chucking in — I'm out

    All Fours — card game in which there are four chances to score a point

    play for love — no stakes

    round game — each plays his own hand

EXERCISING

    gym stalls — gym bars

    physical jerks — exercises

    somerset or **somersault** — somersault

FAIRS

    Cock Shy — a game stand where one used to throw something at a live cock; not a living one these days

    Prick the Garter or **Fast and Loose** — a cheating game where a dupe is invited to put a stick in the loop of a coiled belt so it can't be pulled away

FISHING

    breaking strain — test strength of the line

    burn the water — spear salmon by torchlight (flashlight)

    close season or **close time** — closed season

    cock-a-bondy — fishing fly for angling

fish garth or **enclosed fish weir** — area on a river for holding fish

fly fisher — fly fisherman

free fisher — one who has the right to fish in certain waters

kiddle or **stake fence** — a picket fence set in a stream for catching fish

live box — live fish container

HIKING

rucksack/haversack — backpack or knapsack (from German **"rücken,"** meaning back)

trekkers — hikers

KITING (kite flying)

PAINTING

sketching block — sketch pad

POTHOLING (spelunking)

RIDING (Horseback Riding) "Riding" is considered a "more upmarket" (more refined) name as it assumes one has a horse or has access to one

hacking — informal riding and exercising horses

hacking jacket — tweed coat for informal **riding**

SHOOTING

a **"shot"** — a person who shoots; he/she can also be a **good shot** or a **keen shot**

pea rifle/air gun/rifle — BB gun or other small caliber rifle

pengun — popgun made of a feather

shooter — a gun

shooting range — rifle range

SWIMMING, BATHING OR DIVING

a ripping bathe — great swim

diving kit — scuba outfit

the shingle — a pebble beach

baths or **swimming baths** — pool or swimming pool

corporation swimming baths — town pool

fancy dive — swan dive

frogman suit — wet suit
go brown — get tan
high board — diving board
pond master — swimming pool manager
to bathe — to swim

CONTEST SPORTS
GENERAL EXPRESSIONS

aftergame or **revenge** — a second game played in hopes of reversing the score of the first

bear the bell or **to carry off the bell** —have or gain first place

break a lance with — challenge for a contest

catapult — slingshot

changing room — locker room or drying room

cup tie — one of a series of games to determine the winner of a cup; the whole series is the **"Cup Competition"** ending with a **"Cup Final"**

draw cuts — cast lots

gymkhana — originally a horse show in India; today a meeting or show, primarily of horse contests with perhaps some athletic events

home and dry — home free

joint first — first place tie

marks — points for scoring

nil — zero

pitch — field

"Shot!" — short for **"Good Shot!"**; can mean any skillful stroke in any game, not just shooting

Well held! — Good catch!

Well taken! — Great!

BOAT RACING:

bumping race — race where boats bump each other

to pull for — to row for

BOXING:

bottle holder — boxer's attendant

the fancy — boxers

GOLF:

> **four ball** — a game played with two against two with four balls, the best ball counting
>
> **rub on the green** or **rub of the green** —refers to a chance of outside interference with the ball
>
> **target golf range** — driving range

HORSE RACING Horse races are run clockwise in the U.K.; in the U.S. they go counter-clockwise. The most famous horse race in the U.K. is the **Derby** (pronounced darby) and thousands flock to view the race at **Epsom Downs** in Epsom (Surrey), about 15 miles from London. It's such a big event that Parliament takes the day off and the race is presided over by the **Queen**. It was named for the **Earl of Derby**, who in 1780, offered a prize for an annual race. It's a horseshoe shaped course and the distance is **four furlongs and 29 yards** (one mile). Only three-year-old horses are permitted to race and there's a large entrance fee. The usual attire for men used to be grey suits and top hats, and for women, fancy dresses and fanciful hats like those worn at N.Y. City's Easter Parade. Today, anything goes but only outside the **"Enclosures."** One must be formally dressed in **Tattersall's** or the **Royal Enclosure**, the exclusive sections. Other famous races are the **Royal Ascot, the Oaks** and **the St. Leger**.

HORSE RACING WORDS

> **punters** — people who bet with bookmakers
>
> **race glasses** — binoculars
>
> **to nobble** or **to pull a bit of a flanker** — to dope a horse
>
> **the off** — the start of the race
>
> **the parade ring** — the ring in which the race entrants are led around before going to the starting gate

POOL

> **snooker** — variation of pool

FOOT-RACING

> **breast the tape** — break the tape

TENNIS

fix up a court — reserve a court

knock up — pre-tennis match practice

lawn tennis — tennis

royal tennis, court tennis or **real tennis** — the ancestor of lawn tennis; a medieval game called **jeu de paume** (game of the palm) which is still played today on an indoor court with pear-shaped rackets and cloth balls

History is past politics,
and politics present history.
—Sir John Robert Seeley, 1834-1895

CHAPTER SEVENTEEN

GOVERNMENT AND POLITICS

The Queen's Powers

The United Kingdom is a **constitutional monarchy**. This means that the queen is actually the **head of state** but the government is run by a cabinet of ministers mostly selected from the **House of Commons**. Parliament had a rough time getting this power away from the reigning sovereigns (see Chapter Eight) and makes a point now of not allowing the reigning sovereign to enter into the House of Commons. However, it does acknowledge that the queen is the symbol of the British government by calling itself **Her Majesty's Government**. The opposition party is **Her Majesty's Loyal Opposition**, and any work done for the government is done **On Her Majesty's Service**.

The queen has a number of **residual powers** which she is careful not to exercise without parliamentary approval. She must approve each bill passed by Parliament for it to become law but never rejects a bill; she can dissolve Parliament, but doesn't; and she can choose a prime minister. The choice is made after many consultations with members of Parliament. As **Head of the Church of England** she can recommend bishops but they are really appointed by Parliament after consultations with the Archbishop of Canterbury.

This does not mean that the queen sits around all day doing nothing, in fact, she is very well informed about the workings of Parliament. Every day the **Red Box** arrives with all the cabinet minutes and cabinet papers which she reads assiduously. She also reads nearly all the newspapers every day and is said to have a sharp and retentive mind. She can advise from her past experiences, having had meetings with all the Prime Ministers of whatever party since 1952. Constitutional History was her main subject of study during her school years.

Tuesday nights the prime minister has a talk with the queen. No one knows what's discussed because the press is never allowed to listen in and she's never had a press conference. She is recognized as the U.K.'s premier diplomat and represents stability when Parliament is out of session. Also, she is greatly loved by her people for herself and because she represents tradition...and **tradition** is the U.K.'s middle name.

Parliament

THE MAJORITY PARTY AND THE SHADOW CABINET
The Prime Minister is the leader of the **majority party** in the Commons. The opposition party is called the **Shadow Cabinet** and it's led by the **Leader of the Opposition**, an official salaried position. In a sense, the Shadow Cabinet is on stand-by, because it takes over when the majority party loses a general election. Its leader then becomes the new Prime Minister. Whenever Parliament is **dissolved**, the be-wigged **Common Crier** announces the dissolution by reading a proclamation from the Queen in a loud voice from the steps of **London's Royal Exchange**. Parliament is dissolved: when it's maximum term of five years is completed; if Parliament no longer supports the policies of the Cabinet; and if the Prime Minister wants the country's opinion on an important issue.

THE COMMONS (The House of Commons) is called the **lower house** even though it is the real governing body of Parliament. Lower means, in this case, **"closer to the people."** Commons has 651 members elected by the people of England,

Northern Ireland, Scotland and Wales and they have sole jurisdiction over finance. They represent **constituencies** (electoral
districts) throughout the kingdom. There are about 635 constituencies in Britain and Northern Ireland. District boundaries
are revised every five years to allow for population changes
because each constituency has to have roughly the same population. An **M.P.** (Member of Parliament) can be elected to a
district in which he does not live. Members receive an annual
salary and get travel and administrative expenses.

The Commons **sits** (is in session) for about 160 days annually
from November to the following October. The sessions begin at
mid-afternoon and some continue through the evening and
even the night. The sittings of Commons or Lords may be
adjourned from time to time by order of that House subject to
the right of the Crown to summom both to meet with not less
than six days notice.

The Commons meets in a long room with a Speaker's chair
at one end and rows of benches going down the two sides.
Members of the **Government** (party in power) sit to the
Speaker's right, the **Opposition** to the left. The leaders of each
side sit on the front benches and are known as the **front bench**.
The rest are called the **back bench** or **backbenchers**. Legislation
proposed by the Government is debated with the Opposition.

GENERAL ELECTIONS By a 1911 law, a general election is
to be held every 5 years; however, in times of crisis like a war,
it can be postponed. Also it can be held at any of the times
mentioned above. Following a general election, a Prime Minister is appointed by the Queen. He must be an elected member
of the House of Commons and is generally the leader of the
party that has the most members in the new House of Commons. He/She can only hold this office as long as he/she has
the support of over half of the members of the House. If the
largest party lacks the majority of members in the House, it may
form a coalition with another party.

THE SPEAKER At the beginning of each **new Parliament**, a
Speaker is elected to preside over sessions. The Speaker must

ignore any party allegiance and if he/she **stands** (runs) for re-election, he/she cannot run on a party ticket, only as **"Mr. or Madame Speaker seeking re-election."** The Speaker decides which amendments to bills will be voted on and can cast a tie-breaking vote. In 1992, the 155th Speaker was elected, Ms. Betty Boothroyd, the first woman Speaker ever. In 1994, she was one of 60 women M.P.s in a 651 member Commons.

THE GOVERNMENT After his appointment, the Prime Minister chooses what is known as the **"Government,"** that is, the members of his Cabinet and other prominent officials...about 100 in all: **the Foreign Office** (State Department), **the Home Office** (Department of Interior), and the **M.O.D. (Ministry of Defence)** under which are **"The Armed Forces of the Crown"** with the **Minister of Defence** in charge or his very senior civil servants. The sub-departments are the **M.O.D.(A) Ministry of Defence (Army)** and **Admiralty**, the **Exchequer** (Treasury Department), the **Labour Office** (Department of Labor), etc. All of these must be members of one of the two Houses of Parliament.

Welsh affairs are handled by a cabinet minister, the **Secretary of State for Wales**, with the advice of a broadly representative council for Wales. **Scotland's affairs** are handled by the **Secretary of State for Scotland**. Scotland continues, as before the union, to have different systems of education, local government, judiciary and law (Roman-French); and its national church is the Presbyterian Church of Scotland. Since March 1972, **Northern Ireland** has had direct rule from London through the **Secretary of State for Northern Ireland**. Northern Ireland has 17 members in the House of Commons. **Civil servants** staff the departments of the government and keep their jobs no matter which party is in power. They help the department ministers form policies and carry them out.

THE LORDS (The House of Lords) is called the **upper house** because it is less subject to control by the voters. It has less power than the Commons, but can review, amend or delay temporarily any bills except those relating to the budget. Its main function is the debating of public issues. It is the **highest court of appeal** in civil and criminal cases, except in Scotland where they have the **High Court of Justiciary**. The House of Lords has about 1170 members and about 800 hold heriditary titles. Others hold non-hereditary life peerages, that is, their children cannot inherit the titles. There are also about 20 **"law lords"** appointed for life who handle legal matters that come to the House, **2 archbishops** and **24 bishops**. Members do not get an annual salary but they do get travel expenses.

The chamber of the House of Lords is very Victorian with stained glass windows, statues of the barons of the Magna Carta, and long red leather sofas on each side of the room. Between the two sides is **"The Woolsack,"** a huge red ottoman stuffed with bits of wool from all over the Commonwealth. It is a reminder that wool was once the source of the nation's wealth. Tradition again! To be **"appointed to the woolsack"** is a great **honour** (honor) as the appointee becomes the Lord Chancellor, head of the House of Lords.

This chamber is where the members of both houses meet when a session of Parliament opens. The Regent attends in state and reads a statement prepared by the party in power which outlines what the government intends to do for the country.

HOW BILLS ARE PASSED Bills can be introduced by any member of either house but the great majority come from the governing party. When a bill comes to a vote, the **Doorkeeper** rings a bell four times and shouts **"Division."** This is a signal for the members voting **"Aye"** to walk out to the West Lobby to be counted and those voting **"No"** to the East Lobby. For a bill to become the **law of the land**, it must pass both houses and be approved by the Crown.

AN "UNWRITTEN CONSTITUTION" The British do not have a written Constitution like ours; rather, they have an **"Unwritten Constitution."** Their **"body of law"** is based on statute (all the laws passed by Parliament), **common law** and **traditional rights** such as those given in the **Magna Carta**. (See Chapter Eight.) Changes come about by new acts of Parliament, informal acceptances of new practices and usages or by judicial precedents. The judiciary cannot review the constitutionality of legislation as does our Supreme Court. It is independent of the legislative and executive branches of government.

TRADITIONS OF THE HOUSE OF COMMONS The House of Commons has a number of ancient traditions such as **never locking any door**. It's a terrible **offense** if one does so. Also **no one must touch the mace** (staff) on the clerk's table. Another no-no is **crossing the line**. Members of the governing party and of the opposition and must not cross the imaginary line down the middle of Commons. A good rule, as it no doubt prevents fist fights during heated debates.

PARLIAMENTARY WORDS AND TERMS

on benefits or **on welfare** — on welfare
C.P. or **magistrate** — clerk of the peace
disabled soldiers institute — veterans hospital
the dole queue — the welfare line
grainage — duties on grain
Home Ruler — advocate of home rule
The House rises. — Parliament adjourns.
I.L.P. — Independent Labour Party
jack-in-office — self-important petty official
jaw factory on the Thames — Parliament (Washington is called "Foggy Bottom")
jerrymander — gerrymander
N.H.I. — National Health Insurance
Ladies' Gallery — House of Commons gallery
lay on a table — table a motion
lieges — subjects of a sovereign
Lord High Steward — an important government officer
M.P. — Member of Parliament
N.C.B. — National Coal Board
N.H.I. — National Health Insurance
Old Age Pension — Social Security

The Old Ship or **Old Blighty** — affectionate names
  for Britain
Pennyland — historic sites valued at a penny a year
Pension Scheme — pension plan
Queenship — the ship of state
Red Box — a minister's official papers box
Stationery Office — Government Printing Office
standard — flag
Strangers' Gallery — Visitors' Gallery
table money — allowance for official entertainment
talk against time — filibuster
to whip — to appeal for contributions
Unionist — opponent to Irish Home Rule
Union Jack — flag of the U.K.
with one voice — unanimous

MORE PARLIAMENTARY WORDS AND TERMS

A backwoodsman is a peer who rarely attends the
  House of Lords.
The Better-Notters (Doves) during WWII were Cham-
  berlain and those who believed in dealing with
  Hitler to prevent war; the **War-Wagers** (Hawks)
  were for war.
The Black Rod is an usher of the Chapter of the Gar-
  ter and of the House of Lords who carries an ebony
  rod.
The Blue Book is a Parliamentary publication some-
  what like Congress' Federal Register which has a
  blue cover.
The Commonwealth Conference was originally the
  Colonial Conference; it's a periodic conference of
  the Prime Ministers and other representatives of the
  U.K. and the self-governing dominions.
Commonwealth Federation is a **scheme** (plan) to fed-
  erate the self-governing parts of the British Empire.
The Government Whip enforces party discipline and

makes sure the members of Parliament attend important sessions.

Home Rule is the self-goverment that was claimed by the Irish Nationalists which included a separate Parliament for internal affairs.

Kissing the book refers to the kissing of a Bible or New Testament after taking a legal oath.

NUPE is the Civil Service's National Union of Public Employees.

The Queen's Tobacco Pipe was a kiln at the London docks for burning contraband goods.

Red Book is a red-bound book containing a court guide of the peerage, a directory of persons in the service of the state and offical regulations.

Social Security allowances are not necessarily only to people over 65. There are other allowances to top up small incomes such as the **Housing Benefit**, the **Invalidity Allowance** and the **Children's Allowance**.

Somerset House is the national repository, since 1837, of births, marriages and deaths. It is now being superseded by **St. Catherine's House**.

A three-line whip is a call on members of Parliament to be in their places for a vote on important legislation. The number of times a message is underlined indicates the urgency of the message.

Political Parties

Political Parties came into being during the reign of Charles II when an **"Exclusion Bill"** was presented to Parliament to bar Charles' Catholic brother James from becoming heir to the throne. Charles dissolved Parliament to prevent passage of the bill and Parliament split into two factions: **Whigs**, those for the bill and **Tories**, those against. Today, the main parties are: **Conservative, Labor, The Social and Liberal Democratic Party** as well as **Nationalist parties** in Northern Ireland, Scotland and Wales.

When Charles II died, James became James II without much fuss but when a son was born, the Tories and Whigs joined forces to set aside the Catholic line of kings. They invited James' daughter **Mary**, a Protestant, and her Dutch husband, **William of Orange** (a noted defender of Protestantism) to become joint sovereigns. James escaped to the continent. **William and Mary** agreed to abide by Parliament's **Declaration of Rights** which made the sovereigns responsible to Parliament and banned Catholics from wearing the crown. It's the famous **Bill of Rights.** Since this was a revolution sans bloodshed, it was called **The Glorious Bloodless Revolution.**

British Election Practices

ELECTION NOTIFICATION The Prime Minister only has to give 17 days advance notice of an election.

SELECTION OF CANDIDATES Instead of primaries, candidates are selected by local **party associations. Party leaders** are chosen only by the members of Parliament of their party, not by the electorate.

ELECTIONTIDE (Election Time) At election time, candidates **wear favours** (lapel ribbons like those awarded at American county fairs) in party **colours** (colors): **red for Labour** (Labor), **blue for Conservative** and **yellow and lavender for Liberal**.

ELECTION CAMPAIGNS It seems unbelievable, but a tourist could tour the U.K. during election time and not know one is going on. Election campaigns last about three weeks and cost very little as compared to American elections because there are strict regulations about campaign expenses. If a party overspends, the election result can be annulled; so there are few newspaper ads, few posters on **hoardings** (billboards) and very few television commercials. These are only allowed in moderation during the final days of a campaign. Candidates are given some free radio time but cannot buy time.

ELECTION TERMS

by-election — an off-year election held during a sitting of Parliament when a Member resigns, dies or inherits a peerage

The Constituency's Women's Association — The League of Women Voters

coordination meeting — organizational meeting

election agent — campaign manager

faggot vote — a vote for party purposes

household suffrage or **household franchise** — universal suffrage

a hundred — the division of a county which has enough land to support 100 families

party tub thumper — party faithful

polling station — the polls

ratified — confirmed

returned — elected

returning officer — auditor

scrutineer — poll watcher

shortlisted candidates — finalists

stand for Parliament — run for Parliament

stump orator — party candidate

stump speech — election oratory

thumping majority — large majority

top hats — politicians

to plump for — to vote for

"The Government"

NO. 10 DOWNING STREET, LONDON The leader of the winning party becomes Prime Minister and lives at No. 10 Downing Street, London. He/She has an indefinite term of up to five years but it's considered **bad form** (bad manners) to stay the full time so 4 1/2 years is usually the limit.

GOVERNMENT DEPARTMENTS

Attorney General — chief law officer for the U.K.

C.O.A. — Central Office of Information
Committee on Safety of Medicines — like our FDA
Home Department — department concerned with
  maintaining the internal peace of the U.K.
Home Secretary — Home Department Head
Home Guard — a volunteer force for national defense
Home Office — Home Department headquarters
Inland Revenue Authority — tax department
Paper Office — record room for state papers
Privy Council — originally the sovereign's private advisory group; today, its functions are performed by
  committees
Rating Authority — Tax Department

Local Government

TOWN AND VILLAGE WORDS

Casual Ward — workhouse for casuals (laborers or
  paupers)
county town — the seat of the county administration
Council Houses — subsidized housing built and administered by a town or county council
footwalk or **pavement** — sidewalk
footway — footpath
job centre (center) — employment office
Paper Day — Grievance Day
Parish Council Office — Town Hall
power cut — power interruption
rubbish tip — garbage dump
Sanitary Authorities — Sanitation Department
street furniture — lampposts, parking meters, etc.

TAX TERMS

charitable status — charitable groups are allowed to
  pay little or no tax on donations or legacies

Community Charge — money collected for the local
  councils
education rates — school taxes
excisemen — tax collectors
house duty or **house tax** — real estate tax
rates and **taxes** — rates are paid locally and taxes are
  paid nationally
tax fiddle — a tax dodge

I hold it indisputable,
that the first duty of a State
is to see that every child born therein
shall be well housed, clothed, fed, and educated,
till it attain years of discretion.
—*John Ruskin, Time and Tide, letter viii*

CHAPTER EIGHTEEN

THE BRITISH EDUCATIONAL SYSTEM/ THE SCHOOLMASTER IS ABROAD

"The Schoolmaster is abroad" means "education and intelligence are widely spread." This is very true today in Britain. Through the efforts of Parliamentarians like Baron Brougham and Vaux (pronounced Brorm and Voh) a movement for compulsory education began in the 1800's. The above quotation is ascribed to him. From 1970 to 1994, a number of Parliamentary Education Acts made nationally funded educational opportunities available to all.

Education Authorities (School Administrators)

British education is administered by three separate systems to allow for differences in tradition: one for England and Wales, one for Scotland and one for Northern Ireland. **The Local Education Authorities (L.E.A.)** administer the **state schools** (like our public schools) and also provide funds for the **volun-**

tary/independent schools (like Eton, Harrow or Rugby) or denominational schools (parochial schools) whose secular studies they supervise. The voluntary schools are similar to our private schools but are known as "public schools."

How Funded?

The great majority of schools in Britain, that are attended by over 90% of school children, are publicly provided for, or assisted by the national government. Only nursery schools are funded by parents. Books and necessary supplies are provided for all children from ages 5 to 16. The private ("public") schools are not funded but do receive public grants making them subject to supervision by the British Department of Education. Universities are autonomous self-governing institutions but even they are aided by public funds. Most technical colleges and other centers of further education are also publicly maintained.

Physical Education and Sports

Physical education and organized games such as tennis, cricket, football (soccer), rugger (rugby football), hockey, lacrosse and netball (volley ball) are part of the curriculum.

Health

The School Health Service provides periodic medical examinations and in cooperation with the National Health Service provides free medical and dental treatment for all children in the county schools. Milk is free and the Schools Meals Service provides a midday dinner at a subsidized price to a great percentage of the pupils in both county and voluntary schools.

Religious Instruction

In Britain, about half of the primary schools are denominational. The Local Education Authorities are reponsible for providing nondenominational religious worship and religious instruction in all schools receiving public funds.

Education System

Children can go to the state **infant schools** from ages four-and-a-half to seven, and the **junior schools** from ages seven to eleven. **Eleven-plus examinations** (examinations given at age 11) used to determine which kind of **secondary school** (high school) a child would attend: the **secondary grammar** which provided classical education for those going on to a university; the **secondary modern** provided practical courses for those not interested in a university education, and the **secondary technical** provided vocational training related to commerce and industry. Starting in the early 1970s, the 11-plus examinations were gradually phased out and **comprehensive schools** (similar to our high schools) were phased in providing all three types of training for those from age 11 to 16.

The National Curriculum

In 1989, the Government of England and Wales began a progressive introduction of **National Curriculum** subjects into the primary and secondary schools. The National Curriculum consists of **core subjects**: English, mathematics and science plus Welsh in Wales; and **foundation subjects**: history, geography, technology, music, art, and physical education. Secondary school pupils also take a foreign language. By 1996-97, the entire National Curriculum will be taught to all pupils.

O-levels

At age 16, pupils take **Ordinary (O-level)** examinations to qualify for a **GCSE (General Certificate of Secondary Education)**. Each subject is taken separately, no subject is obligatory and individual subjects can be taken at different times. O-levels are given in more than 50 subjects from astronomy to zoology. Most grammar, direct-grant and independent school pupils take the O-levels. This explains want ads such as: **"YOUNG MAN, 22, FIVE O LEVELS, SEEKS INTERESTING POSITION."** Another expression used in ads is **Fully Qualified** (graduated).

A-levels

The GCSE will get one into a vocational training school but not into a university. That requires two more years of study at a **6th Form College** before one can **sit A-Levels**, that is take a **GCE (General Certificate of Education Advanced A-Level)** exam, the passing of which opens a university door. The opportunity to study a wider range of subjects was given in the late 1980s to allow students to qualify for **AS (Advanced Supplementary) Certificate. A levels** or a mixture of **A** and **AS levels** are the main qualifications for university entrance today. Scotland and Ireland have similar educational requirements with slightly different certificate names. Those who qualify for university entrance are said to be **going up**, the opposite of what happens when a student break a rule, then he/she is **sent down** or **rusticated**, that is, banned from school for a term or expelled if the offense is serious enough.

To Review

1. One is presumably 16 in one's last year of the Comprehensive School. This is called the **Upper 5th Form** or **GCSE year** because it's at the end of this year that one takes the GCSE exams. This exam shows that one has studied the basic subjects and can go on to vocational training and a job.

2. If one is academically inclined, one goes on to a **6th Form College** for two more years of study as one must be 18 to be able to take the **GCE Advanced A-level** or **AS exams**.

3. Passing grades in these exams opens a university door where one stays for 3 years until age 21, unless one is **reading** (studying) medicine as that takes 5 or 6 years. **Reading a modern language** requires that the third year be taken in the country of that language and the 4th year back in the university.

4. **Final examinations** and **post-graduate studies** follow if one wishes an **MA (masters)** or **PhD. (doctorate)**.

Universities

Britain has 33 universities, including the world famous Oxford and Cambridge which date from the 13th Century. The latter are usually lumped together under the name **Oxbridge**, a blend of **Ox**ford and Cam**bridge.** All universities other than Oxbridge are called **"Red Brick,"** no doubt because the original university buildings were of red brick; so when one hears **"He is red brick,"** one immediately knows he's not an Oxbridge graduate. The **Open University**, which was established in 1969, gives those who cannot attend a university full time an opportunity to obtain an academic degree by means of television and correspondence courses.

University Years

Students **go up** to a university to **read** (major in a particular discipline), as for example, one goes up to **read history** (major in history) or **read biochemistry** (major in biochemistry). The University years are identified as **First Year, Second Year**, etc. In some schools they are known as **Fresher** (Freshman), **Junior Soph** (Sophomore), **Junior** (Junior) and **Leaving Student** (Senior). **Year Out** is the name given to the fourth year of a student **reading** a foreign language.

School Talk

British students have developed a very colorful and descriptive language regarding their studies. **A crack jaw** is a tongue twister, the biology lab is the **bug's lab**, an exclamation point is called **a screamer, devilling** is doing research, a **crit** is a quiz, the **longs and shorts** are Greek and Latin verses, **sums** refer to addition, and the dictionary is **dikker**, for short. When students cram for exams they call it **slogging away at one's studies, swotting up** or **mugging up**.

MORE SCHOOL TALK

A bread study — a branch of study taken as a means of earning a living
A to Zed — A to Z
booky — bookish

clerklike or **clerkly** — scholarly or learned
curriculum vitae — school transcript
full marks — excellent or A-plus
games tunics — gym suits
half term — mid-term
keep a term — regular attendance
kerb drill — fire drill
letterless — illiterate
night class — night school
nil or **naught** — zero
open book — easy-to-read book
pass-out marks — final grades
prep (preparation) — homework or study
prep hour — study hall
private tuition or **personal experienced tuition** — tutoring
sixth form pash — a high school crush, as in, "He had a sixth form pash on his teacher."
spotty devils — an affectionate teacher name for students, as in, "Well, it's back to the spotty devils tomorrow."

School Uniform

Students in nearly all British grammar and secondary schools wear school uniforms: trousers and school jacket with school emblem and tie for boys; skirt and school jacket with emblem for girls. Most are dark in color but some schools require a blue or green jacket.

SCHOOL PERSONNEL

careers master — guidance counselor
coach — tutor
games mistress or **master** — phys ed teacher
headmaster — principal
invigilator — proctor (supervisor of exams)
school master or **mistress** — teacher

supply teacher — a temporary or substitute teacher said to be "on supply," that is, "ready to fill in."

SCHOOL BUILDINGS

dining hall — lunch room
notice board or **letter board** — bulletin board
recreation ground — playground
school time — school day
Speech Hall — Assembly Room
staircase — floor, as in, "There's a chap on my staircase who..."

SCHOOL SUPPLIES

india rubber — eraser
rule — ruler

SCHOOL INFRACTIONS AND DISCIPLINE

gated or **jankers** — detention (Jankers is from army slang.)
gate fine — fine for disobedience
"having a bag of sweets under the desk look" —having a guilty look
play the kip, play the way or **skive off** — being truant

School Events

Open Day is Parent's Night when all the school departments have displays or give demonstrations to the parents. It's also an opportunity to talk to the teachers.

Parent-Teacher Association meetings are similar to American PTA meetings.

Speech Day or **Prize Giving Day** comes usually in October. It's the day when the prizes earned during the previous school year are distributed. Besides the students, their parents and the **headmaster** (principal), wife and school personnel, the ceremony is attended by the **Board of Governors** (School Board) and the **Lord Mayor** and **Lady Mayoress**. Prizes of books are given for excellence in the knowledge of Greek Testaments, Modern Studies, **Declamation** (Oratory), Mathematics, Sports etc. At the end, there are usually several **three times threes**, (three cheers repeated three times for the officials.) A senior student runs to the front of the hall and says loudly **"Three cheers for Mr. "Brown, Hip, hip, hooray!"**

VACATION WORDS

a fortnight's mooch — two-week vacation

Black Monday — any Monday

break up or **break-up day** — the last day of school or vacation

down — short for **"shut down,"** the school is closed, "He was on holiday while the school was **down**."

the hols, the **vac (vacation)**, **summer vac**, **summer hols**, and **the long (long vacation)** — the holidays or vacation

Public (Private) School Talk

A fag is a student who does menial jobs for a student in a higher class.

A form was origianlly a bench that students sat on but it later became the name for the grade the student was in; 4th Form, for example, being equal to our 9th grade. Today forms have gone in the state schools and are now usually called First Year, Second Year, etc. They continue on in **Prep Schools** (Preparatory Schools) which have 1st Form to 6th Form, ages 7-plus to 13-plus. **Public** (private) schools usually have no 1st Form. Students start at 2nd Form (II) and end at Upper Vth at age 16-plus unless one is taking A-levels. Then one goes on to Lower VIth at 17-plus and end with Upper VIth at 18-plus unless one is taking **"Oxbridge"** entrance exams after A-levels.

A prefect is a student monitor.

ETON TALK

a dry bob — a member of the cricket team

a wet bob — a rowing team member
an Eton Mess — a concoction of strawberries served
in kirsch and mixed with crushed meringues and
whipped cream. It is traditionally served on
Speech Day.
chamber fellow — roommate
class fellow — classmate
tuck — food
tuck-box — food from home
tuck shop — pastry shop near a school

GENERAL UNIVERSITY TALK

bulldog — proctor's attendant
don — a fellow or college official
High Table — the don's table in the dining hall
maths — math or math students
"Olympus" — the university staff
passed out — completed the course of study
polymath — one with varied learning
Student Common Room — student lounge
townees — townspeople
viva voce exam —oral exam

MORE UNIVERSITY TALK

To break gates is to sneak back into college after the prescribed hour.

A double-first is a university degree with first- class honors in two different subjects.

An external or extra-mural student is one who takes an examination at a university which he/she has not attended.

A first poster is a top student whose name appears at the top of the list of exam results

Gaudeamus, Gaudy Day and Gaudy Night is an annual college festival. Gaudeamus is Latin for "let us rejoice."

"Going up in bye-term" is entering a university in the middle of the school year instead of October.

"The smell of the lamp" as in "There was the smell of the lamp in his room." means the student was making a great show of how hard he was studying, "burning the midnight oil," so to speak.

To **"sport one's oak"** is university slang referring to keeping one's outer door shut when one doesn't want visitors...presumably the door is made of oak.

To **"take a class"** is to take honors in an exam instead of a mere pass.

Town and Gown refers to the general community and the members of the university.

CAMBRIDGE TALK

"a little go" — a preliminary exam

"a great go" — a degree exam

crackling — four bars of velvet on sleeves of student gowns resembling the crackling on scored legs of pork

punting — boating

registrary — registrar

The Backs — tree shaded grounds on the left bank of the river Cam where students go punting (a flat-bottomed boat propelled by a pole)

OXFORD TALK

The High — the High Street at Oxford

The House — Christ Church, the most prestigious college at Oxford (founded by Cardinal Wolsey)

oxford bags — very wide trousers

Cambridge and Oxford Blues

Blues are students who have been chosen to represent their universities in some major sporting event such as cricket, football (both types), boxing and most of all, rowing. Blue is always a significant color in England. It means someone is the **"top"** or the best. A **Half-Blue** is one who represents his/her university in a minor sport such as lawn tennis (up to fairly recently), and even bridge and tiddleywinks.

Blues and Half-Blues are entitled to wear a blue blazer with a richly embroidered badge on the breast pocket with the University coat-of-arms and underneath the reason for the award such as: **O.U.C.C. 1993-94** (Oxford University Cricket Club) or **C.U.R.C. 1993-94** (Cambridge University Rowing Club).

GRADUATION TERMS

college cap or square — mortar board
diploma do — graduation party
full academicals — cap and gown
Fully Qualified — graduated
Prize Man —winner of an academic prize
School Certificate or School Leaving Certificate — diploma
school leavers — graduates

MORE GRADUATION TALK

A First is a top-ranking degree. One would say, "She took or got a First at Cambridge.") Going down the scale are: **Upper Second** or **(2-1), Lower Second** or (2-2), **Third** (Class) and **Pass**.

A Companion of Literature is an honor instituted in 1961 and conferred by the Royal Society of Literature.

An exhibition is a scholarship award to a university as in "She's won an exhibition." It has nothing to do with the art world. This makes her an **exhibitioner** or scholarship winner.

An honours man is a university degree with honors such as Cum Laude or Magna Cum Laude.

And therfore, at the kinges court, my brother,
Ech man for him-self, ther is non other.
—Geoffrey Chaucer, Canterbury Tales, The Knights Tale, I.
    323.

CHAPTER NINETEEN

RUMPOLE'S BEAT OR CRIME AND PUNISHMENT

The Inns of Court

Mystery buff? Then by all means visit one or more of **"The Inns of Court,"** the haunts of **Rumpole**, John Mortimer's delightful fictional British lawyer. (See Rumpole, later on.)

The **Inns of Court** are four societies which have the exclusive right of **calling to the bar** (giving bar examinations to those who wish to become advocates or barristers-at-law). One who passes these exams is said to have been **called to the bar**. A **barrister** can plead before both a lower and higher court.; while a **solicitor** can plead only before a lower court.

There are four Inns of Court: **The Inner Temple, The Middle Temple, Lincoln's Inn** and **Gray's Inn**. Both temples are just referred to as **"The Temple"** as if they were joined when as a matter of fact they are just near each other between Fleet Street and the Embankment. They have nothing to do with religion. The name "temple" is used because at one time the area the Temples occupy was the headquarters of the **Knights Templars**. The knights took their name from the Temple of Solomon in Jerusalem where they had their base when they were fighting the Muslims during the Crusades. Their order was formed to defend the Holy Places in the Holy Land and to protect pilgrims

271

on their way there. Their Temple Church was destroyed during the London Blitz but was rebuilt. It is a round church like the Holy Sepulchre in Jerusalem. It dates from 1140 and has effigies of the knights who are buried there. Of interest to Americans is that five signers of the Declaration of Independence studied at the Middle Temple: **Edward Rutledge, Thomas Heyward Jr., Thomas McLean, Thomas Lynch Jr.,** and **Arthur Middleton**.

Passing the Bar

At the junction of the present day Strand and Fleet Streets, there was once a stout wooden bar known as **"Temple Bar"** to mark the extra-mural jurisdiction of the City of London, or **"The City,"** as it is commonly known. "The City" is the ancient core of London Proper (Roman Londinium) and encompasses 677 acres and has its own Lord Mayor and police force. The original bar was placed there in the time of the all-powerful Guilds who preserved a degree of independence from the king. Today, there's no obstruction. Anyone can **"pass the bar."** A pedestal surmounted by a griffin marks the old site, however, and when the **queen** visits the City, she always stops at this symbolic point as according to ancient tradition, she must ask permission of the Lord Mayor to enter the City. In a short ceremony, he presents her with the sword of the City. She accepts it graciously but returns it before crossing **"the bar."**

Opposite The Temple are the law courts at the corner of The Strand and Chancery Lane; and midway on Chancery Lane is Lincoln's Inn. Chancery runs into Holborn and at a jog right, is Gray's Inn on Gray's Inn Road.

To "Eat One's Terms"

The Inns serve as universities for law students and are only called Inns because they once furnished permanent residence for their members. To become a **barrister**, one must be affiliated with one of these Inns and it's a rule that they must **"eat one's terms"** or **"eat one's dinner,"** that is, attend a certain number of dinners in their dining halls. It's traditional and a good opportunity to join the old-boys/old-girls network. Each Inn is run by a group of its judges and senior barristers. They are called **Masters of the Bench or Benchers**.

The Inns also have libraries, chapels, gardens, offices for leading lawyers and **The Hall**. The Hall is the center of the member's lives. It's where **mootmen** (student lawyers) conduct **moots** (mock trials) and where they meet to debate or dine. Evenings, they are traditionally summoned to dinner by a porter blowing a silver horn.

Barristers and Solicitors

Lawyers who have been **"called to the bar,"** or admitted to the **Inns of Court** are called **barristers**. They write opinions and do some preparatory work for trials but their primary duties are to act as advocates for people in the **"superior courts"** (high courts). In most cases, they can only act upon instructions of a solicitor who is responsible for the barrister's fee. **Solicitors** are also lawyers but can only present cases in the **"inferior courts"** (lower courts). They can't become judges, only barristers have that privilege, and they don't get to wear wigs and robes.

"Taking Silk"

"Called within the bar" is a step up. It's also known as **"taking silk"** meaning getting to wear a silk robe and wig in court and having **Q.C.** or **K.C.** appended to one's name. **Q.C.** stands for Queen's Counsel when there is a reigning queen and it changes to **K.C.** when there's a reigning king.

Wigs

Wearing wigs began in France at the court of Louis XIII in the 17th century. He wore one because he was bald but it soon became the fashion for both men and women to wear them and it spread to Britain, especially during the reign of Charles II. By 1790, the fashion disappeared from general use. Since wigs had become a symbol of office, the Lord Chancellor, judges, barristers and bishops still wear them. They're all made of South

American horsehair and are very expensive but are meant to last a lifetime. The same design is used for both men and women.

THE LONG ROBE (LEGAL PROFESSION) TERMS

adjudicators — judges
affiliation order — paternity suit
attorney-in-fact or private attorney — attorney
chamber practice — the business of a chamber counsel
in chancery — litigation or an awkward situation
Clerk of the Peace or C.P. — justice of the peace
cross question — cross examine
deed poll — court order
Duty Solicitor — public defender
false impersonation — false pretenses
hard swearing — perjury
High Bailiff — server of writs (summons)
Legacy Duties Rogatory — death duties
lodge an appeal — file an appeal
not in the dock — not on trial
Objection allowed! — Objection sustained!
on one's own showing — according to one's own statement
public attorney — attorney at law
Queen's/King's Bench — a division of the High Court of Justice
situation — a case
succession duty — inheritance tax
swear an information — make a formal complaint
ticket-of-leave — suspended sentence
turn Queen's/King's evidence — turn state's evidence
undertaking — agreement
Westminster Hall — Court of Justice
witness box — witness stand
wrongous — legal or unjust
You may stand down. — You may step down.

MORE LEGAL PROFESSION TERMS

A Bill of Exceptions is a statment of objections by way of appeal against the ruling of a judge who is trying a case with a jury in the Court of Sessions.

A Bill of Indictment is a statement of a charge made against a person.

A Chamber Counsel or Counsellor gives advice privately but does not plead your case in court.

Chancery was formerly the highest court of justice next to the House of Lords; it was presided over by the Lord High Chancellor; it is now a division of the High Court of Justice.

A Cross Action is a suit by a defendant against the plaintiff.

A plaintiff coming into court for a divorce must come into court with clean hands. To accomplish this, he/she must write down any indiscretions and give the paper to the judge, the only one who sees it. Once the case is concluded, the statement is destroyed.

A Queen's Counsel is a barrister or advocate appointed by letters-patent (sheets of parchment on which the patent [privilege] is written). The office is honorary but gives the right of precedence in all the courts.

The Law List is an annual book of information about lawyers and the courts.

Letters Requisitory is an instrument by which a court of one country asks that of another to take certain evidence on its behalf.

Petty Sessions is the court in which magistrates try trivial cases and refer others to a higher court.

The Right of Drip is the right in law to let the drip from one's roof fall on another's land.

Rumpole Talk

Fans of John Mortimer's delightful **"Rumpole of the Bailey,"** know that when he goes to work, he goes to **"Chambers."** Chambers are law firms. The **Head of Chambers** is the head of the firm. For lunch, Rumpole frequents a nearby pub which caters mainly to barristers and solicitors and orders **"plonk,"** the house wine. He calls everyone **"old darling,"** men and women alike. Bailey refers to the **Old Bailey**, formerly the criminal court of London. The word is derived from **"baily or bailie,"** Middle English for the outside wall of a medieval fortress or castle.

MORE RUMPOLE TALK

Be upstanding. — All rise. (in court)
brill — brilliant
bullyragging — bullying
chock-a-block — chock full
getting past it — getting old
Get yourself sorted out! — Straighten up and fly right!
gingering up the evidence — spicing it up
going out to grass — retiring
He's not a PLU. — People Like Us
Hilary term — a session of the High Court named for St. Hilary whose feast day is January 13
I'll catch you up. — I'll catch up with you.
locus in quo — scene of the crime
NSOB — Not Sporting, Old Bean!
set lunch — fixed price lunch
She who must be obeyed. — Rumpole's wife
Steady on. — Take it easy.
steak and kidney pud — steak and kidney pudding
the old darling — the judge
to nobble — to fool
two eggs and a fried slice — two eggs and a slice of bread fried in bacon fat

Words Concerned with the Police and Criminals

THE POLICE: The Police patrol their beats without guns, handcuffs or gas canisters. They only carry concealed wooden **truncheons** (clubs). They consider their job to be keeping the peace. During dangerous assignments, however, they can carry arms but must return them when the assignment ends. They still try to follow the concept of **Sir Robert Peel**, the Home Secretary in 1829, that the police were not a military force, rather, a civilian body mixing with a civilian population. He prescribed a non-military uniform that was practical and dignified with a special helmet which took his name, the **"bobby"** helmet. The helmet's name later became applied to the police.

POLICE NAMES:
Regular: **Police Constable, D.C. Detective Constable, Detective** (Tec), **the M.E.—Medical Examiner** (Coroner) and **W.P.C's—Women Police Constables**
Slang: **bobbies, bluebottles, busies, coppers, pigs. rozzers, slop,** and the **fuzz.**

POLICE TOOLS, STATIONS, WORK AND PRISONS:
barriers — wooden horses to cordon off an area
black fisher — nighttime fish poacher
Black Maria — police van
Borstal System — a detention system for juvenile delinquents named for the first reformatory at Borstal, near Rochester, England
bring to book — book
circularizing — checking out criminal places
copped, hipped or pinched — arrested
dabs — fingerprints
darbies or **gyves** — handcuffs
do a turn — serve a jail term
draughtnet — dragnet
engine room — police station office

fingers, grasser, nose, copper's nark, snout, spiv or **rattler** — stool pigeon

gang breaker — gangbuster

gaol, jug, quod, scrubs, nick, or **chokey** — jail ("Scrubs" comes from Wormwood Scrubs, a large London jail)

gaoler — jailer

home beat — the policeman's beat

identity parade — the line-up

kiss the rod — submit to punishment

narco — narcotics squad

on dab — on report

on remand — in custody awaiting trial

on the roster — on duty

out on license — on parole

peg — file charges against

Pixie — police minibus

police burgh — police district

police office, cop shop station or **the nick** — police station

police outriders — police escort

put a watch on — a stake-out

put one down — lock one up

serials — busloads of police dispatched to demonstrations; each has one inspector, three sergeants and two constables.

shooting range — pistol range

sponging-house or **spunging house** —a bailiff's detention house for debtors; they are in his custody before being sent to prison.

squeaks — small bits of information

the dock — court

The Yard — Scotland Yard

to give one in charge — have someone arrested

Up goes the monkey! — The jig's up!

upperstocks — ankle restrainers

warder — jailer

CRIME WORDS

backhand — bribe
being done — being robbed
bent — crooked
bit of bunch — a flim-flam
bit too smart — bit too tricky.
bullet pocks — bullet holes
bumbaze — bamboozle
burke — stifle (kill)
cabbage, crib, nick or **snaffle** — steal
cheatery — cheating
charley — to act sneakily
claret — blood
converted — embezzled
cooking the books — doctoring the books
copping — snatching
coshing — using a blunt instrument
crack a crib — make a break-in
cushy number — pushover
cut one's stick, do a bunk, hop the twig, cut one's luck, hook it or **scarper** — to cut out, leave, hide
dash — a bribe
dibs and dibstones — money and jewels
dicey — chancey
dodges — tricks
fire raising — arson
foolproof wheeze — foolproof plan
fox up something — cook up something
funk hole — escape hatch
gang-breaker — gangbuster
gallows bird — criminal
have someone on toast, sell smoke or **nobble** — to swindle
heeled — have a gun

high toby — robbery on horseback
hoax calls — false alarms
hoky-poky business — dubious type of business
jemmy — burglar's jimmy (crowbar)
keeping obbo (observation) — keeping watch (a look-out)
kicked the baby — ruined the set-up
local talent — crooks
lolly — illicit money or any money in large quantities
long firm — fake company
make up some gas — make up a lie
nasty piece of work — predator
nip a bung or **cut a purse** — purse stealing
nothing worth nicking — nothing worth taking
oodle — boodle
padding ken — thieves' rooming house
pinch the boodle — steal the swag
pinch the till — rob the cash register
pipe off — case a joint
pocket pickers or **dips** — pickpockets
popped — pawned
put a cheat upon — deceive
put the mug on someone — rub someone out
ramp — a snow job
receivers — fences
rhino — money
ring dropping — pretending to find a dropped ring and selling it
rumbled — caught on to
set on — mug
sham packet — fake package
shifting swag — moving the loot
shooter — gun
shove the queer or **slush** —pass bad money
small fiddle — small bit of larceny
snatchers — shoplifters

spivvery — black market operations
stick it in to someone — overcharge
tip one the wink — give the go-ahead
to knock up — to rob
to pickle — to nab
to shop or **blow the gaff** —to sell down the river
to savage — to loot
wages raid — salary heist
winkled — sneaked

CRIMINALS

a back stall — a look-out for a garrotter
a bustard — criminal
a chummy — small time crook
a crack rope — one deserving to be hanged
a cracksman — safe cracker
a croaker — a killer
child bashers — child abusers
con merchant or **confidence trickster** —confidence man
cut purse, nipper, dip or **pocket picker** — pickpocket
footpad — thief on the highroad
hard face — souless, relentless criminal
hedge creeper or **jack hasty** —sneak
legal fiction — a doubtful character
night intruders — prowlers
pick purse — one who steals from a purse
rampsman — swindler of bookmakers
shifty looking basket — a sneaky pete (Basket is an acceptable euphemism for bastard.)
smasher — one who passes bad money
snatcher — shoplifter
spring heeled jack — one who makes a quick getaway
teddy boys, yobbos, pegs, perishers, roughs, hard boys, street ruffians or young tearaways — hoodlums
too downy a bird — slippery character
twister, flicker, waster or footpad — crook

...when a man is tired of London, he is tired of life;
for there is in London all that life can afford."
—Samuel Johnson, Boswell's Life, vol.iii, p. 178, Letter to
   Boswell, 20 Sept. 1777

CHAPTER TWENTY

"THE SMOKE" HOLIDAY or FIVE DAYS IN LONDON

The best way to communicate my enthusiasm for London or **"The Smoke,"** the name given to it when it used to have a thick **fug** (fog) one could cut with a knife, is to have you join my husband Jerry, our son Josh and myself on a New Year's holiday there. At the time, we were living in Leicester, an hour's train ride north from London. We wanted to see all the usual things that visitors feel obligated to see: the **Changing of the Guard at Buckingham Palace, Westminster Abbey, Parliament, Big Ben, Agatha Christie's play "The Mouse-trap,"** the **Tower**, etc.

This is how we did all this and more in five days.

December 29 We took the early train and ordered breakfast.

"Plain breakfast or full breakfast?" the waiter asked.

A plain breakfast is just rolls or toast, preserves, and tea or coffee but we wanted to experience a **full breakfast** so we answered, "Full breakfast, please" and were given the following menu:

Choice of Chilled Fruit Juices
   or Corn Flakes
   or Porridge with Milk
Grilled Bacon and Fried Egg, Tomatoes, Saute Potatoes
   or Grilled Bacon and Sausage, Tomatoes, Saute Potatoes

or Grilled Kippers
or Boiled Eggs
Preserves, Toast, Rolls
Tea or Coffee

The table was set with a white cloth, paper napkins, cups, plates, forks, spoons and a jar of Frank Cooper's "OXFORD" Marmalade, a bowl of TATE LYLE super cubes (sugar) and a log-shaped pat of butter on a small plate. The waiter serving the toast made a long face when I took only one slice. "Not on a diet are you?"

Then he came holding a pot of hot coffee in one hand and a pot of hot milk in the other. "**White** or **black**, Madam?" If white is chosen, milk and coffee are poured simultaneously.

The third time he appeared with toast, he said, "Come Madam, you must."

It was a gray day and sleeting slightly. On arrival, we took one of those famous **London black taxis** to **The Royal Court Hotel**, an old-fashioned hotel on **Sloane Square**. The porter took us up in a tiny elevator and then through a few winding passageways to our lovely wrapped-around-the-corner-of-the-building room. We later found that this hotel, though quaint and very English, was not the most convenient hotel for the places we wanted to see. A hotel in Russell Square would have been more convenient.

We unpacked and went to snack at the fourth floor restaurant of the **Peter Jones Department Store** from whose windows we could enjoy the intricate workmanship of the undisturbed upper stories of Victorian buildings whose decorative styles are often missed from street level because of modern conversions to the bottom stories.

After our snack we walked to the antique markets on **King's Road**; then to **Leicester Square** by the **tube or Underground** (subway) for lunch at the **Angus Steak House**. Later, we went to see "Camelot" at the Warner West End Theatre. Girl **"candy butchers"** went up and down the aisles selling candy and orange drinks. It made me think of Shakespeare's Day when they sold oranges.

We took the tube back. The long escalator trip to the depths was enlivened by the fiddle playing of some musicians at the bottom. We dropped some coins in their nearby upturned caps. This was one of the safe places to which Londoners hurried during WWII when the sirens sounded the warning that bombings were imminent.

December 30 We awakened to the sussulating sound of tires on wet pavement and the clip-clopping of horses' hooves. I jumped up and ran to the window just in time to see a group of bobbies on horseback going in twos around the road bend. We had the hotel breakfast and then I took the underground to **Oxford St.** and **Selfridge's** where I bought a long Scottish kilt which is so beautiful and so well made that I'm sure it will last long enough for a great granddaughter to wear. The **shop** (store) was very crowded with **queues** (lines) forming for the escalators. There were enormous bargains in everything causing the very polite English to even shove a tiny bit to get at them. I taxied back to the hotel and found my men ready to leave for the **Science Museum** so I walked along the **Serpentine** (Serpentine Lake in Hyde Park) and then decided to see what the **Kings Road, Chelsea** shops offered. Most of the stores featured loud music, psychedelic lighting and revolving clothing platforms. The shoppers were mostly young people in minis and maxis wearing weird make-up and hair styles and white midi-length fringed sheepskin coats. Business was brisk in spite of the high prices.

When I returned, I found Jerry and Josh at the Porter's Desk buying tickets for the New Year's Day playing of **"The Mousetrap."** We were tired from our travels and went to lunch at **"The Old Kentucky"** which was appropriately decorated with minstrel scenes. Jerry and I had the Chef's special: Roast beef, Yorkshire Pudding, roast potatoes and peas and Josh had American Pancake Pizza and salad.

We went to **Madame Tussaud's Famous Wax Works** on the

Marylebone Road near Baker Street. I felt the representations were good but not always accurate. President Lyndon Johnson was too short, for example, and President Nixon's forehead had too large a bulge.

December 31, New Year's Eve Loaded down with cameras and film, we followed that marvelous navigator, Jerry, into the Underground depths and out to **Buckingham Palace** to view the **"Changing of the Guard."** There were tons of people there jockeying for position at the gates. As hundreds of cameras were ready with fingers tensed to start clicking away, a **bobby** strolled by and in very quiet, polite, even tones said, "There's no Changing of the Guard today" and then after a pause added, "if that's what you came to see." Disappointed, we consoled ourselves with a delicious lunch at **"The Dover"** on **Petty France St.**, that's "Petite France" anglicized. Other interesting Anglicizations are the **"Elephant and Castle"** Underground stop which started out as "Infanta de Castile" and the **Marlybone** area which was once **"Marie la Bonne."** The lunch "special" was interesting:

Minestrone or Tomato Soup
Prawns (shrimplike crustaceans) Cocktail
Steak and Kidney Pudding
Peas and Creamed Potatoes or
Escallops (scallops) with Spaghetti
Apple Pie or Custard

I made a note that British salt shakers have only one hole while the pepper shakers are full of holes, the opposite of American salt and pepper shakers. We took the Underground to **Westminster Abbey**. **Big Ben**, the clock tower of the **Houses of Parliament**, was very impressive. It was outlined in shining gold and glistened against puffy white clouds drifting slowly behind it. The carved stonework of Parliament must have kept an army of stonecutters busy for many years. The slang term for Parliament is **"the jaw factory."** Visiting is allowed by prearrangement with the London Tourist Board but since we hadn't prearranged, we crossed the street and entered **West-**

minster **Abbey** through the **Poet's Corner**. Chaucer, Milton, Dryden, and Tennyson are buried there. Chaucer's burial began the tradition of the Poet's Corner. Great statesmen also have a corner on the left side on entering the Cathedral.

Washington Irving noted that when he visited the Abbey, it was very gloomy, dreary and shadowy. Perhaps it was in his day. We found it to be bright, full of visitors and VERY LARGE but not as large as St. Peter's which is MASSIVE. The **kneelers** or **kneeling hassocks** (kneeling pads) were beautiful with colorful needlework designs. We visited the tombs of the **"Royals"** which were under the cathedral in the **"Undercroft"** (Crypt) and then to the **Abbey Museum** where were effigies of the queens and kings dressed in royal splendor but the materials they were composed of were dulled by time. Most of the effigies were on tomb covers. The oldest were carved from wood and the more modern were of marble. Saddest to see was the urn containing the bones of the **murdered princes**, Edward V and his brother. I thought, "So much work was invested in monuments to preserve one's name only to have them become obliterated by time."

The only memorials showing no signs of age were the **brasses**. We watched people making rubbings by kneeling on the tombs. I dislike walking over graves but, as many important people are buried right under pews, it's impossible to avoid. I asked a verger where **Henry VIII** and **George III** were buried. He said they were at **Windsor** and added "There will no longer be full burials at Westminster as there's no more room. The bodies are now cremated and the ashes put into urns." He said **Cromwell** had been entombed in Westminster but three years later, his enemies removed his body and hanged it. Then they cut off the head and placed it on a pike. It is now believed his head is buried at his old college in Cambridge. Sic transit gloria.

We found **Major Andre's tomb**. This was of particular interest to us because Andre had been tried, hanged and buried in Tappan, a town near our Rockland County, N.Y. home. Some years after his execution, permission was granted by the President and Congress to have his remains returned to England. We'd visited the Tappan burial area and had also seen the tiny room in which he had been imprisoned in "The '76 House," now a restaurant. Washington admired him and said he was "more unfortunate than criminal." I copied the inscription exactly as written:

"Sacred to the Memory of Major John Andre who raised by his Merit at an early period of Life to the rank of Adj. Gen. of the British Force in America and employed in an important but hazardous Enterprise fell a Sacrifice to his Zeal for his King and Country on the 2nd of October AD 1780, Aged 29. Universally beloved and esteemed by the Army in which he ferved and lamented even by his FOES. His Gracious Sovereign KING GEORGE the Third has caused this Monument to be erected."

Westminster is so huge it must be almost impossible to keep up with any needed repairs. **Queen Elizabeth I**, for example, was minus her sceptor. **Mary, Queen of Scots' tomb**, was the only one fenced round from floor to ceiling. "To prevent what happened to Cromwell?" I wondered. Both queens had aquiline noses. **Charles II** resembled a dashing Spanish nobleman with mustaches, plumed hat, and curls.

Edward the Confessor initiated the building of the Abbey but not a stone of his church remains above ground. Henry III rebuilt it in the same spot and decided to make it into a church modeled on a French one he liked and the work went on for years. The coronation chair is behind a metal screen and is scarred with initials. The **Stone of Scone**, believed to be the one on which Jacob laid his head and had his dream, has been used since 1296 for every coronation.

We went on to **Trafalgar Square** and bought some food to celebrate the New Year in our rooms. At midnight we looked out on the square and it was very quiet. There were just two men leaving the Kings Arms Pub and weaving their way to the Underground.

January 1 We returned to **Buckingham Palace** for another try at seeing the **"Changing"** and this time we were successful.

People were seven deep at the gates. Those in back were passing cameras to those in front and pleading for them to take photos. At about 11:20 the Palace Guards formed themselves into a tight square in the courtyard while their commander marched up and down and stopped at each corner to stamp his feet, 1,2,3 before turning. In the distance came the sound of pipers and from the barracks up **Birdcage Walk** they came, leading the new Guard. Then for 30 cold, shivery minutes—it can get bone-cold in England—the Guard went though maneuvers sending two to walk up and down from one end of the courtyard to the other and three to the tiny guardhouses, etc. The pipers played Loch Lomand, Auld Lang Syne and the band even played some rock and roll. Like the tide, the crowd seemed to ebb and flow following the guards and pipers down the street. We'd seen the Changing! To warm up, we walked quickly to the **Queen's Gallery**, located on the left side of Buckingham Palace. The portraits were mainly of the Royal family and George III and his family. George III had a huge body and a small head. Once warmed, we walked the full length of **Birdcage Walk**—the road all the Palace gates open on to—and then past the **Guards Barracks** to the **Westminster Area**. (The Regiments of the **Guards Brigade [Grenadier, Coldstream, Scots, Welsh and Irish]** take turns being stationed at the Guards Barracks on Birdcage Walk. (Charles II is believed to have kept birds there, hence the name.) Then turning left 2 blocks and up a short cul-de-sac we arrived at **No. 10 Downing Street**. It's an unpretentious building guarded by just one Bobby. Photographers were across the street and people were having their photos taken near the door and the Bobby. I was one of them.

Next, a long **tube** trip taking the better part of an hour to the **Frames** bus depot at 25/31 Tavistock Place for our afternoon bus trip. Our guide wore a grey checkered cap, grey topcoat and had a quizzical expression. His face was red and he smoked constantly. He certainly knew his London. He had pertinent quotes at his command and had a feel for the job as he made the places we visited come alive. He pointed out places where bombs had hit during WWII and gave a concise history of **Christopher Wren** who built 50 churches after the **Great London Fire**. "All were hit during the WWII blitz," he said. "Some have been restored. Even St. Paul's was hit in 3 places but the restoration has been so good, it's hard to tell where." He also said that Wren at age 84 was dismissed because some said he was slowing down the finishing of St. Paul's to keep his job. We stopped at the **Olde Curiosity Shop**. It was so jammed it was impossible to get inside. On the steps of St. Paul's, the guide said "It's always windy here for a reason. It's the Devil. This is where **barristers** (lawyers) heard their clients out years ago. One man the Devil was after escaped to Doctor's Common. The wind is the Devil waiting here for him to come out."

St. Paul's is very beautiful; the 4th largest church in the world. Britain's famous soldiers and sailors are buried here. There's a large monument to **General Cornwallis**, "The one who lost us the American Colonies," said the guide. "Yes, the seeds were there of defeat and he accepted defeat at Yorktown." Of interest is that the only American born person who was held in the Tower was freed in exchange for Cornwallis. **Henry Laurens**, a South Carolina merchant had been captured at sea in 1780 and held in the Tower for 18 months.

From St. Paul's we went on to the **Tower of London**. We saw the Tower Bridge and went past the long suffering and very patient **Beefeaters**, who, because of their colorful costumes, were asked to be photographed alongside many visitors each day. I wasn't one of them but was tempted. (It is not exactly known where the name **"beefeater"** was derived. What is known is that they used to accompany sovereigns to banquets; also, "beef eater" was a contemptuous name the French gave to the English when they were warring.)

The **Tower of London** is England's most famous historic monument. It covers 13 acres and has 13 towers. In the center is the **White Tower** built by William the Conqueror in 1078. It is now a museum of old arms, armor and instruments of torture. At the block where Anne Boleyn, Lady Jane Grey, the Duke of Essex and others were beheaded, our guide told about the Countess of Salisbury who refused to put her head down. "She ran about like a chicken," he said, "and had to be beheaded as she ran."

We saw **Henry the 8th's palace**, very small compared to most palaces, and the place where the last prisoner of the Tower stayed for 4 days, Rudolph Hess. The **Jewel House** was the only warm place there. There were enormous plates of gold, many gold **salts** (salt cellars), sparkling diamond crowns and the famous **Kohinoor diamond** and the **Star of India**.

We saw the **ravens** that legend has it, if they die off, the tower will fall and with it the British Empire; so there are always eight ravens in residence with the flight feathers on one wing clipped. Since ravens court in flight, none were born in the tower for over 400 years; however, in 1989, one was actually born there and named **"Ronald Raven."** Since then, having been put in the charge of a Beefeater of their own called the **Raven Master**, they've bred quite well.

We went over the moat and past the **Traitor's Gate** and back to the bus. After returning to the bus depot, we taxied back to our hotel, and dressed for our big evening; but first, a Chinese dinner and then on to see one of the **"musts"** of London— **Agatha Christie's "Mousetrap"** at the **Ambassador Theater** in the **Charing Cross** area. The audience enjoyed it all while eating ice cream and chocolates from large candy boxes.

January 2 We awakened with aching legs. We soaked them, had breakfest and decided to sit and rest all morning. Josh worked at designing a transmitter and I read, wrote cards and napped. We went to a restaurant on **Kings Row** for dinner and found we were too early. Dinner isn't served until 6:30. We went a little farther up the road and found a store selling far-out items and bought some British playing cards. An artist there asked if he could sketch us for a fee. Josh balked unless we three were sketched together, so that's what we did. Then back for a delicious dinner.

January 3 Josh decided to stay in so Jerry and I took the **tube** to **Piccadilly Circus** and walked down **Haymarket** past the theater to **Trafalgar Square**, London's most famous square named for **Admiral Lord Nelson**'s great naval victory of 1805. His statue is at the top of a column guarded by Landseer's four bronze lions. (Sir Edwin Henry Landseer (1802-1873) was a famous animal painter and sculptor.) Then on to Hyde Park's **Speaker's Corner.** One soapbox orator said, "I'm Australian." Everyone laughed. "And we're out to annex England." More laughter. "And Rhodesia."

The cold got into our bones so we returned to the hotel to warm up. Later, we took Josh to the **British Museum** to see the famous **Elgin Marbles** which Lord Elgin, British Ambassador to the Ottoman Empire, had shipped to England in 1801. Athens at the time was under Ottoman rule. Lord Elgin was concerned about the damage he saw being done to important works of art, especially the sculptures of the Parthenon, and wanted copies made for posterity. When he asked for permission to do this, he was also told he could "take away any pieces of stone with old inscriptions or figures thereon." The marbles that have his name were in a frieze which ran like a decorative band around the top of the Parthenon and were the work of the greatest of Greek sculptors, **Phidias** (about 500 to 430 B.C.) The Greek government is still trying to get them back. We also saw the **Rosetta Stone**, a thin uneven slab of black basalt which held the key to the deciphering of ancient Egyptian writing; and the over-2000-year-old **Portland Vase**.

The British Museum alone was worth the London trip. We returned to our Leicester home very tired but happy. We had had a superb holiday!

Antiquities are history defaced,
or some remnants of history
which have casually escaped
the shipwreck of time.
—Francis Bacon, Advancement of Learning, bk II, ii, l

CHAPTER TWENTY-ONE

THE JANE AUSTEN ADVENTURE or A FOUR-DAY TRIP TO THE WEST COUNTRY

This adventure is an example of how, with careful planning, one is able to get to a number of "must sees" with the mimimum of wear and tear.

Devon, Cornwall, Stonehenge and Jane Austen's Chawton...how could we fit them into the four free days we'd set aside during a business trip to Europe? During the year that we'd lived in Leicester, England, we just hadn't managed to get to the the **West Country** (Devon, Cornwall and Somerset counties), and had promised ourselves a trip there...someday.

"Someday" had arrived! My husband Jerry was scheduled to attend meetings in Manchester, England, and Split, Yugoslavia. While in England, we thought we could easily see Chawton and Stonehenge on our way to Devon and Cornwall and then visit our friends in Leicester on Jerry's way to Manchester. However, a complication arose when we told my father, who lived with us, about the trip. He wanted to go to Italy. Since we were going to Europe, couldn't we leave him with his nieces and nephews in his old hometown of Borgia in southern Italy while we went about our business and then pick him up later?

Chawton, home of Jane Austen.

How could we refuse my 97-year-old Papa and please everyone concerned? The trip was turning into a travel agent's nightmare.

I had taken Papa to Italy several years before, so I knew he'd be OK if we took him there first, got him settled with the relatives and then went on our way. Our travel agent was magnificent, changing the nightmare into a pleasant dream. Our flights and rental car pick-ups were so well arranged that our our five-week trip went off without a hitch. We flew to Rome, drove to Borgia, left Papa there, flew to London, drove to the West Country, drove to Leicester where I stayed while Jerry went to his meeting; and on his return, we drove to London, flew to Yugoslavia, took a bus trip to Dubrovnik, flew to Italy, picked up Papa and flew home.

Although there were many highlights on that trip: being with our Italian relatives, visiting our Leicester friends, and visiting Jane Austen's home in Chawton; I remember it as **"The Jane Austen Adventure."** Jane Austen's my all-time favorite author,

whose books I reread every so often for inspiration and enjoy-
ment. I just HAD to be in the environment that inspired
"Emma" and "Persuasion." As I said, we had just four days for
this side trip, so we made careful preparations. Using a road
map from our days in Leicester, we circled all the "must sees:
"**Chawton, Stonehenge, Ilfracombe, Plymouth** (Devon), and
Penzance (Cornwall). Our home base would be **Exeter**, not
only because all the places we wished to see would be an easy
day's trip away; but because it is the great city of the West
Country, with many attractions. It was the **Isca Dumnoniorum**
of the **Romans**, parts of whose stone walls still exist in the
Rougemont Gardens there. We arranged for a reservation at
the Rougemont Hotel nearby. I kept careful records of that
memorable trip in case anyone wanted to repeat it.

The first day we picked up our rental car at Heathrow
Airport, took the A30 by way of Staines to Camberly, then
A325S through Farnborough and **Aldershot**, a military base, to
Farnham. Then west on A31 through Alton. At Alton, we went
left on A32 for 1 1/2 miles to tiny **Chawton** (about 48 miles from
London) where **Jane Austen** lived from 1809 to 1817, the most
creative years of her life. Her 17th century home on the main
street is open daily from 11 to 4:30. It's a six-bedroom house
with a good-sized entrance and two sitting rooms the length of
the house. She loved that house and soon after moving into it
wrote:

The many comforts that await
Our Chawton home, how much we find
Already in it, to our mind;
And how convinced, that when complete
It will all other Houses beat.

According to the visitor's book, her admirers are worldwide.
I wondered how many writers like myself hoped to derive
inspiration from her by touching her tiny round writing table
near the squeaking door of the sitting room whose warning
sound gave her time to hide her work from visitors. Why did
she hide it? She shunned publicity and was such a private

Stonehenge.

person that all of her books published during her lifetime had "By A Lady" instead of her name on the title pages. She didn't want to be known as a "writer" as writing was just a small part of her life. She also cooked, sewed, baked, visited relatives and friends, entertained at home, danced at balls, and did water colors. Her secret was kept until her brother Henry gave it away. Jane wrote to her sister Cassandra. "...the truth is the Secret has spread so far as to be scarcely the Shadow of a secret now. Henry heard Pride and Prejudice warmly praised in Scotland...& what does he do in the warmth of his Brotherly vanity & love, but immediately tell them who wrote it!"

The house has many of her personal effects including games that she played with her nieces and nephews and a quilt she worked on with her mother which hangs from one wall of her bedroom. To the rear of the house is the bake house or brew house. There was also the stable for the donkey who pulled her **"governess cart"** (small pony cart). Visitors can picnic in the small garden which was the particular pride of her mother and is kept very much as it had been during their lifetime. We lunched across the street at Cassandra's Cup, a tea room named for her mother. We had delicious ham-and-cheese quiche followed by feather-light butterscotch eclairs stuffed with Devonshire cream. I was reluctant to leave this pretty village and have kept it in my mind's eye ever since.

We returned to A31 by continuing through Chawton and keeping to the right to get on A34 north to A303 toward Andover, which we bypassed; and as we went by Amesbury, **Stonehenge** came into sight on the Salisbury Plain (Wiltshire). How exciting it was to watch it seemingly grow larger as we neared it. The historic monument that we'd read and seen pictured innumerable times was now an actuality. We had to bear right onto A344 to get to the **car park** (parking lot). We bought the tickets needed to get near the ancient stones, now protected by fencing.

It has long been thought that the stones were set up by Druids but radio carbon dating has proven that these stones were

erected before the ancient Celtic priests' time, around 200 B.C..
They hark farther back to the Neolithic or New Stone Age when
farming replaced hunting (4000 to 1,500 BC.)

There are many mysterious circular monuments, known as
henges, in England, but this is the most famous. Not all are set
with stones. Archaeologists still do not definitely know how the
stones were transported to this site as they've established that
some came from 30 miles distant. The **blue-stones** (bluegrey
sandstones) came a greater distance, from Dyfed, Wales, 150
miles away. The thinking now is that these may have been
transported by sea and then overland.

The stones were carefully arranged with an outer ring, an
inner horseshoe and a central altar stone. What is astounding
is that the monument's axis was carefully aligned to point
towards sunrise on June 21st, the longest day of the year. I tried
to visualize that 5000-year-old scene. Thousands of animal-
skin-clad men sweating mightily as they pushed and pulled
these massive stones. What drove them to perform this massive
job? Did they use tree trunks as rollers to get them to this spot?
Did they use the inclined plane to raise the **lintels** (the flat
stones atop the verticals)? The answers have defied explanation
to this day!

Leaving Stonehenge reluctantly, we returned to A303 and
went on to the junction with A30 near Honiton and continued
on to our base, **Exeter**. After getting our room at the Rougemont
Hotel, we walked about the ancient city which was founded by
the Romans in AD 50-55. It boasts of having the narrowest street
in the world, Parliament Street, off the High Street; catecombs
at St. Bartholomew's Church and the oldest municipal building
in England, the Guildhall, built in 1160. Exeter Cathedral, in the
town center is even older, built in 1050; and near it is a small
port to which sea-going ships of up to 300 tons have access by
means of a five and one-half mile canal. Nearby is the famous
Mol's Coffee House which was frequented by **Sir Frances
Drake, Frobisher, Hawkins, Gilbert** and **Sir Walter Raleigh.**

Landscape east of Ilfracombe.

Luckily, these areas were spared during the heavy bombings of WWII which destroyed much of the medieval section.

The second day, we explored northern Devon by heading for **Ilfracombe** on the Bristol Channel. We took A377 to **Barnstaple** and A361 on to Ilfracombe, a large market town, resort and fishing port. It's narrow streets, jam-packed with tourists going in and out of tiny shops, reminded us of Cape Cod's Provincetown. We visited the tiny 14th century medieval **Chapel of St. Nicholas** which tops Lantern Hill. Here wives stared out to sea watching for their husband's ships. It still carries a light. This is a wonderful place for fish. We had excellent lemon sole cooked to perfection with peas, french fries and a tomato, pepper and lettuce salad at the Smuggler's Restaurant. For dessert, we went next door for Cornish ice cream **cornets** (cones) topped with **clotted cream** (a famous Devonshire cream prepared by scalding milk).

Leaving Ilfracombe, we took A399 through **Combe Martin** past the turn-off to Lynton and down the steep, winding gorge

Pilgrim Father: Mayflower Steps, the Barbican (courtesy of the British Tourist Authority).

side to **Lynmouth**. Then out of Lynmouth on A39 for **Porlock** and **Porlock Hill**, a 25% grade. **Warning:** Don't go down Porlock Hill unless you have good nerves. There's an alternative toll road. We climbed out of Porlock and skirted the edge of **Exmoor**, Lorna Doone country. The brooding heather-filled moorland brought to mind Wuthering Heights with it's many **combes** (deep little wooded valleys) much like the "hollers" of West Virginia. Then on past **Minehead** and **Dunster** to **Wiliton** and then onto A358 to **Taunton** and the M5 back to Exeter.

The third day, our goal was **Plymouth** to see the **Mayflower Steps** from which the Pilgrims set sail. We took A38 south, then left onto A380 to **Torquay** to A379 to **Paignton**. Then A385 via **Totnes** and back to A38 to Plymouth. At Plymouth's natural **harbour** (harbor), a very strong wet wind tried its best to blow us into the angry sea as we looked at the massive statue of **Sir Francis Drake**. After he circumnavigated the globe, this is where **Queen Elizabeth I** was waiting to knight him when he disembarked in September 1580. The wind prevented us from properly seeing the great citadel which Charles II had built as a precaution against Roundhead trouble. Its ramparts are 20 feet thick in places. We were cold to the bone and pushed against the wind with our umbrellas to a nearby hotel to be warmed with tea and scones.

Then we drove to the narrow, cobbled alleys of the **Barbican**, the Elizabethan zone of Plymouth. It was very busy and touristy. The Pilgrim's departure point in 1620 is well marked by a **Mayflower Stone** and the names of the Pilgrim Fathers are listed at the nearby Island House. I had a glimmer of how the Pilgrims must have felt as the sails of the Mayflower filled and pulled them away from the known to the unknown being reminded of Brighton, the day after we'd arrived for our year's stay in Britain, and the sinking feeling I had as I looked at the western horizon beyond which were home, family and friends. It had gotten so cold, we were happy we had worn layered clothing and added and subtracted sweaters and pullovers according to the changes in temperature, which varied many times that day. We returned to Exeter via A386 through **Tavistock** and then through **Dartmoor National Park** to A30 and A30 via **Okehampton** to Exeter.

The last day, we went by train to **Penzance**. Exeter's **St. David Station** was a 15-minute walk from our hotel, mostly down hill. There we bought **Cornish Explorer tickets** which would have allowed us, had we had enough time, to change trains as often as we wished all over Cornwall. Here is our experience as noted in my diary:

"We've just boarded the 9:07 to **Penzance** and are on one of those trains that are often seen in British films where one can board right at one's compartment. It's a few minutes into the trip and we're already enjoying the beautiful rolling countryside of Devon. 'Sheep in the fields, cows in the corn,' came to mind. I remind myself that **'corn'** is any grain in Britain and our corn is known as **'maize.'** The conductor has just punched our tickets and we can see the sea at **Dawlish**. There are red sandstone cliffs to the right. At the Dawlish stop, three women join

Penzance Harbor.

us, two sit opposite and one next to us. The two opposite are British and one next to us is American, I can tell from their talk.

"More water, more cliffs. The sun is out. Hearing us talk, the American woman asks us if we are American. 'I'm from Michigan and I'm off to Penzance to see relatives I've never met.' she said. 'I became acquainted with these ladies in Florida.' One of the British women said, 'I live six months in Florida and six in England. I'm married to an American from Columbus, Ohio.'

"We've stopped at **Newton-Abbot** and the sun has hidden behind lowering clouds but there's some blue sky in the distance. We have folding umbrellas with us for just in case. We're going inland now and over the **Dart River. Dartmouth** is nearby, naturally. It's 9:52 and we're stopping at **Totnes**. The English ladies say they are ashamed of this train. 'It's old and dirty. You must try the newer one. It's very pleasant with tables and you can order coffee. You can't on this one so we're getting off at Plymouth and will race across to the tea shop to get some coffee and tea. Can we get you some?' We thanked them but declined the offer. They told their American friend to hold the door open for them.

"The train stops and the women run off. The American is writing to her son and asks us what to put in the letter about what's different in England. 'You're in luck,' Jerry says, 'my wife's been putting together a British-American dictionary.' So I gave her a few examples: **a goods train** is a freight train, a **rearhorse** is a preying mantis, the **never-never** is the installment plan, **smalls** are underwear, **American cloth** is oilcloth, **court shoes** are pumps, **Oh, Queen Anne's dead** means That's old hat, **tights** are pantyhose, **pegs** are clothespins, a **jumper** is a sweater and a **red rag** is a tongue.

"It's 10:23. The ladies made it back in good time and offered us a piece of chocolate. They're very knowledgeable about Exeter. 'You must be sure to see Parliament Street, the smallest street in the world. It's 12 inches across.' We're now into quite a discussion about the differences each have noted about our respective countries. The English woman married to the Ameri-

Pub in the Cotswolds.

can said the first time she was taken out to 'the yard,' she couldn't find it. A **'yard'** in England is a small enclosure of concrete with walls about it. 'My husband drives me mad, always saying, I can't understand you,' she said. 'He says that **not too bad** means quite good. **Not too bad** in England is a derogatory expression. Americans speak so differently. I can't get used to it.'

"11:07 **Bodmin**. It's getting warmer and I've removed a sweater. The American woman is dozing. 11:15 **Lostwithiel**. I see palm trees indicating the presence of the Gulf Stream. We've just passed **St. Austell** where white china clay is mined and pharmaceuticals are made, we are told by one of the British women. Now we're traversing a golf course. 11:50 **Truro**. We've told the ladies that after this jaunt, we're going on to Leicester to visit friends and our old haunts. They said on our way we must visit **Bourton-on-the-Water** and **Broadway** as both have beautiful homes made of warm Cotswold stones. [We did get to both and they were as beautiful as described. We had an excellent lunch in Broadway at the Small Talk Tea Shoppe at 32 High Street. Grilled cheese sandwiches with **jacket potato** (baked potato), tea, apple cake and turnover with cream.]

"12:04 St Just, 12:12 **Camborne**, home of the Camborne School of Mines. There's lots of **tin mining** in this area, we're told, but no coal. The other main means of making a living in Cornwall are fishing and copper mining, hence the favorite Cornish toast to **"Fish, tin and copper."** 12:20 Hayle, we're almost there. We're advised to visit **St. Michael's Mount**. The buses run every half hour but when the tide is in, there's a ferry. It's named for the French Mont St. Michel as it also was a monastery, but not as imposing. This one went into private hands after the Dissolution of the monasteries by Henry VIII. The present family, the **St. Aubyns**, came into possession during the latter part of the 17th century and converted it into a mansion. 12:25 St. Erth and we can see the sand beach on the north side of Penzance. We photographed the ladies just as we arrived ON TIME!

When we got off, the American was met by her relatives. It was not the kind of emotional meeting we were used to seeing in Italy. The English women chatted with them a bit and then went off to St. Michael's Mount. We were hungry and found the Wheel Cafe at 3 Albert St. where Jerry had cod and chips and I had a **Gunster Cornish Pasty** with chips. Pasty, pronounced pah-stee, is a sort of chicken pot pie made with ground beef. The pastry was the original **"lunch box"** for the tin miners as it protected the meat and vegetables from mine dust. It was delicious and very hot. Later, we walked up and down the main street, Market Jew Street, and looked in all the shops. It's not a touristy town and there were no signs of Gilbert and Sullivan's Pirates. Most unusual. Penzance was very vulnerable when the Spanish Armada arrived in 1595. The town was sacked and burnt. The main street goes up a hill and on to **Land's End** but we didn't have time to see its miles of beautiful cliffs and coves...another time. At Aunty's, we bought ginger ice cream **cornets** (cones) topped with Cornish cream and a wee wooden spoon. As we ate, we wandered about the docks and looked at the ships.

At 4:26 we were on the "new train" which has tables and even though we can purchase coffee and sandwiches, we don't like it as well as the old train with its "sort of private" compartments. While waiting for the train to start, I'm going over in my mind the events of the past four days and reliving our experiences.

I wouldn't have missed Chawton. It met all my expectations. Stonehenge? I wished it hadn't been fenced so we could have touched the gigantic stones as a link with pre-history. Plymouth, another link with our immediate past, was an experience I'll always cherish; and Penzance was memorable because of the women we met on the train, and the ginger ice cream cornets topped with yummy Cornish cream. Cornwall with its dramatic cliffs and carved out inlets was so different from Devon with it's lovely Virginia-like undulating hills. Both are absolutely lovely and so much larger than I expected. I really thought this area was like Cape Cod and we could see it all in a day or two; but thinking it over, we accomplished a lot.

We had marveled at the accomplishments of our stone-age ancestors, reveled in the serene atmosphere which inspired Jane Austen's great novels, felt the pangs of leave-taking with our British forefathers, and had a delicious tin-miner's lunch. What more could we want?

Ah, there we go, on the dot! What a civilized country!

APPENDIX

CHAPTER ONE

MORE "HOW'S THAT AGAIN?" WORDS

cotton wool — cotton

dead sick — deathly sick

doesn't amount to a row of beans — doesn't amount to a hill of beans

dog sick — sick as a dog

Don't gnaw more than you can champ. —Don't bite off more than you can chew.

Don't take your fences until you have to. — Don't count your chickens until they're hatched.

dressed to the nines — dressed to the teeth

edgeways — sideways

flogging a dead horse — beating a dead horse

fuzzle headedness — fuzzy headedness

get something pat — get something down pat

goer — go-getter

going full belt — going full steam ahead

got it pat — got it down pat

grass mowings — grass clippings

Hark at him! — Look at him!

Have a good care. — Take care.

have one on — put one on

hog pen — pig pen

home keeping — housekeeping

hotchpotch — hodgepodge

I take your point! — I get the point!

indian ink — india ink
It's above my head. — It's over my head.
It's enough to drive one to a tree. — It's enough to drive one up a tree.
It's just about someone's mark. — It's just about someone's speed.
legged it hotfoot — hotfooted it
like a clock — like clockwork
like a kick in the head — like a kick in the teeth
like a sack of coals — like a ton of bricks
like houses on fire — like a house on fire
make a stand — take a stand
money-spinner — money maker
now and again — now and then
on the trot — on the go
orange boxes — orange crates
out-of-door man — outdoorsman
pay-you-out trick — pay-you-back trick
ponging to high heaven — smelling to high heaven
power to make or mar — power to make or break
pottered — puttered
quarter-wit — half-wit
quick-change performer — quick-change artist
ready for off — ready to go
rough-perfect — near perfect
saleroom — salesroom
set one's face against something — set one's mind against something
sharp as a needle — sharp as a tack
shot-free — scot-free
Smartie-boots! — Smartie-pants!
spot of air — breath of air
square and aboveboard — honest and aboveboard
sunk garden — sunken garden
swing doors — swinging doors
talk like a pen-gun — talk like a machine-gun

talk through the back of one's neck — talk through one's hat

The ball is at his feet. — The ball's in his lap.

The cat's mustache! — The cat's meow!

The rapid set. — The fast set.

throw dust in one's eyes — throw the wool over one's eyes

to a hair's weight — to a hair's breadth

to find one's feet — to get back on one's feet

to get on — to get along

to go over with a swing — to go over with a bang

to kit oneself — to outfit oneself

to set up one's bristles — to raise one's hackles

up to one's eyes in work — up to one's ears in work

weak-minded — simple minded

wear the breeches — wear the pants

Where's the harm? — What's the harm?

MORE -ISE/-IZE WORDS

antagonise — antagonize
apologise — apologize
authorise — authorize
centralise — centralize
criticise — criticize
demoralise — demoralize
dramatise — dramatize
economise — economize
emphasise — emphasize
fertilise — fertilize
fertiliser — fertilizer
fraternise — fraternize
generalise — generalize
hypnotise — hypnotize
idealise — idealize
immortalise — immortalize
jeopardise — jeopardize
legalise — legalize

localise — localize
macadamise — macadamize
materialise — materialize
memorise — memorize
modernise — modernize
nationalise — nationalize
neutralise — neutralize
organise — organize
patronise — patronize
realise — realize
recognise — recognize
revolutionise — revolutionize
romanticise — romanticize
scandalise — scandalize
serialise — serialize
specialise — specialize
stabilise — stabilize
sterilise — sterilize
stigmatise — stigmatize
subsidise — subsidize
sympathise — sympathize
tantalise — tantalize
terrorise — terrorize
theorise — theorize
victimise — victimize

MORE -OUR/-OR WORDS

armour — armor
behaviour — behavior
candour — candor
clamour — clamor
colour — color
enamour — enamor
endeavour — endeavor
favour — favor
favourable — favorable

favourite — favorite
fervour — fervor
flavour — flavor
harbour — harbor
honour — honor
humour — humor
labour — labor
neighbour — neighbor
parlour — parlor
rancour — rancor
rigour — rigor
rumour — rumor
savour — savor
splendour — splendor
valour — valor
vapour — vapor

CHAPTER TWELVE

A MAN OR WOMAN: MORE DESCRIPTIONS

buckie — balky
cack-handed — clumsy
cadgy — begs for favors
cowardly custard — yellow
cross-grained — crabby
gets beet red or **assumes a prawn-like hue** — blushes
gooseberry — fifth wheel
highfed — pampered
high-mettled — lively
halfbred — poor upbringing
rolling — rich
shirty — snippy
sloppy — wishy washy
stagey — showoff
starkers — naked

MORE ANGRY EXPRESSIONS

Don't get cheeky. — Watch your tongue!
Don't get strutty! — Stop showing off!
Don't muck about! — Don't mess around!
Get knotted! —Go stuff your head!
Gorblimy! — Cockney for "God blind me!"
Hold your jaw! — Keep your trap shut!
I don't give a brass button or I don't give a farthing! — I don't give a damn!
Mind your tongue! — Hold your tongue!
Pack it in! — Give up!
Stop your natterin! — Stop the chatter!
Stuff yourself! — Go soak your head!
That's a lot of eye water! — That's a lot of eyewash!

MORE FIGHT TALK

a little bother — a bit of trouble
a punch-up — a fight
a tight corner — a tight situation
bullyrag — badger
bunch of fives — knuckle sandwich
come down upon — give one holy hell
a grumble — a gripe
have a down on — have it in for
having a father and mother of a fight — having a grandfather of a fight
lower one's position — knock one down
narked — peeved
sent packing — sent about one's business
slanging match — argument
tick one off — tell one off
tom-lad bouts— kid fights

MORE INTERESTING EXPRESSIONS
ADVICE:
homespun wisdom — cracker barrel talk

Keep a sharp lookout! — Keep watch!
Keep it under hatches. — Keep it quiet.
Keep one's thumb on. — Keep it under your hat.
keep oneself informed — keep track of things
Mind your eye! — Take care! or Look out!
Mind your head. — Watch your head.
talk one round — make one change one's opinion
ALL AT ONCE!
All at one go!
ALL IS NOT ROSES!
beastly — miserable
beat to sticks — beat to the ground
be hard done by — be treated badly
be in a bit of a cleft stick — be in a bind
be lumbered with — be saddled with
carried the can — was a patsy
going through a skitty patch — being flighty or irresponsible
in bother or **in the cart** — in trouble
It's a swizz! — It's a fizzle!
It's put the lid on me. — That finishes it for me.
It went down the loo! — It went down the drain!
making heavy weather of things — having a hard time
making ducks and drakes of things — messing things up
overshooting — overreaching
running up a score — running into debt
schmozzle — mess
sticky wicket — a difficult situation
strike a bad patch — hit a snag
termless — endless
to chuck things up — to give up
trap-fall — pitfall
throw in — give up
up a gum-tree — up the creek
up the spout — down the drain
was badly dipped — lost a bundle

BALKING:
jibbing
CRAZY OR DAFFY:
as daft as they come — crazy as all get-out
go bonkers, go round the twist or **go off the rails**
laughing academy — booby hatch
CLEAN:
a bit of a wipe round — a mop up
speckless — spanking clean
COSTLY:
posh — rich
pricey
DISLIKE:
take a scunner on
DUMB, FOOLISH OR NAIVE:
simple as an egg
in a canter — without much effort
to take eggs for money — to take empty promises
ENDED:
put paid to — finished or The file is closed.
put a term to it — ended it
windswift — fast as the wind
FAUX PAS:
blot one's copybook — mess things up
blow the gaff — blab
drop a clanger or **make a bloomer** — make a boner
shove one's oar in — butt in
spill secrets on one's plate — dumping all the secrets in
someone's lap
tale-bearing — tattle-taleing
to boob
to make a mix-up, queer the pitch or **throw a spanner into
the works** — to louse things up
FREE:
shot free or **scot free**
FUNNY, FOOLISH OR SILLY:

a wag — a funny fellow
hoax or **josh** — string along
jape or **wheeze** — joke
joke drawings — cartoons
send one funny — make one act oddly
to gammon — to fool
GET THE BETTER OF:
score off
You've got him on a plate.
run one to earth — run one down
GET RID OF SOMEONE:
get shot of someone
GO FAST:
going like old boots — going like crazy
in a brace of shakes — in a jiffy
in a canter — in no time
in a muck sweat
in a tic — in a sec
near cut — short cut
nips like one o'clock — goes off in a flash
sarky — in a hurry
smartish — at a fast clip
straightaway
to beetle — to rush
to go whip and spur
to rabbit — skedaddle
to whip off
was sharp about it — was very fast
GO SLOW:
to oil out
to slope off
toddle off
tick and toy — dilly dally
GOOD!
a shot in the locker — something yet in reserve
be at the top of one's form — be at one's best

be on form — doing very well
I'm keen for it! — I'm all for it!
It's a cert! — It's in the bag!
It's fixed! — It's a date.
Let's make a broadside! — Let's win!
on the first go — on the first throw
turned up trumps — turned out ok
up to standard — up to par
very decently run — well run
was spot on — hit the nail on the head
Well played! — Well done!
GOOD TIME:
Liberty hall! — A place where one can do as one pleases.
IDEA:
The penny dropped! — It just hit me!
think out — think up
I MEAN IT!
And no mistake!
If you take my meaning. — If you get what I mean.
IN DUE TIME:
in the fullness of time
IN SO MANY WORDS:
in terms
the whole strength of it — the whole story
IT DOESN'T MATTER!
So stone the crows!
San Fairy Ann (WWI soldier slang taken from the French "Sans faire rien")
IT'S A WASTE OF TIME!
It's a mugg's game!
IT'S THE REAL THING!
It's up to Dick!
The real McKay! — The real McCoy!
JUST THE SAME:
all the same
LET'S GIVE IT A TRY!

It's neck or nothing. — Let's go for broke.
Let's have at it again!
Let's slog on! — Let's go on to the bitter end.
Let's strike a blow! — Let's take a chance!
until the last shot
LET'S TAKE IT AS IT COMES.
Let's not snatch (grasp) at straws.
Let's take it by numbers.
Stand to! — Be firm!
Try not to flag — weaken
through weal and woe — through thick and thin
LET'S TALK.
I'd like a word with you.
Let's put matters right. — Let's straighten things out.
LOOKS LIKE:
looks like the Blackpool illuminations —lit up like Times
Square
more of a pig — bigger than
She looks zipp-fastener to me. — She's the kind that's
always in a hurry.
LOUD NOISE:
rowededow or **rowdydow**
MANNERS:
has shark manners — is rapacious
It's near the knuckle. — almost indecent
MEANWHILE:
Betimes
NAP, REST OR EXHAUSTION:
a little lie-down
doing sweet-all — doing nothing
doss down — bed down
have a lay-down
kipping down — hitting the sack
knackered — exhausted
pole axed, knackered or **shagged out**
NERVE:

puff
NOT A CHANCE IN A MILLION!
a dog's chance
for nix — nothing
Not a hope!
Not an earthly! — Fat chance!
Not for nuts! — No way!
Not half! — Not on your life!
Not on your nelly!
NOT WORTH A RED CENT:
twopenny-halfpenny, two pennyworth, two pennorth or tuppence
OFF COLOR STORY:
smoking-room story
OLDER:
senior to — older than
when one hears the clock ticking — when one feels one's age
ORDINARY PEOPLE:
suet puddings
OUTDOORS:
abroad
ROT, DRIVEL OR STUFF AND NONSENSE!
Absolute bilge!
Crafting dottle!
Slosh!
Tedious codswallop!
That's a load of madam!
That's rot!
Twaddle!
SAFE:
as safe as houses
home and dry
I'll see you back. — I'll see you safely home.
SARCASTIC:
sarky

SAUCY OR IMPERTINENT:
cheeky
SHOW-OFF:
playing brag
putting on side
snobby
to take one's talent out of the napkin
SKIP IT!
Give it a miss!
SMELL:
It pongs! It stinks!
STUFFY:
stivy
TAKE A LOOK.
Have a dekko. (Urdu word from the soldiers in India.)
Take a butchers. (Shortened from Butcher's hook, rhyming Cockney slang...hook sounds like look.)
TALKING TOO MUCH:
Let's not make a meal of this. — Let's not make too much of this.
nattering — chattering
rabbiting — talking too fast
split — tell on
talkee-talkee or talky-talky — chitter-chatter
talk the hind leg off a donkey
the same kind of chat — same kind of talk
to fob one off — to change the subject
tongue work — tongue wagging
to the backbone through and through —talk through one's hat
TECHNICAL:
light-tight — impervious to light
ticking over nicely — moving along well
THINGS ARE BAD!
a bit sweeping — a bit much
a box-up — a foul up

a crashing howler — a bad mistake
All is not beer and skittles.
TO UNDERSTAND:
to twig
tumbled to — caught on
TOO MUCH!:
on the bow hand — wide of the mark
too much on one's plate — overwhelmed
UNEXPECTED:
after-clap — an unexpected sequel when something is supposed to be finished
caught on the hop — caught in the act
WAVING A HANKIE:
flipping a wiper
WHAT'S THE DIRT?
What's the bumpf?
What's the griff?
WON'T WORK
won't do a blind bit of good

BIBLIOGRAPHY

Academic American Encyclopedia. Grolier Inc., Danbury, Connecticut, 1993.

Amazing Britain, (For the British Travel Authority, American Airlines and Saga Holidays). Mill House Books Ltd, Great Britain, 1992

"A Very British Christmas," *Britain.* December 1992.

Baker, Margaret. *Christmas Customs and Folklore,* Shire Publications of Tring, 1968.

Baker, Margaret. *Folklore and Customs of Rural England.* Rowman and Littlefield, Totowa, N.J., 1974.

Baker, Russell. *The Good Times.* William Morrow and Company, N.Y. 1989.

Bolton, W.F. and Crystal, D. *The English Language,* Vol. 2. Cambridge at the University Press, 1969, pp183-202.

Boutell's Heraldry, revised by Brooke-Little, T.P. Frederick Warne, London and N.Y., 1983.

Britain Bed and Breakfast. British Travel Authority, 1993.

Britain 1993, An Official Handbook. HMSO Publications Center, P.O. Box 276, London SW8 5DT.

British Broadcasting Company Pronouncing Dictionary of British Names. Oxford University Press, London, 1971.

British Christmas Customs. British Information Services, August 1971.

Brown, James W. and Brown, Shirley N. *Before You Go to Great Britain,* The Shoe String Press, Inc., Hamden, Conn., 1986.

Burton, Elizabeth. *The Pageant of Elizabethan England.* Chas. Scribner's Sons, N.Y. 1958.

Burton, Elizabeth. *The Pageant of Georgian England*. Chas. Scribner's Sons, N.Y. 1961.

Bushell. *Cricket: The Gentlemen's Game*, London Press Service, 1985.

Carey, G.V. *American into English*, William Heinemann, Ltd, Melbourne, 1953.

Chamber's 20th Century Dictionary. William Geddie, ed. W. & R. Chambers, Ltd., Edinburgh and London, 1970.

Claiborne, Robert. *The Roots of English*. Times Books, Division of Random House, N.Y., 1989.

Colliers Encyclopedia, MacMillan Education Co., N.Y., 1990.

Crowl, Philip A. *The Intelligent Traveller's Guide to Historic Britain*, Congdon & Weed, Inc., N.Y., 1983.

Crookston, Peter, *Village England*, Hutchinson & Co., London, 1980.

Customs. *Her Majesty's Customs and Excise*. January 1993.

"Debate Is Unleashed, but Wild Animals Lose the Day in Parliament," (The Hunt in England), *Philadelphia Inquirer*, 2/15/92

Delaney, Mary Murray. *Of Irish Ways.*, Dillon Press Inc., Minneapolis, Minn., 1973.

Dyer, James. *Discovering Archaeology in England and Wales*. Shire Publications, Tring, Herts, 1969.

Fowler, H.W. , Fowler F.G., Allen, R.E. *The Concise Oxford Dictionary of Current English*. Clarendon Press, Oxford, England, 1990.

Godden, Rumer. *On Words from the Writer's Handbook*. Burack, A.S., ed. The Writer Inc., Boston, Mass., 1974.

Health Information for International Travel, U.S. Department of Health and Human Services, 1992.

Hogg, Garry. *Customs and Traditions of England*. Arco Publishing Co., Inc., N.Y. 1971.

Hudson, Kenneth and Nicholls, Ann. *The Cambridge Guide to the Historic Places of Britain and Ireland.* Cambridge University Press, Cambridge, 1989.

Hamlyn All Colour Cook Book. The Hamlyn Publishing Group, Limited, London, 1970.

Horan, Christopher. *English Country Cooking.* St. Martin's Press, N.Y. 1985.

Jane Grigson's British Cookery. Atheneum, N.Y., 1985.

Keating, Frank. "On the Village Green," *Britain.* May 1991.

Key Officers of Foreign Service Posts. US Department of State, Spring 1993.

Kightly, Charles. *The Customs and Ceremonies of Britain,* Thames. *London, Insight City Guides.* APA Publications, 1990.

London Plus, Britain and Europe. British Airways Holidays, 1993.

Map of Roman Britain. Ordnance Survey, Chessington, Surrey, England, 1956.

Marsden, Barry M. *Discovering Regional Archaeology.* Central England, Shire Publications, Tring, Herts, 1970.

Modell, David. *The Terrier Men.*

National Holidays 1993, 1994. British Information Services, May 1993.

Newman, Judith and Stein, Ellen. "Mistress of an Unruly House," *People,* February 28, 1994, p44.

Nicholson's Historic Britain. Robert Nicholson Publications, Limited, London, 1982.

Oxford English Dictionary. The, Oxford University Press, 1971.

Powell, Anton. *London Walks.* Holt, Rinehart and Winston, N.Y., 1981.

"Stonehenge," PBS. November 25, 1993.

Reaney, P.H. *The Origin of English Place-Names*. Routledge and Kegan Paul, London, 1960.

Royal Britain. *Your Vacation Planner*. British Tourist Authority, New York, 1993.

Sampson, Anthony. *Anatomy of Britain*. Harper & Row, N.Y. 1962.

Secret Britain. The Automobile Association, Basingstoke, Hampshire, 1986.

Simon, Kate. *England's Green and Pleasant Land*. Alfred. A. Knopf, N.Y. 1974.

Stimpson, George. *A Book About a Thousand Things*. Harper & Brothers, N.Y., 1946.

The Encyclopedia Americana. Grolier Inc., Danbury, Conn., 1990.

The New Encyclopedia Brittanica. Encyclopedia Brittanica, Inc., 15th edition, Chicago, 1991.

Theroux, Paul. *The Kingdom by the Sea-A Journey Around Great Britain*. Houghton Mifflin, Boston, 1983.

Touring Britain and Ireland. The Automobile Association, Basingstoke, Hampshire, 1991.

Traditional Britain. Martin, Mark. Golden Hart Guides, Sidgwick and Jackson, London, 1983.

United Kingdom, Background Notes from the United States Department of State. Bureau of Public Affairs, 1990.

Webster, Noah, *An American Dictionary of the English Language*. Johnson Reprint Corp., N.Y. & London, 1970.

Wilks, Brian. *Jane Austen*. Hamlyn, London, 1978.

Winks, Robin W. *An American's Guide to Britain*. Charles Scribner's Sons, N.Y., 1983.

World Book Encyclopedia. World Book Inc., Chicago, 1994.

Wright, Edmund. *The American Guide to Britain*. Salem House Publishers, Topsfield, Massachusetts 1987.

INDEX

INDEX

Ireland
Daniel O'Connell, 128
Government of Ireland Act, 128
holidays, 212
Home Rule, 128
honours, St. Patrick, 131
Republic of Ireland Act, 128
St. Patrick's Day, 215
Iron Age, 112
iron smelting, first success with
coke, 71

James I, 124
James II, 126
Joan of Arc, 122
John I, 119
Johnson, Dr. Samuel, 78, 103

Kipling, Rudyard, 103

Lady Jane Grey, 123
languages, 27-33, 115
law, 271-276
barristers and solicitors, 273
law societies, 271-272
wigs, 273-274
Leicester, 106-110
Londinium, 73
London, 73-81
London Bridge, 73-74

Magna Carta, 101-102, 108, 119
Mary I, 123
Mary, Queen of Scots, 123, 264
Milton, John, 102
Model Parliament, 120
money, 53-54

Neolithic Period/New Stone Age,
111
Normans, 117
Northern Ireland, 98,
Belfast, 104-105

Secretary of State for Northern
Ireland, 250
Northmen, 116

Offa's Dike, 116

Papists (Catholics), 123
Parliament, 120, 124, 127-128, 248-254
government departments, 256-257
"Unwritten Constitution," 251-252
Penzance, 305-306
Philip, Prince, 128
Picts/Caledonians, 113
Pilgrims, 124
Pitt, William, 127
Plymouth, 300-301
police, 277
politics
elections, 249, 255
political parties, 254-255
Tories, 126
Whigs, 126
Portland Cement, 72
post offices, 47
Public Record Office, 78
pubs, 141-147
hours, 143
jargon, 145-147
offerings, 143-145
Puritans, 123-124

Reaney, Dr. P.H., 66
recreation, 227-245
children's games, 198-199
religion, 183-185
school religious instruction, 260
restaurants, 80, 151-155
Restoration, The, 126
Richard I, the Lionhearted, 119
Richard II, 121
Richard III, 122
Romans, 106-107, 113, 115

327

HIPPOCRENE LANGUAGE AND TRAVEL GUIDES

These guides provide an excellent introduction to a foreign country for the traveler who wants to meet and communicate with people as well as sightsee. Each book is also an ideal refresher course for anyone wishing to brush up on their language skills.

LANGUAGE AND TRAVEL GUIDE TO AUSTRALIA, by Helen Jonsen
Travel with or without your family through the land of "OZ" on your own terms; this guide describes climates, seasons, different cities, coasts, countrysides, rainforests, and the Outback with a special consideration to culture and language.
250 pages • $14.95 • 0-7818-0166-4 (0086)

LANGUAGE AND TRAVEL GUIDE TO FRANCE, by Elaine Klein
Specifically tailored to the language and travel needs of Americans visiting France, this book also serves as an introduction to the culture. Learn the etiquette of ordering in a restaurant, going through customs, and asking for directions.
320 pages • $14.95 • 0-7818-0080-3 (0386)

LANGUAGE AND TRAVEL GUIDE TO INDONESIA (Coming soon)
350 pages • $14.95 • 0-7818-0328-4 (0111)

LANGUAGE AND TRAVEL GUIDE TO MEXICO, by Ila Warner
Explaining exactly what to expect of hotels, transportation, shopping, and food, this guide provides the essential Spanish phrases, as well as describing appropriate gestures, and offering cultural comments.
224 pages • $14.95 • 0-87052-622-7 (503)

LANGUAGE AND TRAVEL GUIDE TO RUSSIA, by Victorya Andreyeva and Margarita Zubkus
Allow Russian natives to introduce you to the system they know so well. You'll be properly advised on such topics as food, transportation, the infamous Russian bath house, socializing, and sightseeing. Then, use the guide's handy language sections to be both independent and knowledgeable.
293 pages • $14.95 • 0-7818-0047-1 (0321)

LANGUAGE AND TRAVEL GUIDE TO UKRAINE, by Linda Hodges and George Chumak
Written jointly by a native Ukrainian and an American journalist, this guide details the culture, the people, and the highlights of the Ukrainian experience, with a convenient (romanized) guide to the essentials of Ukrainian.
266 pages • $14.95 • 0-7818-0135-4 (0057)

(Prices subject to change.)

COMPANION GUIDES FROM HIPPOCRENE

COMPANION GUIDE TO BRITAIN, *by Henry Weisser*
Highlights are cited and explained clearly, describing what is best to see in London and the provinces: castles cathedrals, stately homes, villages, and towns. This essential practical guide lists history, geography, politics, culture, economics, climate and language use.
_____250 pages • 0-7818-0147-8 • $14.95

COMPANION GUIDE TO AUSTRALIA, *by Graeme and Tamsin Newman*
With helpful tips on preparing for your trip, this cheerful guide outlines the distinctive characters and main attractions of cities, describes picturesque countryside, and links the things tourists like to do with the history and character of the Australian people.
_____294 pages • b/w photos and 4 maps • 0-87052-034-2 • $16.95

COMPANION GUIDE TO MEXICO, *by Michael Burke*
Along with the usual tips on sites, this guide outlines contemporary realities of Mexican society, religion and politics.
_____320 pages • b/w photos • 0-7818-0039-0 • $14.95

COMPANION GUIDE TO POLAND (Revised), *by Jill Stephenson and Alfred Bloch*
"This quaint and refreshing guide is an appealing amalgam of practical information, historical curiosities, and romantic forays into Polish culture."—*Library Journal*
_____179 pages • b/w photos, maps • 0-7818-0077-3 • $14.95

COMPANION GUIDE TO PORTUGAL, *by T.J. Kubiak*
Learn about the land, the people, their heritage and much more with this guide to the unexpected bounty of Portugal.
_____260 pages • maps • 0-87052-739-8 • $14.95

COMPANION GUIDE TO ROMANIA, *by Lydle Brinkle*
Written by a specialist in Eastern European geography, this modern guide offers comprehensive historical, topographical, and cultural overviews.
_____220 pages • 0-87052-634-0 • $14.95

COMPANION GUIDE TO SAUDI ARABIA, *by Gene Lindsey*
Gene Lindsey, an American who has spent much of the last decade in Saudi Arabia, traces the history of the region, religion, development, harsh environment, foreign policy, laws, language, education, technology, and underlying it all, its mindset.
_____368 pages • maps • 0-7818-0023-4 • $11.95

THE HIPPOCRENE MASTERING SERIES

MASTERING ARABIC
Jane Wightwick and Mahmoud Gaafar
320 pages, 5 1/2 x 8 1/2
0-87052-922-6 $14.95pb
2 Cassettes
 0-87052-984-6 $12.95
Book and Cassettes Package
0-87052-140-3 $27.90

MASTERING FINNISH
Börje Vähämäki
278 pages, 5 1/2 x 8 1/2
0-7818-0233-4 $14.95pb
2 Cassettes
0-7818-0265-2 $12.95
Book and Cassettes Package
0-7818-0266-0 $27.90

MASTERING FRENCH
E.J. Neather
288 pages, 5 1/2 x 8 1/2
0-87052-055-5 $11.95pb
2 Cassettes
0-87052-060-1 $12.95
Book and Cassettes Package
0-87052-136-5 $24.90

MASTERING GERMAN
A.J. Peck
340 pages, 5 1/2 x 8 1/2
0-87052-056-3 $11.95pb
2 Cassettes
0-87052-061-X $12.95
Book and Cassettes Package
0-87052-137-3 $24.90

MASTERING ADVANCED GERMAN
278 pages, 5 1/2 x 8 1/2
0-7818-0331-4 $14.95pb
2 Casettes
0-7818-0332-2 $12.95
Book and Cassettes Package
0-7818-0348-9 $27.90

MASTERING ITALIAN
N. Messora
360 pages, 5 1/2 x 8 1/2
0-87052-057-1 $11.95pb
2 Cassettes
0-87052-066-0 $12.95
Book and Cassettes Package
0-87052-138-1 $24.90

MASTERING ADVANCED ITALIAN
278 pages, 5 1/2 x 8 1/2
0-7818-0333-0 $14.95
2 Cassettes
0-7818-0334-9 $12.95
Book and Cassettes Package
0-7818-0349-7 $27.90

MASTERING JAPANESE
Harry Guest
368 pages, 5 1/2 x 8 1/2
0-87052-923-4 $14.95pb
2 Cassettes
0-87052-938-8 $12.95
Book and Cassettes Package
0-87052-141-1 $27.90

MASTERING POLISH
Albert Juszczak
288 pages, 5 1/2 x 8 1/2
0-7818-0015-3 $14.95pb
2 Cassettes
0-7818-0016-3 $12.95
Book and Cassettes Package
0-7818-0017-X $27.90

MASTERING RUSSIAN
Erika Haber
278 pages, 5 1/2 x 8 1/2
0-7818-0270-9 $14.95
2 Cassettes
0-7818-0270-9 $12.95
Book and Cassettes Package
0-7818-0272-5 $27.90

MASTERING SPANISH
Robert Clarke
338 pages, 5 1/2 x 8 1/2
0-87052-059-8 $11.95pb
2 Cassettes
0-87052-067-9 $12.95
Book and Cassettes Package
0-87052-139-X $24.90

$24.90

MASTERING ADVANCED SPANISH
Robert Clarke
300 pages, 5 1/2 x 8 1/2
30 b/w photos
0-7818-0081-1   11.95pb
2 Cassettes
0-7818-0089-7 $12.95
Book and Cassettes Package
0-7818-0090-0

In praise of the Mastering Series:
- "Truly the best book of its kind."

- "Your book is truly remarkable, and you are to be congratulated."
  —a field editor for college textbooks.

  All prices subject to change.
  Ask for these and other Hippocrene titles at your local booksellers!

HIPPOCRENE HANDY DICTIONARIES

For the traveler of independent spirit and curious mind, this practical series will help you to communicate, not just to get by. Common phrases are conveniently listed through key words. Pronunciation follows each entry and a reference section reviews all major grammar points. *Handy Extras* are extra helpful—offering even more words and phrases for students and travelers.

ARABIC
$8.95 • 0-87052-960-9

CHINESE
$8.95 • 0-87052-050-4

CZECH EXTRA
$8.95 • 0-7818-0138-9

DUTCH
$8.95 • 0-87052-049-0

FRENCH
$8.95 • 0-7818-0010-2

GERMAN
$8.95 • 0-7818-0014-5

GREEK
$8.95 • 0-87052-961-7

HUNGARIAN EXTRA
$8.95 • 0-7818-0164-8

ITALIAN
$8.95 • 0-7818-0011-0

JAPANESE
$8.95 • 0-87052-962-5

KOREAN
$8.95 • 0-7818-0082-X

PORTUGUESE
$8.95 • 0-87052-053-9

RUSSIAN
$8.95 • 0-7818-0013-7

SERBO-CROATIAN
$8.95 • 0-87052-051-2

SLOVAK EXTRA
$8.95 • 0-7818-0101-X

SPANISH
$8.95 • 0-7818-0012-9

SWEDISH
$8.95 • 0-87052-054-7

THAI
$8.95 • 0-87052-963-3

TURKISH
$8.95 • 0-87052-982-X

(All prices subject to change.)

TO PURCHASE HIPPOCRENE BOOKS contact your local bookstore, or write to: HIPPOCRENE BOOKS, 171 Madison Avenue, New York, NY 10016. Please enclose check or money order, adding $4.00 shipping (UPS) for the first book and $.50 for each additional book.

HIPPOCRENE INTERNATIONAL LITERATURE

THE DEDALUS BOOK OF BRITISH FANTASY: The Nineteenth Century
Brian Stableford, Editor
Beginning in 1804, this anthology traces the development of the genre through the
stories and poems of Coleridge, Keats, Dickens and Disraeli.
416 pages, 5 1/2 x 8 1/2
0-7818-0212-1
$14.95pb (403)

THE DEDALUS BOOK OF DECADENCE: Moral Ruins (Revised)
Brian Stableford, Editor
A striking anthology that plumbs the depths of perversity, this unique collection
features over 40 stories by authors such as Baudelaire, Poe and Wilde.
288 pages, 5 1/2 x 8 1/2
0-7818-0181-8
$14.95pb (101)

THE SECOND DEDALUS BOOK OF DECADENCE: The Black Feast
Brian Stableford, Editor
More tales of the macabre from some of Britain's and France's greatest authors.
356 pages, 5 1/2 x 8 1/2
0-7818-0110-9
$14.95pb (105)

Available Spring 1995:

DEDALUS BOOK OF SURREALISM I

DEDALUS BOOK OF SURREALISM II

(All prices subject to change.)

TO PURCHASE HIPPOCRENE BOOKS contact your local bookstore, or write to:
HIPPOCRENE BOOKS, 171 Madison Avenue, New York, NY 10016. Please enclose
check or money order, adding $4.00 shipping (UPS) for the first book and $.50 for
each additional book.